Barbara Woods,
Karon Oliver and Philip Banyard

Fourth Edition
Psychology

OCR GCSE

HODDER
EDUCATION
AN HACHETTE UK C

The authors and publisher would like to thank the following for permission to reproduce photographs in this book:

Figure 1.1 © c.Universal/Everett / Rex Features; Figure 1.3 © Kimberly Reinick – Fotolia; Figure 1.4 © Reuters/ Corbis; Figure 1.7 With kind permission by Albert Bandura; Figure 1.8 © Bettmann/Corbis; Figure 2.8 (all three images) © George Mather / School of Psychology, University of Lincoln, UK; Figure 2.15b © bradcalkins – Fotolia; Figure 2.17 (both images) Courtesy of Harvard University Archives, Call # HUG 4229.20, Box IV, Folder "Size consistency in a picture."; Figure 2.20 With kind permission by Richard L. Gregory; Figure 2.21b © Xavier MARCHANT – Fotolia; Figure 3.1 © soupstock – Fotolia; Figure 3.4 © micromonkey – Fotolia; Figure 3.11 © fotomorgana - Fotolia.com; Figure 4.1 © From the film *Obedience* © 1968 by Stanley Milgram; © renewed 1993 by Alexandra Milgram; Figure 4.2 © Yuri Arcurs – Fotolia; Figure 4.4 © Joe Gough – Fotolia. com; Figure 4.6 © Hulton Archive/Getty Images; Figure 4.7 © Paul Ekman Ph.D./Paul Ekman Group, LLC; Figure 4.8 © Stephen Bonk – Fotolia; Figure 4.11 © Karon Oliver; Figure 5.4 © Archives of the History of American Psychology, The Center for the History of Psychology, The University of AKRON; Figure 6.1 © Cresta Johnson – Fotolia.

Every effort has been made to obtain necessary permission with reference to copyright material. The publishers apologise if inadvertantly any sources remain unacknowledged and will be glad to make the necessary arrangements at the earliest opportunity.

Orders: please contact Bookpoint Ltd, 130 Milton Park, Abingdon, Oxon OX14 4SB. Telephone: (44) 01235 827720. Fax: (44) 01235 400454. Lines are open from 9.00–5.00, Monday to Saturday, with a 24 hour message answering service. You can also order through our website www.hoddereducation.co.uk

If you have any comments to make about this, or any of our other titles, please send them to educationenquiries@hodder.co.uk

British Library Cataloguing in Publication Data
A catalogue record for this title is available from the British Library

ISBN: 9781444168310

Published 2012

Impression number   10 9 8 7 6 5 4 3 2
Year   2016, 2015

Hachette UK's policy is to use papers that are natural, renewable and recyclable products and made from wood grown in sustainable forests.

The logging and manufacturing processes are expected to conform to the environmental regulations of the country of origin.

Illustrations by Barking Dog Art and Typeset by DC Graphic Design Limited, Swanley, Kent

Printed in Italy by Printer Trento for Hodder Education, An Hachette UK Company, Carmelite House, 50 Victoria Embankment, London EC4Y 0DZ

Contents

How to use this book

This book is divided in to 6 chapters, the first five focus on the different approaches to psychology and the final chapter focuses on reseach. In each of the approaches chapters (1–5) the first half focuses on the Unit B541 material for that approach, and the the second half deals with the Unit B542 material. Chapter 6 links to the final Unit, B543, giving you an introduction to how psychological research is conducted and then describing how to plan, undertake and analyse research.

Each of chapters 1 to 5 contain two pieces of actual psychological research (the Core Studies), information on how they were conducted, the results and conclusions as well as mention of some of their limitations.

Throughout the book important terms are picked out and defined either in the text or in a box nearby, make sure you know what these terms mean! There are also numerous features to help you learn:

Further your understanding
Extra information on a topic, helping you understand background and context that go beyond the basics.

DISCUSS...
Ideas to encourage you to think more deeply about a topic. Why not discuss them in class to see what everybody else thinks?

QUESTIONS
Questions appear throughout the chapters, you'll find the answers at the end of the book (pages 214–19). They'll help you test your knowledge on a particular topic.

HOMEWORK
Points you can look up and research at home that will help you really understand a topic.

KEY CONCEPTS
Helping you relate everything you've learned back to the OCR specification and what you will need to know in the exam.

Clarification and explanation
Throughout the text important points will be clarified and cross references given to other material in the book that might help you understand a topic.

Applications of research

This box will outline what you need to know about how the research in a topic can be applied to real world issues.

CORE THEORY

IN THE EXAM

These boxes outline what you will be expected to know about each of the core theories, to help you keep track of your learning.

You need to be able to:
This will make sure you know what you need to help you aim for top marks in your exams!

Exam-style questions

At the end of each unit throughout the book there is one full exam question based on that topic. The questions are taken directly from OCR past papers and there is a good cross-section of the types and structure of question you might face in the exam. The author has also written sample student answers as well as comments that highlight common student mistakes and contain tips on how you can aim for top marks.

OCR past papers and markschemes are a really useful resource when you're revising for your exams, and more are available on the OCR website www.ocr.org.uk.

Exam structure

Studies and Applications in Psychology

The first five chapters of this book cover two papers:

- Paper One (Unit B541): Studies and Applications in Psychology 1
- Paper Two (Unit B542): Studies and Applications in Psychology 2

Each paper has five sections and one topic is selected from each of the five approaches.

In the first paper the topics will be:

Approach	Topic	Core Study
Biological psychology	Sex and gender	Diamond and Sigmundson (1997)
Cognitive psychology	Memory	Terry (2005)
Developmental psychology	Attachment	Hazan and Shaver (1987)
Social psychology	Obedience	Bickman (1974)
Individual differences	Atypical behaviour	Watson and Rayner (1920)

In the second paper the topics will be:

Approach	Topic	Core Study
Biological psychology	Criminal behaviour	Mednick *et al.* (1984)
Cognitive psychology	Perception	Haber and Levin (2001)
Developmental psychology	Cognitive development	Piaget (1952)
Social psychology	Non-verbal communication	Yuki *et al.* (2007)
Individual differences	The self	Van Houtte and Jarvis (1995)

The format of the questions for *both* paper 1 and paper 2 are as follows:

Four multi-part questions are worth 15 marks each.

- Three out of the four 15-mark questions contain only short-answer questions with some parts being worth up to four marks (see pages 14–15 for examples).
- The fourth 15-mark question also comprises short-answer questions but the last one is worth six marks (see pages 180–1 for examples).

The fifth multi-part question is worth 20 marks.

- This section will contain a number of different parts which become more challenging with the last question being an essay-style question worth 10 marks (see pages 50–51 for examples).

The short-answer questions may include stimulus questions, for example, completing tables, multi-choice, matching concepts and interpreting a source (which is a piece of text describing a situation or piece of research – see page 14, question 1).

Different topics can be assessed by the different question styles so you cannot predict which approach will be examined in either the 15-mark or the 20-mark questions. For example, one year the 20-mark question may come from the biological approach and the next year it may be from the social approach.

Research in Psychology

Chapter 6 deals with the third paper:

● Paper Three (Unit B543) Research in Psychology

This paper lasts for 1 hour and is worth 40 marks (20 per cent of the total GCSE marks).

This question paper has two sections:

● **Section A (worth 25 marks):** You will need to answer a series of questions based on and around a source that describes a piece of research. The questions will test your knowledge of the research process (see page 209 for an example).

● **Section B (worth 15 marks):** You will be given a 'stimulus' which will be a description of something that needs to be investigated. You will be asked to plan an investigation based on this stimulus and will be told what sort of investigation you will need to plan which could be either an experiment, a questionnaire, an interview or an observation (see page 212 for an example).

How to tackle the exams

First of all, read the question and then read it again. When you are in an exam, nerves might make you misread the question. Don't write about what you want to write about because you don't know the answer – it won't earn you any marks. If you write a letter to the examiner, it may make them laugh or feel sorry for you, but it won't gain you any sympathy marks. However, it may make your fellow students think you know the answer if you are writing furiously!

If you are going to use psychological terms in your answer, make sure the examiner knows that you understand what that term means.

These are the things to look out for:

● Always look at the number of marks that are available for answers.
When a 2-mark question says 'Explain what is meant by …' or something similar, for 2 marks, you need to explain in a little detail rather than giving a one word answer.

If you are asked to explain the difference between two things for 3 marks, you will need to explain what each thing is (1 mark each) and then outline the difference between them for the last mark.
If you are asked to describe and evaluate for 10 marks, 5 marks are available for description and 5 for evaluation.

● If a question says 'Briefly … ' you don't need to write a really long essay. Again, look at the number of marks that are available.

● If you are asked about one strength or weakness don't write about two.

● Look at whether the question asks you to describe and evaluate or whether it just says one or the other.
Lots of candidates lose marks by thinking they don't know enough evaluation, so they will put additional descriptive information in. The trouble is, even though the additional information might be correct and interesting, this will not earn extra marks because the examiners have to mark to strict criteria to make the examination fair.

● If you are asked to describe a study (rather than the core study), it is possible to use a study that you have been taught in lessons.

You must make sure that you know enough details about the study before you start answering as you may not earn all the marks available if you only know basic information about the study. It is worth checking whether there are additional questions about the study you are describing that you can't answer before you start to write.

● When you are asked to describe one of the core studies – don't forget to mention the main points, for example, if you were describing an experiment you would mention the following:
  a) Aim   b) Sample   c) Any controls
  d) Method   e) Any measurements
  f) Results   g) Conclusions.

● Use diagrams or illustrations if they help, but make sure you label them clearly.

1 Biological psychology

The subject of biological psychology looks at the role that biology plays in our behaviour and experience. The questions psychologists ask are often focused on whether our lives are shaped by the way we are made or by the experiences we have.

On a simple level we know that the things we eat and drink, such as coffee or alcohol, will affect the way we see the world and the way we behave. We also know that damage to the brain and nervous system can have an effect on behaviour. The action of chemicals and the structure of the nervous system are the two main themes of biological psychology. However, the questions most frequently asked are how much our biology makes us what we are, and what other factors intervene to affect our behaviour?

Unit B541: The first section looks at the interaction between biology and psychology by considering sex and gender. The core study relating to this issue is an article reporting the long-term follow-up to a case where a little boy had his penis accidentally cut off when he was a baby and was consequently raised as a little girl.

Unit B542: The second section looks at the interaction between experience and biology by considering criminal behaviour. The study at the end of the chapter considers whether genetics or environment have a greater impact on criminality.

Sex and gender

Overview

'Is it a girl or a boy?' is one of the first questions a new parent asks. The answer will affect how the baby is treated and how the child views her/himself. Our society has different expectations of men and women, and the growing child soon learns what they are. But to what extent are these differences due to our biological make-up? This section first considers the biological differences between males and females, and evolutionary change in males and females, and then reviews several explanations for how children come to adopt the attitudes and behaviours that their society considers appropriate to their sex.

Definitions of sex and gender

The words sex and gender are sometimes used as though they mean the same thing, and sometimes as though they have different meanings. They do have different meanings, as explained below.

- Sex refers to the biological aspects of the individual which do not vary. For example, a child's sex is identified at birth by its genitals. Although this might seem like a very simple way of distinguishing between boys and girls, there are a number of people – about 1 in 2,000 – who are born with both types of genitals.
- Gender refers to the psychological and cultural aspects of maleness or femaleness. The term was first used in this way by John Money (see the core study on page 8). It refers to your social roles (what you do) and also your sense of who you are (your identity).

Masculinity: Men are traditionally considered to be masculine if they are strong, bold and fearless – the protector and provider of the family. In the past, men who chose to stay at home and look after children while their wives worked, or those with professions such as ballet dancing, were not considered to be masculine.

Femininity: Women are traditionally considered to be feminine if they are gentle, sensitive and nurturing. Being competitive and aggressive are qualities that would make a woman appear more masculine.

Androgyny: If a person does not appear to be either masculine or feminine in appearance and could be mistaken as either gender, we say they are androgynous. They can also demonstrate both masculine and feminine traits in approximately equal portions.

Gender roles today are very different from those of past generations, and both men and women display characteristics that we could consider as characteristically more masculine or more feminine. This does not mean that society is becoming full of people who are androgynous (or of indeterminate gender). What it suggests is that society has changed and that we no longer criticise people in the same way for taking on different roles. For example, some girls choose typically male-dominated careers, and vice versa. However, they may still be very feminine in their appearance and behaviour. Many people today choose clothes to exaggerate their gender identity. For

▲ Figure 1.1 Billy Elliott

example, men could wear skirts or wear their hair in a bob just as easily as women, but Western society might see that as a little strange and might think that they were trying to look female.

CORE THEORY: biological theory

IN THE EXAM

Candidates should be able to:
- outline the role of chromosomes in typical gender development
- outline the role of gonads and hormone production in typical gender development
- describe basic evolutionary sex differences in human behaviour
- explain the criticisms of the biological theory of gender development.

Biological theory
The role of chromosomes in typical gender development

When an egg is fertilised, the child's sex is determined by the sperm that fertilises the egg. This is because the man's sperm contains one chromosome, which will either be X or Y, whereas the mother's egg always contains the X chromosome. Therefore, if the man's sperm contains the X chromosome, the baby will then have XX, which will be female. If the sperm contains the Y chromosome, the baby will have XY chromosomes, which will be male.

These two chromosomes are needed for the development of the internal and external sex organs. Babies are formed with the *possibility* of being either a girl or a boy, as both have a pair of body parts called gonads.

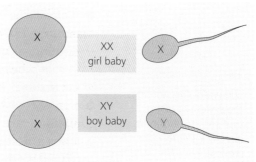

X   XX girl baby   X

X   XY boy baby   Y

▲ Figure 1.2

Further your understanding

Gonads are the underdeveloped reproductive glands (ovaries or testes). Initially the gonads of an embryo are no different in males and females. The 'indifferent' gonads will become testicles if the embryo has a Y chromosome, but if no Y chromosome is present, they will become ovaries.

The role of gonads in typical gender development

If the fertilising sperm contains the X chromosome, the gonads will develop into ovaries. However, if the sperm contains the Y chromosome, the gonads will develop into testes, which start to produce the chemical testosterone – a hormone. It is at this point that the genetic influences on sex cease and hormones take over the biological sex determination.

The role of hormones in typical gender development

Until the seventh week of development in the womb, all babies' genitals (the external sex organs) look the same. After that time, testosterone is responsible for a change in the external sex organs of boys, as a penis and scrotum develop. The ovaries in the female foetus produce oestrogen and progesterone, which lead to the development of the womb and the vagina. In fact, both sexes produce these hormones, but in different quantities.

If the hormone levels are unusual in the womb, this can have a number of repercussions. For example, low levels of testosterone result in the child appearing to have female external genitals at birth, even though the child may have XY chromosomes. Different levels of hormones are also considered to affect the development of the brain of a foetus and recent research suggests that sexual orientation as an adult can be affected by the levels of sex hormones while in the womb.

In order to remain healthy, both males and females produce the hormones testosterone and oestrogen, although in very different quantities. Hormone imbalances in growing children can significantly affect their development. Testosterone is responsible for a number of changes in the bodies of males, including an increase in hair growth, a deepening of the voice, and increased muscle and aggressive behaviour.

The endocrine system is the system of glands that secrete hormones directly into the bloodstream. The testicles, which are part of the endocrine system, secrete testosterone.

- Women who have higher than normal levels of testosterone will become more masculine in their appearance and behaviour. This can be caused by disorders of the endocrine system or it may be due to choice for female bodybuilders, who use anabolic steroids (synthetic versions of the male sex hormone testosterone).
- Men who have low levels of testosterone will experience loss of muscle and lack of strength, low sex drive, tiredness and depression. If their levels of oestrogen increase so that they are higher than normal (remember, both men and women produce both hormones, but in differing quantities), they may even exhibit some female sex characteristics, such as the development of breasts and a reduction in facial hair.

Basic evolutionary sex differences in human behaviour

Biologically, we are programmed to ensure the continuation of our species. We therefore have to reproduce and survive, which means that men and women will have different behaviours to ensure that this is the case.

Evolutionary theorists argue that although we still have the same biological sexual functioning, our mating behaviours have gradually evolved in response to the changes in our environment, which in turn allow us to continue to survive as a species. This adaptation suggests that gender rather than sex is socially constructed.

Human-like creatures have been around for about 2 million years and through most of that time they were foraging and scavenging for food. Around 50,000 years ago people changed their behaviour quite dramatically and quite quickly. They started painting on cave walls, they started to bury their dead and they started to use tools much more creatively. This last point meant they could start to hunt larger animals. To do this efficiently meant they had to travel in groups and this would be difficult with children. A division of labour probably developed for females to move about less and nurture the young, and for males to take on more of the hunting. Men developed superior navigation skills, which would have made them more effective hunters. Women, on the other hand, have a preference for landmarks, which would help them to gather food closer to home and, at the same time, reduce their chances of encountering danger.

In evolutionary terms, even women's better verbal skills would make sense, because while strong men could fight in order to protect their family, women would have to use language as a way of defending themselves – through arguments, persuasion and manipulation.

Women today often look for different things in a husband. It is not essential in Western cultures for men to be physically powerful, as power today can come from money, knowledge and economic status. Women also want men who are nurturing and caring, and who are willing to share the child rearing, as many of women have their own careers. The underlying principle of selection is there, however, and women have been shown to favour men who have the health to father healthy children and the resources to provide for them.

Criticisms of the biological theory of gender development

If our biological sex differences were the only factor responsible for the differences between men and women, our roles would not have changed over the generations and we know that they have.

QUESTION ?

1. What is the biological explanation as to why men are more likely to be sexually promiscuous than women?

By environment we mean not only where and how we live, but also the structure of our society, our lifestyles and so on.

HOMEWORK

Search the internet for 'cross-cultural studies of gender roles' and note the differences in the roles of men and women in three different cultures.

> Learning by observing others is known as social learning theory and is discussed in more detail later in the chapter on page 23.

Males and females behave very differently in different cultures, suggesting that socialisation is responsible for differences in gender development rather than biological differences.

Biological theory does not take into account the fact that children observe the behaviour of others and then copy the way they behave.

If biological differences are all that mattered, why do transvestites (also known as cross-dressers) find that dressing in the clothes of the other gender makes them feel more comfortable? If the issue were purely biological, they would only feel comfortable with gender reassignment surgery, rather than simply dressing as the opposite sex.

CORE THEORY: psychoanalytic theory

Candidates should be able to:

- consider psychoanalytic theory as an alternative theory, with specific reference to the role of the Oedipus/Electra complex in gender development.

Psychoanalytic theory and gender roles

An alternative theory that can be used to explain gender development is the psychoanalytic theory of Sigmund Freud. According to Freud, human behaviour is driven by instinctive biological drives.

One of these drives is called the libido and it is the drive behind our desire for physical pleasure. This pleasure might be something we eat, something we smell or something we touch, for example. One pleasurable aspect of behaviour is sex, so the libido is often described as the sex drive. The way we cope with the libido is what underpins the development of our gender role, and this is influenced by our parents.

Freud proposed the following ideas, suggesting that all these feelings happen in our unconscious mind, so we are not actually aware that they are going on, although they will affect the way we behave. Although the theory might seem quite strange, Freud was trying to explain how a child makes sense of the confusing feelings they experience. One aspect of this development concerns the longing that children have for exclusive close emotional bonds with their parents.

At about 4 years of age, according to Freud, the child's libido creates a desire for the opposite-sex parent. However, the child also fears that the same-sex parent will be very angry when this desire is discovered. This conflict between the child's emotion and their fear fills them with anxiety.

A boy experiences the Oedipus complex because of his desire for his mother and fear that his father will castrate him by cutting off his penis. In order to prevent this from happening and as a way of reducing his

> Freud named the Oedipus complex after the Greek tale about Oedipus, who was the son of the king and queen of Thebes. He was rejected by his parents and raised as a foundling by the king and queen of Corinth. When he grew up he was involved in a fight with a man who was actually his father. Later he married a woman who turned out to be his mother. The name Electra also comes from Greek mythology.

castration anxiety, he begins to adopt his father's behaviours, speech and attitudes. According to Freud, this is how the male gender identity appears.

A girl experiences the Electra complex when she develops unconscious longings for her father. This is because her father has a penis, which represents power, and she too wants a penis (known as penis envy). She believes she has already been castrated by her mother as punishment because she desires her father. Therefore she is not as frightened of her mother as little boys are of their fathers. The girl learns her gender role by identifying with her mother in an attempt to possess her father vicariously.

> When you do something vicariously, it means you seek to experience the event through the actions of someone else. For example, a mother who always wanted to be a ballet dancer but never did, may push her child in that direction and gain pleasure from her child's achievements.

Evaluation of the psychoanalytic explanation

Although psychoanalytic theory has had a huge impact on ideas in the wider world as well as in psychology, it is difficult to gain evidence to support or disprove it. This is because it is very difficult to measure and test our instinctive drives. Another factor is that because our drives and the causes of our anxiety are in the unconscious, we cannot observe or test them.

◀ Figure 1.3

QUESTION ?

2. What happens if a child does not have either a mother or a father? Do you think this will affect the child's gender development?

CORE STUDY: M. Diamond and H.K. Sigmundson (1997)

M. Diamond and H.K. Sigmundson (1997) Sex reassignment at birth: long-term review and clinical implications. Archives of Paediatrics and Adolescent Medicine 151, pp. 298–304

Background

This case study focused on an 8-month-old baby boy who was one of a pair of identical twins born in Canada. During a regular circumcision operation, an accident occurred that resulted in his penis being badly damaged through burning. The parents were not sure what to do and by chance they saw psychologist John Money on the television talking about how boys could be turned into girls. As a result, the parents contacted Money, who advised them to raise John (pseudonym given to him by Money) as a girl, as he believed that gender was determined by upbringing.

At the time John Money had two controversial beliefs:

- that gender was based on upbringing – that is, that by bringing a boy up as a girl, he would be just like a girl
- that in order to have a healthy psychosexual development, it was important for someone's genitals to look normal – that is, as he no longer had a normal-looking penis, if John were raised as a boy, he would not have a normal psychosexual development and might become quite 'disturbed' and wonder what gender he should really be.

Psychosexual development refers to the changes in our bodies, both physically, when we are becoming sexually mature, and mentally, as we begin to think about sex and become aware of our own sexuality.

Diamond and Sigmundson reported the case study of John in their article 'Sex reassignment at birth: long-term review and clinical implications', after they become involved with John and his family. By the time they wrote the article, John (real name: David Reimer) was an adult, living as a man. Diamond was an authority on sexual matters and Sigmundson was the head of the psychiatric management team in the area where John's family lived.

Further your understanding

John's real name was Bruce Reimer (his brother was Brian). John Money named Bruce as John/Joan in his reports. Later Bruce changed his name to David, as he explained that his life had been a struggle like that between David and Goliath in the Bible.

You need to be able to …
- describe Diamond and Sigmundson's case study of the castrated twin boy raised as a girl
- outline the limitations of the study.

For more on case studies, see Chapter 6, page 200.

QUESTION ?

3. People often want to change their appearance to make themselves look different in some way. For example, some women seek to have their breasts enlarged. What reasons could we give to explain why some women may choose to have this operation?

The authors of the article challenged the doctor's beliefs by showing that biology is a better explanation of gender than socialisation alone.

Describe the study

Money reported the case of David Reimer in 1975 and suggested that, following the decision to raise John as a girl, he adjusted well to his life as Joan. The problem was that no one could verify if this was really true, as Money restricted other people's access to John/Joan and his family.

The information gathered by Diamond and Sigmundson came from the following sources:

- a review of the original medical notes and therapists' impressions
- interviews with the adult John, John's wife and his mother.

QUESTION **?**

4. Do you think this 'retrospective' evidence would be accurate?

At the age of 17 months, John had surgery to remove his testes and he became known as Joan, and was then raised as a girl.

Money claimed that Joan adapted well to being a girl, but Sigmundson found that this was far from the truth. Joan struggled with being a little girl throughout his childhood. Between the ages of 9 and 11, he became very upset and unhappy and considered suicide. He had no friends and was teased about his looks and was called a 'caveman' and a 'gorilla', which resulted in him fighting with the girl who called him the name. As a result, he was expelled from school.

▲ Figure 1.4
David Reimer
1965–2004

John/Joan's mother provided the following information:

- Joan was often more boisterous than her twin brother, enjoying rough-and-tumble play. She would get involved in fights.
- She would ignore the girls' toys she was given and would play with her brother's toys, or with gadgets and tools.
- She disliked dresses and would rather dress up in men's clothing.
- She would mimic her father rather than her mother, such as pretending to shave rather than applying lipstick.
- Joan was good-looking, but when she started to move or talk it was obvious that she was a boy.

John provided the following information:

> *There were little things from early on. I began to see how different I felt and was, from what I was supposed to be. But I didn't know what it meant. I thought I was a freak or something …*

> *I looked at myself and said I don't like this type of clothing, I don't like the types of toys I was always being given. I like hanging around with the guys and climbing trees and stuff like that and girls don't like any of that stuff. I looked in the mirror and [saw] my shoulders [were] so wide, I mean there [was] nothing feminine about me. I [was] skinny, but other than that, nothing. But that [was] how I figured it out. [I figured I was a guy] but I didn't want to admit it. I figured I didn't want to wind up opening a can of worms. (quoted in Diamond and Sigmundson 1997, p. 302)*

When John reached puberty (age 12), he was given hormones to help him develop breasts and a more female shape. This made him more unhappy, so he threw away the tablets and refused to wear a bra. His father finally admitted to him that he had been born a boy, and when he was 14 he told his doctor that he had always felt like a boy. From this point, he started to live as a male and was given male hormones; he had his breasts removed and underwent surgery to reconstruct his penis between the ages of 15 and 16.

John had never been interested in boys when living as a girl, but he was interested in girls and had his first sexual relationship when he was 18. At the age of 25 he met and married a woman who was older than him, and adopted her children. He explained that, once he was a male, he felt that his attitudes, behaviour and body were finally 'in harmony'.

Sadly, John took his own life when he was 38 years of age. He had been deeply upset about his unhappy childhood and had suffered from depression. His twin brother had experienced mental health issues through most of his adulthood and also took his own life.

Conclusions

The conclusions we can draw from this case study are that:

- babies are not psychosexually neutral at birth and gender is based more on biology than upbringing; John was raised as a girl but still felt like a boy
- healthy psychosexual development does not depend on the appearance of a person's genitals, but is more dependent on what is known as the gender defined by chromosomes; John's genitals looked like those of a girl, but he still considered himself to be more like a boy.

Limitations

This study was a case study, only investigating the case of one individual. As with all case studies, this individual may not be representative of other individuals, who may have responded very differently, being successfully raised as girls. Perhaps having a twin brother made the situation more difficult for John.

QUESTION ?

5. What do you think John meant by his attitudes, behaviour and body being in harmony?

DISCUSS...

Do you think it is possible that John may have suffered from depression or other mental health issues even if he had not had his penis damaged and been raised as a girl? Perhaps there was a genetic link?

Both Money and Sigmundson had been involved with John, so they may not have been really objective in their descriptions and beliefs about the case. For example, John said he felt unhappy being a girl, but this was not reported by Money, who kept John and his family away from outsiders.

Much of the evidence was retrospective, with the researchers looking back over old information, which may have been misinterpreted or some aspects might have been missing.

Perhaps John's parents' knowledge that he was really a boy had an effect on the way he was brought up; if he had been born a girl, they might have behaved differently. This may have resulted in some of John's confusion.

Applications of research into sex and gender:
equal opportunities for the sexes

Candidates should be able to:

- explain how psychological research relates to equal opportunities for the sexes – for example, sex typing in education, gender roles at work, natural differences in choice of leisure activities.

Equal opportunities for the sexes

In the past, a person's future was often decided by gender, with women generally being considered child-bearers who were less intellectual, and men taking up academic or management roles or roles dependent on greater physical strength. Today both men and women have much greater choices, with many choosing subjects and employment that were not traditionally available, in academic or management roles, or in skilled professions, such as female firefighters and male midwives. In fact, discrimination on the basis of gender is now illegal. However, it seems that we have not yet reached gender equality, and one role for psychologists is to continue to try to understand whether males and females actually have different strengths that could impact on their success in education and their future careers.

Sex typing in education

In past decades, schools frequently channelled girls towards subjects that were thought to be more related to their gender, such as cookery, textiles and childcare. On the other hand, boys were encouraged to take subjects such as science, maths or technological subjects, where they could then take on an apprenticeship in building or mechanics.

HOMEWORK

Use websites such as those of the newspapers the Independent and the Guardian to look for articles comparing the numbers of women and men who are employed in top jobs. Consider executive roles, banking, legal professions and Members of Parliament. Do you think that there is gender equality?

There is some psychological research suggesting that women and men do have different strengths. Boys tend to be better at visual spatial tasks and are less interested in reading and writing in school, while girls are more interested in subjects that involve language. These strengths seem to be reflected in the subjects boys and girls choose to study in school, with more boys going for technical and science subjects, and more girls choosing subjects related to social sciences or the arts (Equal Opportunities Commission 2007). The Department for Education and Science (DfES 2007) reported that this becomes more obvious at A level.

Boys	Girls
Maths	English
Physics	Psychology
Business studies	Art
Geography	Design
Physical education	Sociology
	Media/film/television studies

Table 1.1 Department for Education and Science Statistics (2007) on the most popular A level choices for boys and girls. Data protected by Crown Copyright.

HOMEWORK

Ask your family whether the boys or girls began to speak at an earlier age. Listen to the kinds of conversations mothers have with their sons and daughters and see if you can see any differences.

DISCUSS...

Are there are any other ways that the knowledge of students could be assessed?

There is currently no conclusive evidence to suggest that these choice differences are due to differences in ability alone, so perhaps they are more to do with socialisation. There is some evidence to suggest that girls develop language skills and speak earlier than boys, but this may be because mothers talk more to girls than to boys. Evidence from brain scans has shown that girls' brains work harder than boys' in language tasks and that they rely on different parts of the brain. Perhaps, because the subjects are taught in different ways, boys find the subjects that are less language-based and more practical in nature easier to study, and vice versa.

Although girls are generally doing better in all subjects than boys in both GCSEs and A levels, we cannot be sure that there are really gender differences in ability. It is interesting that in the past, boys achieved the highest academic results. This does not mean that girls are now cleverer than boys, however; it may suggest that in the past, examination and career success were not seen as being important for girls. Today, girls are encouraged to achieve and they may be given the advantage because the means of testing is language-based. Perhaps by developing different ways of assessing knowledge, boys will do as well as girls in examinations.

Gender roles in work

Although girls achieve higher grades than boys at school, the subject choices they make often mean that they do not receive the same financial or social rewards as boys. In fact, women tend to be concentrated in low-paid, gender-stereotyped and often part-time jobs.

Pregnancy and motherhood also impact on women's careers. When a woman takes maternity leave, she might feel less confident on her return to work, as things within the work environment may have changed while she has been away. Research indicates that women not only tend to take responsibility for childcare arrangements, but also try to juggle their career with running the home, and this may affect their desire for, or chances of, promotion at work.

DISCUSS...

What is your view on mothers or fathers working when their children are very young?

Employment	% of women	% of men
Health and social care	79	21
Childcare workers	98	02
Receptionists	95	05
Cleaners	76	24
Senior police officers	10	90
Judiciary	09	91
Directors and chief executives	17	83
Private-sector managers	30	70

DISCUSS...

What is the best way for women to be helped with childcare arrangements?

◀ Table 1.2 Gender bias in paid employment

Source: Equal Opportunities Commission (2006). Data protected by Crown Copyright.

Leisure activities

In these times of work-related stress and high levels of unemployment, psychologists could be employed to find out how we encourage people to take part in a variety of leisure activities. We know that leisure activities for all age groups seem to reflect the same stereotypical gender roles. Girls tend to choose more passive or domestic activities, such as reading, studying, helping around the home, shopping, visiting relatives or taking part in organised activities. Boys, on the other hand, tend to be involved in more active and aggressive pursuits, such as doing hobbies or participating in competitive sports, and seem to prefer unorganised or unsupervised activities.

Data from the National Office of Statistics, surveying people over the age of 16 in 2006/7, indicate that these gender differences continue into adulthood.

Women enjoy shopping more than men. They also prefer activities such as reading, arts and crafts, while men enjoy more physical activities, such as DIY and sport and exercise. Men also enjoy computer games more than women.

With regard to sport, there are again gender-related differences, with women enjoying swimming and working out in the gym. Men also enjoy working out in the gym, but, compared to women, they prefer more outdoor activities.

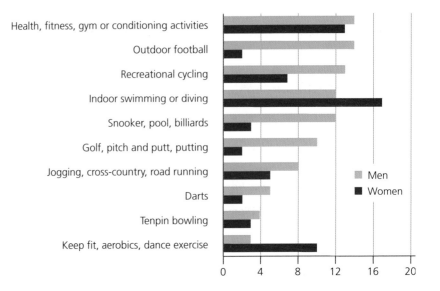

Figure 1.5 Selected sports, games and physical activities among adults, by sex (2006/7, England) ▶

Source: National Statistics website: www.statistics.gov.uk (2008). Crown Copyright material is reproduced with the permission of the Controller of HMSO.

Exam-style question – Biological psychology: Sex and gender

These questions are taken from the OCR B541 Psychology paper, from January 2010. For more past and sample papers plus answer exemplars visit the OCR website. OCR have not seen or commented on the quality of the sample answers.

> **Sons & Daughters**
> *Lucy and Jim are 5 year old twins. Although they have been brought up very similarly, they have quite different relationships with their mother. Lucy is very jealous of her mum. For example, she gets upset with her mum for kissing her dad. Jim is very affectionate towards his mum. For example, he is constantly asking her for cuddles.*

1. Using the source,

    (a) identify an example of the Oedipus complex; [1]

    Jim is very affectionate towards his mum. (1)

    (b) identify an example of the Electra complex. [1]

    Lucy gets upset with her mum for kissing her dad. (1)

2. Identify whether the following statements are true or false.

    A person's sex depends on how masculine or feminine they are. [1]

    TRUE   (FALSE) *(1)*

    Two people can be the same sex but have a different gender. [1]

    (TRUE)   FALSE *(1)*

Androgyny means to have many masculine and feminine traits. [1]

⟨ TRUE ⟩   FALSE *(1)*

3. Outline the **findings** of Diamond & Sigmundson's (1995) case study of the twin boy raised as a girl. [3]

Joan did not feel comfortable with her feminine identity (1) and started living 'as a man' when 'she' discovered 'she' had been born a boy (1) showing that the impact of the environment on gender could not outweigh the effect of biology (1).

The candidate gets three marks here as they provide the main findings of the study and explain them in a way that shows what happened to Joan/John over time.

4. Explain one limitation of Diamond & Sigmundson's study. [3]

Because the case only looked at one boy (1) it is difficult to generalise the findings (1).

This is a three mark question so giving one brief sentence may not be enough to earn all the marks. Here the candidate could have further explained that Joan may have been particularly masculine and not representative of all boys, whereas others may have adapted to their new gender more easily. We could not be sure unless this was tested with further research.

5. Describe the role of hormones in gender development. [4]

The male hormone testosterone (1) is responsible for making males more aggressive than females (1), whereas the female hormone oestrogen (1) is related to feminine behaviours, such as sensitivity and emotionality (1).

The candidate has read the question which asks about hormones (plural) so it is necessary to mention more than one. The answer has identified two hormones and has gone on to focus on the psychological role that these hormones have in gender development. If the candidate had focussed on the physical role alone the examiner might have thought this was a biology exam rather than a psychology exam!

SECTION TOTAL [15]

Criminal behaviour

Overview

Reports of crimes appear in the papers or on television every day. The victims' relatives, the police, criminal psychologists, psychiatrists and members of the legal profession all try to understand the reasons why some people turn to crime. One question they frequently ask is whether people are born criminals or whether their behaviour is the result of their upbringing and experience.

Definitions of crime

Defining crime is not as easy as you may think, but perhaps the best definition is 'behaviour that is prohibited by the criminal code'. Of course, this is not the end of the story, because different societies have different criminal codes. So the definition of a criminal act is affected by the country in which it is committed, the culture and even the era in which it takes place. In order for a behaviour to be considered a criminal act, the person doing it needs to have shown intention – that is, that they meant to carry out that behaviour rather than it simply being an accident – and to have done it voluntarily.

- Country: Some countries will view an act as criminal, whereas in another country, the same act may go unnoticed – for example, in some countries adultery is considered a punishable crime.
- Culture: Some cultures say it is illegal for a man to have more than one wife, but in parts of the USA and in some Muslim countries it is common practice to do this.
- Circumstances: It is a crime to kill another human being, but it may be very different during times of war or if you do it to defend yourself.
- Era: Before 1972, homosexuality was considered a criminal offence, but this is no longer the case, with homosexual couples having the same legal rights as heterosexual couples.
- Age: The age of criminal responsibility varies from country to country, so a child may be convicted of a crime in one country, but be seen as below the age of criminal responsibility in another.

> This section still focuses on biological psychology, but it will be examined in the second examination paper you sit.

KEY CONCEPTS

crime, measures of crime, criminal personality

The OCR examination requires candidates to be able to:

- outline the problems of defining and measuring crime
- explain the concept of a criminal personality.

> The legal definition of crime is 'an act that breaks the law of the land'.

Further your understanding

In the examination, mention that there are a number of definitions of crime. Provide at least one definition and then explain (using examples) why it is so difficult to define.

DISCUSS...

Do children differ in their ability to accept responsibility depending on which country they live in?

QUESTION ?

1. Use the internet to see if you can complete the following table, showing the age of criminal responsibility in different countries.

Country	Age
Scotland	
England, Wales and Northern Ireland	
USA (some states)	
Canada, the Netherlands	
France	
Germany, Austria, Italy, Japan, Russia	
Scandinavian nations	
Spain, Portugal	
Brazil, Peru	

Measures of crime

It is very difficult to measure crime accurately. First of all, we need to agree on what we mean by crime; as we have seen, this varies across countries, cultures and so on. In the UK, our crime statistics come from police records or surveys such as the British Crime Survey, but these cannot provide a completely accurate picture because some crimes are not always reported, such as street robbery or sexual assault. Sometimes people do not realise that they have been the victim of a crime, as they may not have noticed that things have been stolen or damaged.

Is there a criminal personality?

By personality, psychologists generally mean the characteristics that account for relatively consistent patterns of thought and behaviour.

What gives us our personality? Is it inherited or is it the result of our experiences? Most psychologists believe that personality is an interaction between both these elements, with biological inheritance influencing the way that we manage our life chances. If you ask most people, they will probably say that they have broken the law at some point in their life in minor ways, such as littering or breaking the speed limit, but very few people actually commit serious crimes such as robbery or murder.

Some psychologists have suggested that criminals have a different type of personality to non-criminals, which results in unusual thinking patterns and, subsequently, more unusual or antisocial behaviours.

Further your understanding

The British Crime Survey on the Home Office website provides lots of interesting information about crime and criminal acts.

www.homeoffice.gov.uk/
science-research/research-
statistics/crime/crime-
statistics/british-crime-
survey

HOMEWORK

Consider four different criminal activities and how they are viewed by different cultures. Examples might be smoking in public places, littering, theft, homosexuality, drinking alcohol or owning a firearm.

QUESTION ?

2. Why do you think that some people choose not to report crimes?

17

Further your understanding
You can test your own personality online by typing 'personality tests' into a search engine.

Using assessments such as the Eysenck Personality Inventory (EPI), which is a pencil-and-paper test, where participants answer a series of questions that are then scored, it seems that certain personality profiles are associated with crime.

Hans J. Eysenck, who constructed the EPI, held the view that people with certain features of personality (which he believed are inherited) are more likely to become involved in antisocial behaviour if they experience a certain type of upbringing. He concluded that people who score highly on certain traits are more likely to be associated with violent crime.

The conclusion from some psychologists is that there is a type of criminal personality that displays the following characteristics:

- self-centred
- finds it hard to see things from other people's perspective
- has no concept of guilt
- has a poor grasp of reality
- has high levels of aggression and hostility, which may not always be obvious.

It would be really convenient to be able to give someone a personality test and then decide whether they were a criminal or not. However, things are not that easy, and many factors will influence a person's life, including their family and their environment. Most people in their lives do something that is against the law, and some people do it a lot more often than others. The question is whether the people who do it a lot more often are actually a different type of person (a criminal) or just an ordinary person who does criminal things more often. And then there is the question of getting caught. Some people do many things that are classed as criminal but do not get caught and are therefore not classed as criminal, whereas someone else might carry out just one criminal act but get caught and therefore be labelled a criminal. Who is the most criminal out of two such people?

CORE THEORY: biological theory

Candidates should be able to:

- explain the role of heritability in criminal behaviour
- explain the role of brain dysfunction in criminal behaviour
- explain the facial features associated with criminals
- explain the criticisms of the biological theory of criminal behaviour
- consider social learning theory as an alternative theory, with specific reference to vicarious reinforcement of role models in the learning of criminal behaviour.

Biological theory

The role of heritability in criminal behaviour

In the past, researchers looked at the family trees of criminals and, as a result, concluded that criminal tendencies run in families. More recent studies have also shown that a small number of repeat offenders often do come from the same family. Therefore research has tried to identify whether criminality is inherited by passing on a 'criminal gene' from one generation to the next.

Psychologists have investigated whether criminal traits are inherited by looking at pairs of twins. Identical twins share the same genetic material, so if criminality is inherited, both twins should become criminals. This evidence would be stronger if the twins were reared apart, so that both had the same genetic inheritance but different life experiences. There are very few cases of this happening, so research evidence cannot be certain that the findings show a genetic basis for criminal behaviour.

Reginald and Ronnie Kray were probably the most famous criminal twins; they were involved in organised crime in London's East End in the 1950s and 1960s. They had an older brother, Charlie, who was also a convicted criminal. However, they shared life experiences, so we cannot conclude that they carried a 'criminal gene'.

In the absence of research on identical twins reared apart, another way of considering whether criminal behaviour is inherited is to compare children of criminal parents who have been adopted with their criminal biological parents and their non-criminal adoptive parents. The core study at the end of this section by Mednick and colleagues (1984) compares adopted criminals with their biological and adoptive fathers, and concludes that there must be a genetic link as the adopted children are more like their biological parents than their adoptive parents.

> Heritability refers to how much a trait, such as criminality, comes from genetic rather than environmental influences.

> **Further your understanding**
> Look up the story of the Kray twins on the internet.

The role of brain dysfunction in criminal behaviour

Researchers have considered that criminal behaviour may be the result of brain dysfunction, rather than heritability. Brain dysfunction is where the brain is not working properly; this may be due to some kind of brain damage or to an abnormal brain structure.

Brain damage

The brain is made up of a number of different areas, some of which are responsible for controlling the way that we think, act, memorise and problem-solve. From studies of people with brain damage due to accidents, it has been possible to map the functions of these different areas.

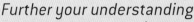

Further your understanding
The case of Phineas Gage (1823–60)

Phineas Gage's case is often used to illustrate how damage to the brain can cause changes in behaviour which may ultimately result in criminal actions.

Phineas, a mild-mannered and considerate man, worked on the railways as a construction foreman. One day he was involved in an accident at work which resulted in a large iron rod entering his cheek, passing behind his left eye and leaving the top of his head. Although he remained conscious and retained his memory, he damaged his prefrontal cortex. After the accident his personality changed from being hardworking and respectful to being impulsive, unpredictable and rude.

Although Phineas never actually committed a criminal act, it helped scientists to clearly understand the serious implications of damage to the brain.

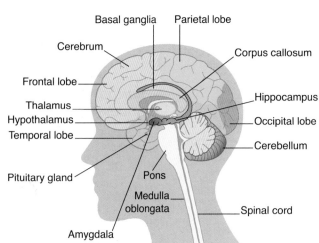

▲ Figure 1.6

Further your understanding

Psychopaths are people who do not seem to have any regard for others, who can be responsible for the most horrific acts but who show very little remorse for their actions. Many of our most famous criminals, such as Fred West, have been identified as psychopaths.

- Frontal lobe: The frontal lobe, also known as the cortex, is the part of the brain that helps us in thinking and planning, decision-making and problem-solving. It also helps us to moderate our social behaviour and suppress any antisocial responses. Damage to the frontal cortex of the brain can affect a person's social behaviour and make them impulsive, aggressive and uncaring. An example of this was the case of Phineas Gage (see Further your understanding).
- Temporal lobe: The temporal lobe contains the language centres and also has a part in memory formation. Psychopaths have shown abnormal brainwave activity in their temporal lobes and limbic systems.
- Limbic system: The limbic system contains a number of primitive brain structures that are related to survival. These structures are involved in many of our emotions and motivations, such as fear, anger and sexual behaviour.
  - The hippocampus is part of the limbic system and is involved in forming new memories. Psychopaths who are caught and convicted are more likely to have an asymmetrical hippocampus (with the right side being larger than the left side).
  - The amygdala is said to be the 'seat of emotion' and has a significant role in our ability to show empathy to others. Professor James Blair of the National Institute of Mental Health compared the activity in the amygdala of psychopaths and non-psychopaths. Blair showed both groups pictures that were emotionally disturbing or shocking. The psychopaths showed no heightened amygdalic activity to the scenes, whereas the non-psychopaths showed a higher level of amygdalic activity.

- Corpus callosum: This is a tract of fibres that forms a bridge between the two halves (or hemispheres) of the brain. One side of the brain specialises in language and logic, and the other in more abstract or creative thought. Murderers have a less active corpus callosum than non-murderers, which may impact on communication between the two hemispheres.

Facial features associated with criminals

In 1876, Italian criminologist Cesare Lombroso suggested that 40 per cent of criminals were 'born criminals' and claimed it was possible to identify them from their skull and facial features. He collected the physical measurements of criminals and non-criminals using specialised tools, and conducted post-mortem examinations, concluding that the physical appearance of criminals is different to that of non-criminals.

Lombroso claimed that criminals had the following physical characteristics:

- a head that was different in size and shape to the heads of those of the same race
- asymmetry of the face
- eye defects or peculiarities
- large jaws and cheekbones
- ears that were either very small or that stood out from the head like the ears of a chimpanzee
- twisted, upturned or flattened nose in thieves
- aquiline or beak-like nose in murderers
- swollen nostrils and a pointed tip to the nose in other criminals
- fleshy, swollen and protruding lips
- cheeks that look like they have pouches in them, like a hamster
- a chin that was either receding, excessively long or short and flat (as in apes)
- abnormal teeth
- lots of wrinkles
- hair that was more like the hair of the opposite sex.

Lombroso also suggested that criminals had excessively long arms. These features, he concluded, suggested that criminals were reverting to a primitive type of man, with physical features similar to those of apes.

Criticisms of the biological theory of criminal behaviour

Biology (nature) versus nurture

It can never be proved that criminal behaviour is inherited because criminal families also share a common environment and life experiences. It may be that these are the causes of crime rather than genetics. There are also many people who have the biological factors that may predispose them to criminal behaviour, but who, nevertheless, never become criminals.

Further your understanding

Brain damage can be caused by tumours rather than trauma. When he was 25 years old, Charles Whitman, a student at the University of Texas, shot and killed 14 people (including his wife and mother), and wounded a further 31. He was only stopped when he was shot by police marksmen. His body was sent for post-mortem, where it was discovered that he had a cancerous tumour in the hypothalamus region of the brain. It was this tumour that had affected Whitman, resulting in his criminal behaviour.

HOMEWORK

Look up Cesare Lombroso's museum of criminal anthropology on the internet.

HARROW COLLEGE
Learning Centre

21

The only way it might be possible to separate nature and nurture is to raise twins from the same family in social isolation and then look at their behaviour as adults. However, most twin studies into criminal behaviour have only a very small sample size because of the problems involved in obtaining access to twins involved in crime.

Criminal genes

There are many different types and levels of crime and this suggests that there may be different genes for different activities – for example, a thieving gene, a murdering gene, a fraudulent gene. Is this likely?

HOMEWORK

Search the internet for genetic disorders, research them and use the following table to consider whether the sufferers look unusual in any way.

Genetic disorder	Symptoms	Appearance (usual/unusual)

Brain abnormalities

No one specific area of the brain has ever been identified as actually causing criminal activity, although we know that certain areas might increase the likelihood that people will become criminals. On the other hand, people with similar brain abnormalities do not go on to become criminals. Even the case of Whitman, who was later found to have a tumour, showed that he may also have been affected by his early childhood experiences, because his father was very tyrannical and did not allow him to play or socialise with other children.

Criminal appearance

Despite the interest in Lombroso's suggestions, there is no evidence to support his theory that criminals look physically different to non-criminals. The criminal sample he used included people with a number of genetic problems. Such genetic problems can cause significant learning difficulties, together with an unusual appearance. Therefore these people may have been involved in criminal activities because of their learning difficulties rather than because they were actually 'born criminals'.

Social learning theory

Social learning theory proposes that we learn by observing other people and imitating their behaviour, which is why it is also called observational learning. We are more likely to imitate someone if the outcome of their behaviour is positive – for example, John threatens to hit Jack unless he gives him his sweets; Jack then hands over his sweets to John. The observer may be more likely to copy that behaviour than if the outcome was negative, where Jack, instead of handing over his sweets, went and told the teacher and John was then excluded from school.

In this instance, by watching John receive a reward for behaving in a certain way (getting the sweets), the result acts as a vicarious reinforcement. Although our observer did not receive the reward directly, simply by watching the positive outcome of John's behaviour may be a good enough reinforcement to make our observer behave in the same way in the future.

> *Vicarious reinforcement is where a person is not directly rewarded for doing something, but sees someone else being rewarded, which in turn increases the likelihood that they will do the same.*

Social learning theory and criminal behaviour

It has been suggested that people could learn criminal behaviour by imitating antisocial or criminal acts. This would be an alternative explanation of why crime runs in families, with children imitating parents, especially if they are seen as being successful criminals. This theory also links to the nurture debate.

In social learning theory, anyone whose behaviour is observed is called a role model. You have probably heard people say, 'He's not a good role model', when talking about someone whose behaviour is unacceptable. Psychological research has shown that the type of people who are most influential as role models for children are those who are:

- similar – such as someone of the same sex, same age, same family or with the same interests as the child
- powerful – such as a relative, teacher, pop star, sports star, cartoon hero or heroine
- caring – such as a parent or teacher
- reinforced – if the child sees that the model's behaviour leads to pleasant consequences (such as gaining approval), they are more likely to copy it.

QUESTION ?

3. Think of three other types of vicarious reinforcement that you have seen which may have influenced your own behaviour.

Further your understanding

Remember, the nurture debate focuses on whether children are influenced more by the environment in which they are brought up than by their biological inheritance (genes).

Bandura's research on aggression

One of the most famous studies which looked at how children learn by observing was carried out by Albert Bandura and his colleagues in 1961. Some children were in the same room as an adult role model hitting and kicking a large inflatable doll (called a 'Bobo doll'). Afterwards the child was allowed to play with a range of toys, including the Bobo doll. Other children saw the adult role models behaving without any aggression.

Observing the children playing later through a one-way mirror, Bandura found that the children who had seen the aggressive role model imitated their aggressive acts towards the Bobo doll, and the boys were generally more aggressive than the girls. However, there were other children who did not copy the adult role model, although they could explain exactly what the adult had done when they were asked, which suggests that children may learn certain behaviours by observing but do not always copy what they have seen.

DISCUSS...

- Why do you think that only certain programmes are broadcast on television after the 'watershed' at 9pm?
- Why do computer games have age ratings on them?
- Why are there age ratings for films shown at the cinema? Do you think these are effective? Have you ever ignored the age rating on a film?

Figure 1.7 ▶ Pictures from the original study by Albert Bandura

CORE STUDY: S.A. Mednick, W.F. Gabrielli and B. Hutchings (1984)

S.A. Mednick, W.F. Gabrielli and B. Hutchings (1984) Genetic influences in criminal convictions: evidence from an adoption cohort. Science 224, pp. 891–4

Further your understanding

This study focuses on the nature/nurture debate.

Is there really a criminal gene (nature) or is criminality to do with the way you are brought up (nurture)?

Background

If criminal behaviour runs in a family, it might be possible to argue that each child has inherited the genes for criminality.

What would happen if the child from the criminal family were adopted and raised by a family of non-criminals?

- If they had inherited the genes for crime, they would still become criminals. This suggests that criminality is due to nature.
- If they did not become criminals, it would be possible to argue that the environment that the rest of the family members shared could explain their criminal behaviour – they probably share a 'culture of crime'. This suggests that criminality is due to nurture.

Describe the study

The aim of this adoption study was to investigate whether people become criminals because of their genes or because of the environment in which they are brought up.

Population

The authors looked at records for adoptions that had taken place in Denmark between 1927 and 1947. They found that almost 14,500 children had been adopted by people who were not their family members. They also looked at court convictions to see if these adoptees had criminal records.

Sample

The authors then reduced the number of adoptees if any of their birth information was missing or if they were adopted by single women. This left a sample of just over 13,000, with slightly more women than men included in that sample (approximately 6,000 men and 7,000 women).

Method

Information on the remaining adoptees' adoptive and biological parents was collected. The data were compiled and put in a table (see Table 1.3).

You need to be able to …

- describe Mednick *et al.*'s adoption study into the genetic basis of criminal behaviour
- outline the limitations of the study.

Look at Chapter 6, page 189 when considering choice of participants for research.

QUESTION ?

4. What other behaviours could be studied by considering whether they are due to nature or to nurture?

QUESTION ?

5. Why was it important that the adopting parents who were chosen for the study were not family members?

Procedure

The authors compared the records of the people who had been adopted

- with the criminal records of their biological parents
- with the criminal records of their adoptive parents.

They did not include the female adoptees in the analysis because they had very low levels of conviction.

Results

On analysing the data, the authors found the following:

- The biological fathers had more convictions for criminal offences than the adoptive fathers.
- The adoptive fathers had a lower level of criminal activity than the population as a whole.
- 72.7 per cent of the adopted sons had criminal convictions.
- 13.5 per cent of the sons of non-convicted biological parents who were adopted by non-convicted adoptive parents received a criminal conviction.
- 14.7 per cent of the sons of convicted adoptive parents and non-convicted biological parents received a criminal conviction.
- 20 per cent of the sons of convicted biological parents and non-convicted adoptive parents received a criminal conviction.
- 24.5 per cent of the sons of convicted biological parents and convicted adoptive parents received a criminal conviction.

	Non-convicted biological parents	Convicted biological parents
Non-convicted adoptive parents	13.5%	20%
Convicted adoptive parents	14.7%	24.5%

The authors were interested in looking at whether siblings who were adopted into different families showed similar levels of criminal conviction, supporting the idea that there is a genetic component to crime.

Relationship between siblings	Concordance rates (how likely they were to both be convicted)
Unrelated (different mother and father)	8.5%
Half-brothers (one different parent)	12.9%
Full brothers (same mother and father)	20%

QUESTION

6. If the authors had used the data on the female adoptees, how would it have affected the results?

DISCUSS...

Perhaps high levels of crime within the family meant that the children had to be taken away from parents and as a result, they were adopted. Perhaps the children had already had some experience of living in a criminal family. Would this have affected the results of the study?

◄ Table 1.3
Comparing the conviction rates of the sons of convicted and non-convicted biological and adoptive parents

◄ Table 1.4
Concordance rates between siblings and convictions

The results suggested that the more closely related the brothers were, the more likely they were to be convicted of a crime.

Authors' observations

The authors recognised that the adoptees were taken from their parents at different times and had different experiences while growing up. They suggested that these differences did not affect their chances of becoming criminals because most of the children were removed from their parents when they were very young:

- 25.3 per cent of the adoptees were placed in an adoptive home straight away
- 74.7 per cent were placed in orphanages (50.6 per cent were adopted in the first year and 12.8 per cent in the second year)
- 11.3 per cent were adopted after the age of 2 years.

Conclusions

A significant correlation was found between the biological parents and their adopted sons for property crimes but not for violent crimes. The more criminal convictions the biological parents had, the more likely they were to have sons who became criminals, even though they were raised with adoptive parents who did not have a record of crime. This provides strong evidence for the likelihood of there being a genetic component to crime that is passed on from parents to their biological children (the link between full siblings and criminal activity also supports this idea).

If there had been no relationship between the convictions of the biological parents and their adoptive sons – that is, their adopted sons did not break the law – this would suggest that the environment in which the biological parents lived must have made them more likely to turn to a life of crime.

Limitations

Participants

The authors only used the data of convicted criminals. Do you think these data were representative of the population as a whole? What about those involved in criminal activities who had not been caught and convicted?

DISCUSS...

Do you think the authors were correct when they said that the children's early experiences would not have affected them in any way? Is this the case for all the adopted children?

Another word for correlation is a relationship between two things. See Chapter 6, page 200.

HOMEWORK

What sort of social or environmental circumstances may make a person turn to crime?

Perhaps some of the adoptive parents had been criminals but had not been caught.

The authors did not include the data from the women in the sample due to their low level of conviction. Perhaps the women had actually got away with crimes – that is, were not convicted – because they were not perceived by the judges to be capable of criminal activities.

How can we be sure that the early experiences of the criminal adoptees did not affect them? After all, a child going into a children's home is going to have very different early experiences to one being adopted straight away.

Ethics

There were no real ethical concerns with this study as the data were historical, although in reality the participants had not given permission for their records to be analysed.

Methodology

The study was retrospective, so none of the participants could be interviewed to check the accuracy of the data.

General

It is difficult to see how a factor for 'being a criminal' can exist because there are so many behaviours that can be judged to be criminal, and some of these are perfectly acceptable in some cultures but not in others. Think about someone who steals money from others – if you are a market trader and you swindle someone out of a few pounds you might well end up in court; on the other hand, recent events have suggested that if you are the head of a major UK bank and you pay yourself hundreds of thousands of pounds while at the same time driving the bank to near-bankruptcy, you will not end up in court, and may receive a large payout to leave your job.

QUESTION ?

7. Retrospective studies are studies that look back on things that have happened in the past. Are these data always accurate? If not, why not?

DISCUSS... 💬

Do you think the authors should have ignored the women's data?

Applications of research into criminal behaviour:
crime reduction

Candidates should be able to:

- explain how psychological research relates to crime reduction – for example, biological perspective on the use of prisons, implications of research for crime prevention, reinforcement and rehabilitation.

Crime reduction

Psychological research has identified that there may be a genetic component to crime, although this cannot be proved without doubt. There are always factors that can influence the way that people behave which may relate to their home environment, their parents, their schooling, their friends, the things that they see around them and the opportunities they have to get involved in crime. It is impossible to control all these things in order to really find out whether someone is a born criminal or not.

DISCUSS...

What happens if we identify crime as being genetic? Should we just lock people in prison for ever?

And what happens if we can identify babies who are born with a 'criminal' gene? What should we do with them?

HOMEWORK

Can you think of a better way to investigate whether someone is a born criminal or not?

Design a piece of research, similar to that of Mednick *et al.*, to investigate whether criminality is inherited. You will need two groups of people who have all been adopted, and you will need to think of all the things you will have to control in order to be able to compare the two groups.

For this piece of 'fantasy' research, you do not have to consider ethics.

Write down the ways that you could control some of the different factors that might affect the children. You could fill in a table like the one below and include anything else that may be important.

	Group 1 (criminal biological parents)	Group 2 (non-criminal biological parents)
Age at adoption		
Age of young person now		
Siblings (living with them or separately)		
Details of birth parents (e.g. together, divorced)		
Details of adoptive parents (e.g. criminals/non-criminals)		
Schooling		
Environment		
Ability		
Any other factors		

Remember, in the real world we must make sure that any research we do is completely ethical.

The biological perspective on the use of prisons

If people are 'born criminals', the only answer would be for them to be locked up for ever, as any sort of rehabilitation would be pointless.

Further your understanding

Broadmoor, Rampton and Ashworth are high-security psychiatric hospitals in England; Carstairs is a similar institution in Scotland. They house the most dangerous patients, most of whom have been convicted of serious crimes or are considered to be too ill to plead. During their stay, prisoners may receive medication, together with additional therapies such as counselling. In the past, institutions like these 'treated' prisoners using surgical interventions called lobotomies. These operations removed the parts of the brain that were thought to be responsible for criminal behaviour.

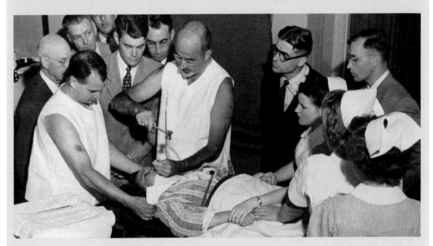

△ Figure 1.8 Prisoner at Vacaville Penitentiary in California being prepared for a lobotomy in 1961. At the time, many psychiatrists believed that 'criminal' behaviour was lodged in certain parts of the brain, and lobotomies were frequently carried out on prisoners

DISCUSS...

Should criminals who are 'mentally ill' be imprisoned with others who have no 'excuse' for their behaviour?

See operant conditioning in Chapter 5, page 153.

Research has shown that some criminals act the way they do because of chemical imbalances in the brain, which results in what we would describe as a 'mental illness'. Perhaps we should consider them to be mentally ill rather than describing them as criminals, and give them medical treatment in a hospital environment rather than a prison.

In Chapter 4 (page 122) we discuss the use of prisons as a way of punishing criminals. The chapter also mentions the fact that there is a high rate of recidivism (reoffending). If criminality is due to biological factors, then prisons are possibly the only way to keep society safe, because rehabilitation will not work. However, psychological research has shown that we can go on learning through our lives, especially when we are given the right rewards. Rehabilitation programmes in prisons aim to help change the behaviour of criminals by re-educating them into a new way of behaving, and rewarding that behaviour as a way of helping them learn.

Implications of psychological research on crime reduction

Psychological research has indicated that most criminality is due to a mixture of both nature (biology) and nurture (social and life experiences). Psychology cannot influence biology directly, but it can influence our understanding and treatment of criminals.

Today the management of convicted criminals uses psychological interventions, which may involve looking at thoughts, feelings and patterns of behaviour using techniques like cognitive behavioural therapy (CBT). Counselling can also help prisoners to cope with any anxiety or trauma that has been the result of early experiences. They also learn life- and work-related skills, the aim being to allow them to be rehabilitated and to return to society without the need to continue criminal activity.

> *See Chapter 5, page 179 for an explanation of CBT.*

Exam-style question – Biological psychology: Criminal behaviour

These questions are taken from the OCR B542 Psychology paper, from January 2011. For more past and sample papers plus answer exemplars visit the OCR website. OCR have not seen or commented on the quality of the sample answers.

1.
> **Criminal Features**
> *Doris witnessed a mugging and so was asked to give a description of the attacker to the police. She said he had large ears, a crooked nose, high cheekbones and a pointed chin. The police officer said that, apart from the pointed chin, she had described a typical criminal.*

Using the source:

Identify **three** facial features associated with criminals. [3]

1. *large ears (1)*
2. *crooked nose (1)*
3. *high cheekbones (1)*

The candidate has noted that the source suggests the pointed chin is not a typical criminal feature.

2. Identify whether the following statements about Mednick *et al*'s (1984) study into criminal behaviour are true or false. [2]

Mednick *et al* studied six generations of one family in their study.

TRUE   ⟨ FALSE ⟩ *(1)*

Mednick *et al* found evidence that criminal behaviour is inherited from families.

TRUE   FALSE   *(1)*

3. Describe the role of brain dysfunction in criminal behaviour.   [3]

The corpus callosum is less active in criminals compared to non-criminals so the two halves of the brain may not communicate as well. (2 marks only)

For full marks the candidate would need to explain the link between the brain dysfunction and specific behaviours. Do you think this answer would be better?

The corpus callosum which is like a bridge between the two halves of the brain (1), *is less active in criminals compared to non-criminals. The two sides of the brain do different things (one side is logical and the other side creative) so if these two sides cannot communicate as well as they should* (1), *this might affect the way the person thinks or behaves and make them more likely to engage in criminal activities* (1).

4. Give **two** criticisms of the biological theory of criminal behaviour.   [2]

Make sure you look at the number of marks each question is worth. You need to remember that if the question asks for two points or two criticisms, you need to make two points. If the question has three marks, this should tell you that you need to elaborate your answer and not just give a very brief one word or short sentence answer.

It is unlikely that there is only one gene that covers the whole range of criminal behaviour (1). *Not all criminals look different from non-criminals* (1).

5.
> **The Case of Katie**
> The police have recently arrested Katie for shoplifting. Katie told the police that she had copied her older sister, Sophie. She said that Sophie had always got away with it. She had also seen Sophie with lots of stolen make-up and clothes.

Using the source:

(a) Name the person who is a role model for criminal behaviour.   [1]

Sophie (1)

(b) Identify **one** way in which criminal behaviour was vicariously reinforced.   [1]

Katie saw Sophie getting lots of make up.(1)

6. Describe **one** way that psychologists suggest that crime could be reduced.   [3]

If criminals are seen to be punished (1) *then this will act as a deterrent to others as they learn vicariously* (1) *that imitating that behaviour will have negative consequences* (1).

Here the candidate has earned three marks by giving a reason, using psychological theory, to explain why custodial sentencing might work.

SECTION TOTAL [15]

2 Cognitive psychology

Cognitive psychology helps us to understand our brains and the internal processes that help us to think, remember and generally interpret the world, rather than looking only at our behaviour and our biology. It is a way of studying the internal 'cogs' in our brain. As it is difficult to see how people's brains work, the only way that cognitive psychologists can try to figure out these processes is by asking people to do different tasks and then to draw conclusions from the results.

Unit B541: The first section focuses on how we take in and store information in our memory. In particular, we will consider how we tend to remember the first and last pieces of information we are given, but often forget the information in the middle.

Unit B542: The second section considers how our brains interpret information that comes through our senses and focuses specifically on information that comes through our eyes. Psychologists have investigated the extent to which visual perception develops as a result of our experiences, or whether most of our visual abilities are innate, and this is a major theme of this section. The study relating to this part of the chapter considers how information stored in our memory can influence our judgement of size.

UNIT B541

Memory

Overview

Without memory we would be unable to do many of the things we take for granted – to use words, to dress ourselves, to recognise a familiar voice, even to recognise our own face in the mirror. Without memory, everything we experience would seem to be experienced for the first time; it would be completely new to us. As well as providing a background to some of the work on memory, the first part of this chapter considers the reasons why we forget and some ideas for helping us to remember, which is particularly useful for students who are about to sit exams!

Information-processing

The information we receive from the outside world enters through our sense receptors, but this information comes in a form that is not easily understood. For example, the sound waves that enter our two ears would mean nothing unless we had learned to interpret what they signify. It is the same with the information that enters our eyes in the form of light waves.

DISCUSS...

We have several senses, including:
- hearing
- seeing
- smelling
- tasting
- touching.

Fill in the following table.

Sense	Sense receptor
Hearing	
Seeing	
Smelling	
Tasting	
Touching	

Other senses include heat, cold, pressure, pain, motion and balance.

In order for the information that enters through our senses to mean anything to us, it has to go through a number of stages, and psychologists have tried to understand how these processes work. In order to do this, they have suggested that the brain could be compared to a computer, which processes the information it receives.

Encoding – putting the information in
Information enters through our senses and is changed (or encoded) so that we can make sense of it. Light waves are converted into images of what we have seen (see the section on perceptual abilities, page 58); sound waves are converted into words or music – for example, the words are converted into meanings or the music into a tune. Once encoded, the information has some kind of meaning and can then be sent on to the next process.

Storage – storing the information
The encoded information is stored as a memory that we may need at some time in the future. This memory contains lots of information – for example, our memory for a word will include what it sounds like, what it looks like and what it means.

Retrieval – getting the information back
We retrieve information when we access it from where it has been stored in our memory. Sometimes we cannot remember the information at all – it is no longer available. At other times, we know we know something but just do not seem to be able to get hold of it from our memory – it does not seem to be accessible to us (see below).

Output – doing something
Once we have retrieved the information from memory, this 'output' may result in us choosing to make some sort of response or take some sort of action, or may even involve working out what we should do next.

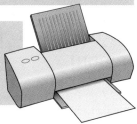

◀ Figure 2.1

QUESTIONS ?

1. Describe what is meant by information-processing.
2. What are the stages of information-processing?
3. Describe what each stage of information-processing means, using the creation of a text document.

Further your understanding

Availability – when we actually forget something, the information is no longer available to us. No matter how hard we try, we just do not seem to have it in our memory any more. An example of this is how we may learn something at school, such as the date of an event in history, and we can remember it for an examination, but at a later time we have no memory of what the date was.

Some psychologists believe that we do not actually forget anything, but simply cannot access the memory any more, while others believe that the memory trace has gone because we no longer need to remember it.

Further your understanding

Accessibility – when we know we know something, but just do not seem to be able to get at the information. Sometimes it is possible to 'hook' the information out of memory by using a retrieval cue.

Have you ever gone to pick up something from another room, but when you get there you cannot remember what it was? Returning to where you started from often enables you to retrieve the information from your memory. Returning to the same context acts as a retrieval cue. (See page 48 for more information on retrieval cues.)

CORE THEORY: multi-store model of memory

Candidates should be able to:

- distinguish between sensory store, short-term memory and long-term memory, with reference to duration and capacity
- describe the processes of attention and rehearsal
- explain how forgetting occurs through decay and displacement
- explain the criticisms of the multi-store model of memory
- consider the levels of processing theory as an alternative theory, with specific reference to the importance of deep processing in memory.

The multi-store model of memory

Have you ever noticed that if you look up a phone number, you can remember it just long enough to dial it and then it seems to disappear from memory. On the other hand, some information will stay with you for ever. Psychologists have identified that we have a short-term memory, where we only manage to store information for a very short time, and a long-term store, where information is stored for long periods, if not for ever. This distinction between different types of memory is the basis of the multi-store model.

The key features of the multi-store model of memory

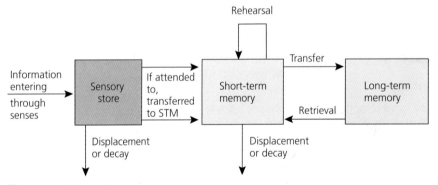

▲ Figure 2.2 The multi-store model of memory

The multi-store model suggests that memory has three different stores, which are separate, and that information can go from one store to the next. Where that information is finally stored will affect how long we can remember it.

Input

Information comes into the senses in the form of words, images, sounds, smells or touches and enters sensory memory.

Sensory store

Sensory information is held as a 'fleeting' memory within the sensory receptors, not at a central location, so there is only a limited capacity. The sensory store also has a very limited duration, lasting for about half a second.

From this information, we select what we want to retain to process further, while all the other information is lost. This process is necessary as we are bombarded with so much information that we would go into a state of overload if we tried to process all that information at the same time. Look around the room that you are in. There are probably many different things to see and hear. If you have to 'process' the information about each one – for example, deciding what it is, what it does, where it came from, what it sounds like or feels like – you would spend far too long doing this and would not achieve anything else.

The information that enters sensory memory must somehow be processed in order to allow us to select what we want to pay attention to, although psychologists are not sure exactly how this happens. What we do is to somehow select the information that is of interest to us, relevant to us or unusual, although we are not aware of this happening. Although sensory memory seems to work outside our consciousness, we can sometimes bring it into conscious awareness. For example, when someone says something to you and you have not really paid attention, you ask them to repeat what they said, but just before they say it again, you remember what it was.

Although we do not know the capacity of sensory memory, we do know that the sensory information we have paid attention to is passed into short-term memory (STM). The remaining unimportant information simply decays and is lost.

Short-term memory

Short-term memory (STM) has a very limited capacity. That means that it can only store a very small amount of information, and new information that enters the STM pushes out (or displaces) information already held. Short-term memory also has a limited duration, which means that it is not stored for very long. However, the information is generally stored for long enough to enable us to use it – for example, retaining a phone number long enough to dial it, although it may be forgotten soon after. It is also the memory store that allows us to have a conversation with another person. You cannot remember the entire content of a conversation, but will be able to remember enough to respond.

Information can be held in STM only for up to 30 seconds; in order to make sure it is maintained there, we need to rehearse it, which means (if it is a word or number) repeating it over and over again or (if it is an image such as a pattern or a human face) constantly looking at it.

If the information is rehearsed for more than 30 seconds, it will be transferred into long-term memory.

Displacement is the process where stored information is displaced by subsequent information. Imagine this process with short-term memory, which has approximately seven 'slots' where information can be stored. If we take in an eighth piece of information, the first piece of information will, in effect, fall out of the memory as there is no more room to store it.

In long-term memory, displacement happens when new information overwrites the original information. This can happen with information we learn at school. When you first learn a subject you might be quite young, so you will be given only very basic information. As you get older you may go through the topic again in more depth, and the new information may overwrite the very basic information you were given as a young child – the original memory will have been displaced.

DISCUSS...

Finding out the capacity of short-term memory

George Miller (1956) originally investigated short-term memory capacity. You can have a go at assessing short-term memory capacity for yourself in class.

Take the following list of digits and read them, line by line, to one of your friends. Read them at a rate of one number per second (no faster). Ask your 'participant' to repeat the numbers back to you once you have finished saying each line. You will find the average range of memory is between 5 and 9 digits (shown in red below).

7										
6	8									
9	3	5								
4	2	1	3							
5	8	7	3	1						
6	2	8	5	9	7					
9	4	3	8	2	6	5				
2	8	6	4	9	5	3	7			
8	6	9	4	6	3	2	4	8		
9	5	7	5	6	3	2	9	4	3	
2	4	7	6	9	5	8	3	6	3	2

When your participant has reached the limit of their memory, try asking them what the first digit was that they were given. They are unlikely to remember the first digit because it will have been displaced by later information.

Chunking: In order to make the capacity of our STM larger, you could try 'chunking' the information. This means putting bits of information together to make a chunk.

The numbers 1 9 4 4 1 9 8 4 1 0 6 6 could be chunked into three pieces of information – 1944, 1984, 1066.

The letters h e r o n e m u g u l l h a w k p i g e o n s w i f t could also be chunked – heron, emu, gull, hawk, pigeon, swift.

If you repeat your experiment, you could try chunking the numbers you read out into twos, as the following example shows:

```
 7
68
93     5
42    13
58    73     1     and so on
```

See if there is a different outcome in the actual number of digits your 'participant' remembers.

Long-term memory

We seem to be able to remember some of the things we learn or experience as we grow up for very long periods, and some of that information stays with us for the whole of our lives. This information will have been transferred to long-term memory (LTM). Information taken into long-term memory is information that is meaningful to us (semantic information), someone's spoken words or music (acoustic information) or visual images (iconic information).

The duration of LTM is not clear, but it may be unlimited. However, part of the information may be lost, it may become distorted or it may be overwritten with updated information. This suggests that our long-term memories are not actually like a video or DVD recorder, where the information that is taken in stays exactly as it was. You have probably realised, when trying to remember something that happens on a regular basis, that you mix up memories of one event with the next. Retrieving information in LTM may be difficult and sometimes we may need to have some sort of cue to help us recover it.

Psychologists believe that long-term memory capacity is unlimited; there has never been a case on record where a person is actually unable to take in any more information, although sometimes it might feel like it, such as when you are revising!

Stages	Sensory memory	Short-term memory (STM)	Long-term memory (LTM)
Encoding	Mainly acoustic (as heard) or iconic (as seen)	Mainly acoustic or iconic	Mainly semantic (by meaning), acoustic or iconic
Storage capacity	Not known	7 (+ or – 2 items)	Unlimited

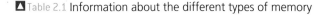 Table 2.1 Information about the different types of memory

QUESTIONS ?
4. Why do we forget things?
5. What can be done to try to prevent forgetting?

Table 2.1 Information about the different types of memory (cont.) ▶

Stages	Sensory memory	Short-term memory (STM)	Long-term memory (LTM)
Storage duration	Iconic – less than 1 second Acoustic – 3 to 4 seconds	Up to 30 seconds	From minutes to years
Retrieval	Only possible immediately; information is retrieved in its original form, but may be incomplete	Only possible immediately; information is retrieved in its original form	Possible at any time; can use links with other material to retrieve; information may be different each time it is retrieved

Criticisms of the multi-store model

The multi-store model gives a simple description of memory processes, but there are a number of criticisms that suggest that it is really too simple to explain how complex our memories are.

The model was created using research that lacked ecological validity

> Ecological validity refers to whether something is valid in the real world rather than just being the product of an experiment. In this case the information we have to remember in our lives is much more varied than simple word lists or numbers.

The model was constructed using research that focused on memory for new facts, such as lists of words or numbers. This is why the model seems to explain how we remember a telephone number until we can dial it, but cannot explain many of our everyday experiences of memory.

We often remember things without using rehearsal. The model suggests that we have to rehearse things in order to transfer them into long-term memory, but it is not the only way. We are often able to recall information that we did not rehearse, such as a smell or the look of something. We may find it difficult to remember something that we have rehearsed really well (like a phone number). You may read this page a number of times but not be able to remember any of it!

STM is just a passive holding place

STM seems to be more complex than just a 'holding' store. We can work on the information in STM, such as doing complicated mental arithmetic problems.

LTM stores different types of information

> **DISCUSS...** 💬
>
> Can you think of examples of any of these different types of memories you have stored in your LTM?

Our LTM stores different types of information, such as information about events (known as episodic memory), different types of general knowledge (semantic memory) and sounds (acoustic memory). It also stores our knowledge of how to do things (procedural memory) and knowledge of what we know we know (declarative memory).

The levels of processing theory

Perhaps the reason why we transfer information from short- to long-term memory is more to do with the amount of processing we apply to the information. If the stimulus has a lot of meaning to us, we will take more notice of it and think about it more than other pieces of information.

The levels of processing theory suggests that the reason why we remember some things better than others is due to this amount of processing. If the information (which could be an event or something we are told) is important to us, interests us and we think about it a great deal, we would be processing it much more deeply than if we simply noticed it and then moved on to something else. The theory suggests that there are different ways in which we process information:

- iconic processing: what something looks like – this is shallow processing
- acoustic processing: what something sounds like – this involves more processing than iconic processing, but not as much as semantic processing
- semantic processing: what something means – the information is processed in greater depth than with the other methods.

> ### Further your understanding
>
> Make sure you are able to explain what is meant by deep processing in memory. It might be helpful to compare shallow and deep processing in order to help you give a clear answer.

HOMEWORK

This activity will help you to understand the levels of processing theory by testing it out for yourself on several participants.

Compose a list of 21 words – for example, house, egg, shoes. Divide the list into three so that you have seven words in each list.

For the first seven words, you should have a question that asks something about what the word looks like – for example, is the word in capital letters or lower case? (this is iconic processing).

For the second seven words, find some words that rhyme and some that do not rhyme, which means the words will have to be processed using acoustic processing.

For the last seven words, you should ask participants something to do with the meaning of the word, which means they will use semantic processing.

Put the words in random order on a sheet similar to the example given below.

Please answer the following questions and then complete the task at the bottom of the page.

1. *Is the word in capital letters?*	*EGG*
2. *Does the word rhyme with spell?*	*Shoes*
3. *Do people live in it?*	*House*
4. *Do we wear them on our feet?*	*Gloves*
5. *Is the word in capital letters?*	*Book*
6. *Does the word rhyme with tree?*	*Knee*

etc.

Please count backwards from 20 to 1.

Now turn over the page for the next instruction.

> On the next page the instruction will be: Please remember as many of the words written in red as you can from the previous page.

At the bottom of the page, as shown in the example above, the participant is told to count backwards from 20 to 1 and then turn over; on the back of the page, they are asked to try to remember as many of the words as they can. The counting task stops them from continuing to rehearse the information, so the words they remember will only be those they have transferred into long-term memory.

When they cannot remember any more, add up the number of words from each category, so that you have the total number of words that were iconically processed, acoustically processed and semantically processed. Did your participants remember more semantically processed words than words from the other two groups?

The levels of processing theory does not differentiate between STM and LTM, but simply suggests that all information goes into a store and that whether it is remembered or forgotten depends on the levels at which we processed it in the first place. However, the only way we can test the theory is by looking at the results of memory tests such as the one above. Unfortunately, we cannot be absolutely certain how we processed the information in the first place, because some of the words may be more important to us than to other people – for example, we may have had an egg for breakfast that morning, or we may be about to move house. Therefore the theory can only remain a theory.

Serial position effect

Laboratory experiments have demonstrated that if people are given a list of words to learn, they tend to remember the first things on the list (primacy effect) and the last things on the list (recency effect), but forget much of what is written in the middle of the list. This happens to us when we are given information – we often remember the first and last things we have been told, but the rest of the information gets lost.

If we gave people a list of 20 words and asked them to try to remember as many as they could, the results would look like those presented in Figure 2.3.

The curve is known as a U-shaped serial position curve. This curve illustrates the primacy and recency effects.

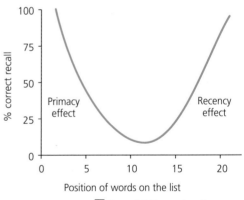
▲ Figure 2.3 Example of a U-shaped serial position curve

- The primacy effect can be explained by participants having longer to rehearse the information before the end of the learning period, which would allow them to transfer the information into LTM.
- The recency effect is explained by the last words in the list remaining in STM.
- The information in the middle of the list would not have had enough rehearsal to transfer it to LTM, but would have been displaced by more information coming into STM due to the limited capacity of STM.

CORE STUDY: W.S. Terry (2005)

W.S. Terry (2005) Serial position effects in recall of television commercials. Journal of General Psychology 32, pp. 151–63

Background

If we are likely to remember the first and last pieces of information we are given, this will have implications for commercial breaks on television. Perhaps viewers are more likely to remember the first advertisements shown and the last ones before the programme starts again, and forget the ones in the middle.

Previous research into the subject had been conducted by asking people about advertisements they had seen in their own homes. This research showed that they remembered more of the first advertisements they had seen (the primacy effect).

The aim of this research was to see if the same results would be found by carrying out a controlled experiment in a laboratory.

> **QUESTIONS** ?
> 6. What is the name of the curve that Terry was investigating?
> 7. What would be the most effective way of getting someone to remember all the items in a list rather than just the first and last items?

Describe the study

Terry conducted three laboratory experiments using independent groups.

Experiment 1 – Recall and then delayed recall test

Participants

Thirty-nine undergraduate college students were tested in small groups in a classroom.

Materials

Terry put together lists of television commercials that were made 10 months before the experiment. There were 60 commercials altogether, divided into four lists.

> *Further your understanding*
> Terry chose commercials that were 10 months old so that they were not too familiar to the students.

> You need to be able to …
> • describe Terry's experiment on the serial position effect in recall of TV commercials
> • outline the limitations of Terry's study.

> *Field studies versus controlled experiments: see Chapter 6, page 195 for an explanation of the strengths and weaknesses of these methods of investigation.*

> *Independent groups: see Chapter 6, page 189 for a description of independent groups.*

Procedure

The students were told that the study was to test their memory for brand names immediately after they had been shown the adverts. They watched half the adverts and were then asked to remember as many of them as they could in any order (free recall). Then they saw the rest of the adverts. Before they were asked to remember the rest of the commercials, they were asked to do another task which involved writing. This is known as a distractor task and was used to delay recall.

Further your understanding

When psychologists ask people to remember information in any order, this is a technique called free recall. Psychologists also use recognition, which involves trying to identify something we have seen before from a larger array.

QUESTION ?

8. According to the multi-store model, where would we store information that is:
- immediately recalled?
- delayed in recall?

Results

Terry found that when students had to recall the adverts immediately, more items were remembered from the beginning and the end of the sequence, which supports the idea of primacy and recency effects.
He also found that:

- more adverts were remembered from the end of the list with immediate recall
- more adverts were remembered from the beginning of the list when recall was delayed.

Experiment 2 – Recall test

Participants

A different group of 27 students were tested in small groups.

Materials

A comedy programme with three commercial breaks was used.

Procedure

Students watched the programme with the commercial breaks and were then asked to remember the commercials they had seen.

Results

The adverts seen at the beginning of each break were the ones most often remembered (primacy effect).

Experiment 3 – Recognition test

The author wondered if the students might remember the brand names from the commercials if he showed them a list of products once they had seen the commercials, because he thought they may have remembered the commercial but not be able to remember the product name.

Materials

A television programme with three commercial breaks was used.

Participants

Another group of 23 students took part.

Procedure

The students watched the television programme and were then shown a list of products and asked if they recognised any of the products they had seen advertised.

Results

The students remembered more of the products from the first commercials they saw in each commercial break (primacy effect).

HOMEWORK

What were the differences in the three experiments? Fill in the table below to help you.

	Materials	Participants	What kind of recall (immediate/ delayed etc.)	Results	Were the commercials stored in LTM or STM?
Experiment 1					
Experiment 2					
Experiment 3					

Why did Terry use these three different designs in his investigation?

Discussion

The results of these three experiments show that, in general, the commercials from the beginning of the lists were the ones most often remembered. He used these three different designs to see if the effect was the same, by presenting the commercials in different ways and using a disruptive (distractor) task.

An explanation for these results would be that the students were able to transfer the commercials they had seen at the beginning of each group into their long-term memory by using rehearsal. They would not have been able to rehearse the ones shown in the middle of each group as more commercials were being shown and they had to pay attention to the new ones, resulting in them forgetting the middle commercials. However, the last ones shown remained in the participants' STM so they were able to recall them. We must remember that the capacity for STM is quite small, which may explain why they were unable to remember many of the commercials seen at the end of the group.

Not surprisingly, Terry found that the students remembered more of the commercials from the end of the list with immediate recall, but fewer when recall was delayed by doing another task.

They were also more able to remember more from the beginning of the list when STM was disrupted by the distractor task, probably because information stored in STM would have been displaced by the new information from the task (because STM has a very limited capacity to store information).

Conclusions

The results of these laboratory experiments support the findings of previous research that was conducted in a more naturalistic way. They also suggest that advertisers need to try to get their advertisements placed at the beginning or end of the commercial break rather than in the middle, and, if possible, to have them placed at the beginning for the best likelihood that people will remember the content of the commercial.

Limitations

Laboratory experiments

Laboratory experiments on memory are usually not ecologically valid because the results found in a laboratory are not necessarily the same results you would find in real life. Terry did try to make parts of the study as lifelike as possible – for example, he showed the commercials during the screening of television programmes, which is where you would expect to see them in real life.

Participants

The participants were not necessarily representative of the population as a whole, the sample was quite small and there were not equal numbers of males and females.

DISCUSS... 💬

Working on your own or with a small group, plan a piece of research investigating which commercials in a group you manage to remember.

Things to consider:

- Who are you going to test?
- How are you going to gather commercials? Can you record them onto a computer, video or DVD, or access them from sites such as www. visit4info.com?
- How many commercials will you use?
- Are you going to use recognition or recall when finding out which commercials are most remembered?

Materials

Perhaps a greater number of the commercials appealed to one gender rather than another, but the author does not explain whether he took this into consideration. For example, if some of the adverts were for cosmetics, perhaps the females would be more likely to be interested than the males.

Demand characteristics

The students may have been affected by demand characteristics. They may have been more motivated to remember than other people because they were studying at the time and may have been taking part in these studies as part of their course. Perhaps they would have wanted to help Terry by really trying to do as he asked. On the other hand, perhaps they did not take the research seriously.

Ethical considerations

Although the participants were not asked to give informed consent, the researchers were asking participants to do something they commonly do – watch television, and to watch regular programmes and advertisements. Therefore, for this particular study there were no serious ethical concerns. The low level of secrecy about the hypothesis was unlikely to create any harm or distress.

Applications of research into memory:
memory aids

Candidates should be able to:

- explain how psychological research relates to memory aids – for example, use of cues and retrieval failure, use of imagery and meaning, mind-mapping and organisation.

DISCUSS...

Do you think students should be tested using recognition or recall in examinations?

What method is used in GCSE psychology?

Improving memory

When trying to remember stored information, we have to bring it back into our conscious awareness. Sometimes information can be easily remembered, but at other times we seem to struggle to recall it. This difficulty with accessing information that we know is called a retrieval failure. The information is 'there', but we just cannot seem to get at it! Psychological research has helped us to understand the way that we take in information and has identified ways that we can improve our memory, which is obviously very helpful in preparing for examinations.

DISCUSS...

Work with a friend and try to think of all the mnemonics you have learned to help you remember things. Go to www.fun-with-words. com/mnemonics.html for more examples.

Further your understanding

How many times have you gone upstairs to get something and forgotten what you went to get? The only way you can remember is to come back down again and go to the same place where you were when you first decided to go and get the object in order to try to remember what it was.

QUESTION

9. Describe the three levels of processing we use to take in information according to Craik and Lockhart.

Use of cues

Cues are like hooks that can help us retrieve information. For example, if you cannot remember the name of an object, the person you are with might give you the first letter of the word you have forgotten, which will act as a cue to help you remember. We often use this technique to remember things like the colours of the rainbow (red, orange, yellow, green, blue, indigo and violet) by remembering a mnemonic phrase such as 'Richard Of York Gave Battle In Vain'.

The reason cues work is because when we learn something, we do not just take in the information on its own, we also store other associated information, such as the situation we were in, the time of day, the associated sounds and smells. These kinds of cues are called context-dependent cues – the cue will be the context in which you first experienced the information, and by reinstating that context you will be able to remember the information.

Some evidence to support the idea of context-dependent learning came from Godden and Baddeley (1975), who asked participants to learn a list of words either on land or 20 feet under water. The participants who had learned the words under water recalled more when under water, and those who had learned on land recalled more when on land. Try imagining yourself back in the classroom if you cannot remember something in your examinations, because the context may act as a retrieval cue.

Use of imagery

Research has shown that we remember information better if we can also form an image of it. Some examples of the use of imagery to help recall are explored below.

The method of loci uses a familiar place or location to help you remember. If you have gone shopping but have forgotten your shopping list, in order to try to remember what is on the list, you could walk round your kitchen in your mind's eye and imagine each cupboard in turn, picturing what is in each one. Memorising the location of the objects would help you to remember what you have forgotten.

Another way to use imagery is by linking an image with a word. When learning a new language you could create an image that sounds like the new word. Figure 2.4 shows some examples you could use when learning French.

Use of meaning

Craik and Lockhart (1972) indicated that processing information for meaning is the deepest form of encoding. Therefore, when you process information for meaning, you are more likely to store that information. (Remember the activity on page 41 of this chapter.)

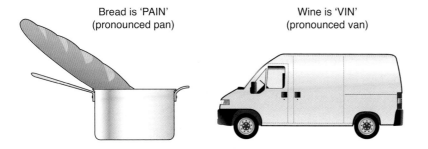

Bread is 'PAIN'
(pronounced pan)

Wine is 'VIN'
(pronounced van)

Organisation in memory

Information is remembered better if it is organised in a logical or structured way. In order to organise the information, you have to think about it and this means that you will be processing the information for meaning, which, in turn, means that you are more likely to remember it. This method also means that you are making links between parts of the information, and these links can act as cues to help you remember.

Below are two examples of organisational techniques.

Hierarchical organisation

This involves starting with a general category, which is then divided into several sub-categories, which are in turn subdivided into more specific information.

HOMEWORK

Look at Chapter 6, page 184, which provides details of a piece of research you can carry out, looking at how effective hierarchical organisation is to help us to remember a list of words.

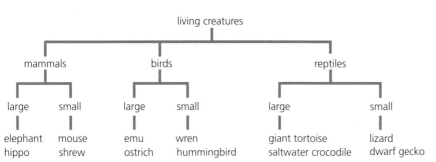

◀ Figure 2.5 Example of a hierarchical structure

Mind-mapping

Mind maps are a kind of diagram that is used to represent information, starting from a central key word or idea. The ideas branch from the centre and are linked together in a tree structure, with the central ideas leading to more and more minor concepts. They involve pictures and colour, and are therefore a helpful tool to support learning, especially for people who find it easier to remember visual rather than spoken information.

1. Start in the centre of a blank page (turned lengthways) so the map can develop in all directions.
2. Use a word or a picture for the central idea. The central idea is usually represented with an image or picture in order to trigger the imagination.

HOMEWORK

Try to draw mind maps for each of the topics you have covered so far in this course.

Search the internet for examples of mind maps by typing 'mind maps' in to your search engine and then selecting 'Images'

3. Use colours to make the map more interesting to look at.
4. The main branches are connected to the central image, and the second- and third-level branches are connected to the first and second levels and so on, giving the mind map a kind of hierarchical structure.
5. The branches should be curved rather than straight, because curved lines are more interesting to the brain.
6. There should be only one key word per line.
7. The map should include lots of pictures because they often convey more meaning than words.

Exam-style question – Cognitive psychology: Memory

These questions are taken from the OCR B541 Psychology paper, from June 2010. For more past and sample papers plus answer exemplars visit the OCR website. OCR have not seen or commented on the quality of the sample answers.

1. Complete the diagram below to show the stages of information processing in memory. [2]

| Input | → | Encoding | → | *Storage* | → | *Retrieval* | → | Output | *(2)* |

2. Explain the difference between accessibility and availability problems in memory. [3]

Accessibility problems in memory mean you have stored something but can't retrieve the information (1). Availability problems in memory mean that you actually don't have that information stored any more and that the memory trace has gone (1). Both result in a person forgetting, but one is permanent if the data is unavailable the other may be temporary if the data is inaccessible (1).

This candidate will get full marks because they have described both, and explained that they both result in forgetting.

3. Terry (2005) investigated students' recall of TV commercials in a laboratory experiment. Outline **one** limitation of the **procedure** used by Terry. [2]

People don't normally watch TV commercials under controlled conditions like the ones in the study (1), so this limits the ecological validity (1).

These limitations are well explained and show the examiner that the candidate understands the points they are making.

4. Outline the **findings** of Terry's study. [3]

All three experiments showed that the commercials shown at the beginning of the experiment were the ones most often remembered.

The first experiment with no distractor task, showed that the student participants remembered the commercials from the beginning and end of the lists rather than the ones in the middle. They had stored some information in LTM and the last commercials they saw were stored in STM.

The other two experiments showed that the students remembered most of the commercials from the beginning of the lists (stored in LTM) if there was some kind of distractor task to disrupt their storage of information in short term memory. (3)

This is a good answer which not only gives the findings but also explains to the examiner why this happens.

5. Describe and evaluate the multi-store model of memory. [10]

The question says describe AND evaluate so that means 5 marks each. You can't get 10 marks for a description, no matter how good it is! It might help to use the headings 'Describe' and 'Evaluate' to remind you.

Describe:

Information enters the sensory memory from our senses and then if we pay attention to it, it is transferred to STM. If we don't pay attention to it, it will either be displaced by other information coming in through the senses or it will decay. Once it is in the STM we have to rehearse it which means repeating it over and over again for it to go into LTM. STM only lasts for about 30 seconds and if we don't rehearse the information, it will be lost because the capacity of STM memory is small (between 5 and 9 pieces of information). We can increase our STM.

If we want to get the information back we have to retrieve it from LTM. LTM has unlimited capacity but we may forget things that we don't use over time or they might get distorted or overwritten. (5)

Evaluate:

The model is very simple and our memory seems to be much more complicated.

This model was put together by doing research on things like remembering lists of words or numbers and not real life memories so it is not ecologically valid (valid in the real world). It doesn't seem to explain how we can remember things that are visual and it doesn't explain that we often remember things without rehearsing them. It does not explain how we can rehearse how something looks. We can rehearse something lots of times but still not be able to remember it.

STM is not just a place for storing information for a short time because we can often do things like mental arithmetic by using our short term memory.

LTM stores lots of different types of information such as sounds and smells and general knowledge and events and this model doesn't explain how all these different types of information are stored. (5)

This is a good clear answer. A diagram might help explain the way memory works but will only get marks if it adds extra information to the answer. The candidate did not need to write about increasing the STM because that was not part of the question. This answer is clear enough to get the candidate full marks. They have described and then evaluated and the evaluation illustrates the weakness of the model.

SECTION TOTAL [20]

Perception

Overview

When we take in any sort of sensory information, whether it is through our eyes, ears, fingertips, nose or mouth, it is necessary for us to process and identify what it is – to perceive it.

Most people will agree that our most important sense is the sense of sight. In fact, vision is the strongest of our senses, and research has shown that we will be more influenced by the things we see than the things we hear, smell, taste and touch. Cognitive psychologists have taken a great deal of time to try to understand how we see and interpret the things around us and whether these abilities are innate or learned.

KEY CONCEPTS

sensation, perception, depth cues

The OCR examination requires candidates to be able to:

- describe the difference between sensation and perception using shape constancy, colour constancy and visual illusions
- explain depth cues, including linear perspective, height in plane, relative size, superimposition and texture gradient.

Sensation and perception

Any sensory input, such as light waves into the eyes, pressure on the skin, chemicals in the mouth, gases inhaled into the nose or sound waves picked up by the ears are all sensations. However, we need to interpret these sensations into something meaningful and this is the process of perception.

To consider how amazing the process of perception is, consider what happens when we look at something. The light rays enter the pupils of each eye, but because light travels in straight lines, the light crosses over as it passes through the lens in our eyes, projecting the image on to the back of the eye (see Figure 2.6). Not only is the image small, blurred and upside down, but as we have two eyes, there are two images and yet we only see one image.

From this crude sensory input, we actually see one clear, three-dimensional coloured image, which is the right way up. This process of turning these crude images into something that is interpreted and then understood is called visual perception, which is the subject of this part of the chapter.

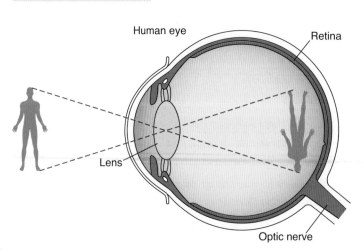

Human eye · Retina · Lens · Optic nerve

◀ Figure 2.6 Images are inverted on their way to the retina at the back of the eye

Further your understanding

The sensory information for vision comes from the light waves that strike the retina. These are changed into electrical signals that are transmitted to the brain. We then make sense of this information. The brain is also able to fill in any gaps in our sensation in order to make an object appear whole.

HOMEWORK

Try making a pinhole camera, which works in the same way as your eyes.

You will need:

- a shoebox with lid
- a sheet of black sugar paper or a roll of tinfoil
- a sheet of tracing paper or a piece of greaseproof paper
- adhesive tape and scissors
- a needle or drawing pin.

Cut two holes at either end of the shoebox as follows: trace round a cup at one end of the shoebox and cut out the circle. Cut a rectangle about 8 x 12cm at the other end.

Now cut out a square of sugar paper or tinfoil, making sure it is bigger than the circle you cut in the box. Tape this to the inside of the box to cover the hole. Using your needle or drawing pin, make a small hole in the centre of this paper/foil.

Cut out a piece of tracing paper or greaseproof paper so it is larger than the rectangle you have cut out at the other end of the box. Tape this to the inside of the box so it covers the hole. This will work as the screen.

Now tape the lid to the box, making sure that the lid fits securely; your pinhole camera is ready to use.

Point the tinfoil end of the camera towards the window or a light and look at the screen. You should see an upside-down, back-to-front image. You can make the image clearer by putting a blanket over you and the back of the camera.

DISCUSS...

Look at a wall in front of you and, while looking at it, wave your hand from side to side in front of your face. You are still able to see the wall, even though the image on your retina changes from wall to hand to wall to hand. The brain fills in the missing information that has been disrupted by the moving hand.

Similarly, are you aware that the image you are focusing on is actually being disrupted on a regular basis by your blinking?

Visual constancies

As we move about in our world, and as the objects we look at move about, the sensory information we receive is constantly changing, but what we see does not appear to change. The following are examples of visual constancies.

Shape constancy

One example of the power of the brain to interpret information is demonstrated by shape constancy. When you look at a door, the shape of the door changes as it opens, yet we do not see it as changing shape, simply as changing position (see Figure 2.7). This is because we have stored in our memories lots of information about doors. We know that they are solid and that they do not actually change shape or size, even when they are open.

QUESTION

1. Think of another object that has 'shape constancy'. Try to illustrate your answer by drawing the object from different positions.

Figure 2.7 **The different images that fall on the retina as we see a door open** ▶

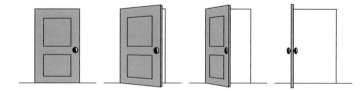

Colour constancy

The redness of a tomato seems the same whether we see it in bright sunshine or deep shade; this is an example of colour constancy. We actually judge colour by comparing an object with the intensity of the colours surrounding it, often making allowances for the difference in light. We also know what the colour should be, so we perceive the tomato's colour as red, regardless of its actual appearance.

The images in Figure 2.8 show a bowl of fruit photographed in three different lights: artificial light, hazy daylight and clear blue sky. The colours vary according to the light, but if we look at the pictures, one at a time, we see the correct colour for each fruit. The contrast is only obvious when we see all three together.

  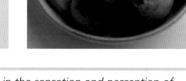

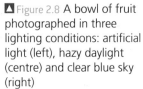 Figure 2.8 A bowl of fruit photographed in three lighting conditions: artificial light (left), hazy daylight (centre) and clear blue sky (right)

The following table shows the difference in the sensation and perception of shape and colour constancies.

▼ Table 2.2

	Sensation	**Perception**
Shape constancy	Different retinal images	Seen as a consistent shape
Colour constancy	Different wavelengths of light entering the eye	Seen as the same colour no matter how much light is available

Visual illusions

In visual illusions our perception seems to play tricks on us, because of the way our brains misinterpret the information that the eyes receive. There is a kind of mismatch between the sensation and what we perceive, so that what we perceive is not necessarily what we see.

> ### Further your understanding
> There are many different types of visual illusions. If you type 'visual illusions' into a search engine, you will find lots of examples.

> *Visual illusions can often be explained by understanding how we interpret different depth cues (see page 56).*

The following are examples of some of the more well-known visual illusions.

Geometric illusions

1. The Ponzo illusion: The image on the retina is of two horizontal lines of equal length, yet we perceive the higher line as longer than the lower one.
2. The Necker cube: The image on the retina is a two-dimensional line drawing, but we perceive a three-dimensional cube. Which is the front: the shaded area or the unshaded area? It appears to jump from one position to the next.

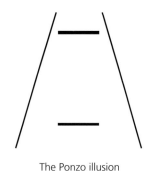
The Ponzo illusion

▲ Figure 2.9
The Ponzo illusion

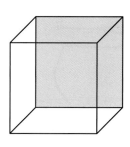
The Necker cube

▲ Figure 2.10
The Necker cube

Fictitions

Illusions such as the Kaniza triangle suggest that something is there that is not actually there. The brain tries to interpret the white shape as a whole object.

Impossible objects

How many shelves are present in Figure 2.12? Here we use our knowledge of what shelves are like to interpret the picture.

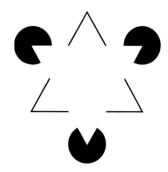

▲ Figure 2.11
The Kaniza triangle

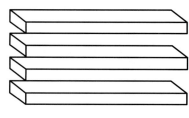

▲ Figure 2.12

▲ Figure 2.13 **The Hermann grid**

▲ Figure 2.14 **The duck rabbit**

Figure 2.15 **In both the illustration and the photograph, the parallel lines appear to converge as they recede into the distance** ▶

Moving illusions

The Hermann grid appears to have black dots appearing where the white lines cross each other. This is because of the overactivity of the receptive cells on the retina.

Ambiguous figures

The illusion in Figure 2.14 could be either a duck or a rabbit. If you are more interested in ducks, you may see the duck first. If you like rabbits, then that will be the first thing you see. Motivation and interest are the major factors influencing the first thing we see in an ambiguous figure.

Depth cues

The image that falls on the retina is a flat, two-dimensional image, so how can we see the world in three dimensions? How do we perceive depth? The answer is that we have to invent it ourselves. Our brains do this by combining the information we see and the information we have stored in our memories to convert the two-dimensional images into an image with depth – a three-dimensional image – but as we have seen with visual illusions, occasionally we can get it a little wrong!

Depth cues are available in our environment and we learn what they mean. Therefore we use them to help us interpret how near or far different objects are from us. The following are some of the depth cues we use.

Linear perspective

When we look at train tracks that we know are parallel, they appear to converge as they stretch into the distance. We use this linear perspective as a depth cue whenever we see parallel lines.

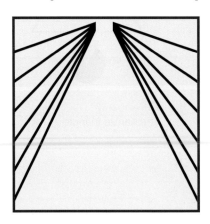

Height in the plane

The closer to the horizon an object is, the greater the distance from the viewer. The elephant in Figure 2.16 is seen as being further away from us than the antelope, as the elephant is nearer the horizon.

Relative size

Our brains interpret larger objects as being closer and smaller objects as being further away. A good example is given in Figure 2.17. We know humans are approximately the same size, so in the first image we interpret the woman on the right as being further down the corridor, as the retinal image is smaller. However, we do not actually see her as being the size of a gnome. Our brains compensate for distance by increasing the perceived size of an object. It is only when you put the two images side by side that you can see how much the brain has compensated for distance.

▲ Figure 2.16

Superimposition

Because we know that an object near to us will block our view of an object behind it, we automatically decide that the hidden object is further away.

Texture gradient

Imagine you are looking at pebbles on a beach. You can see the ones near you clearly and they look quite bumpy and uneven. The further away you look, the smoother they seem, until they appear to blend together in an even texture.

▲ Figure 2.17

QUESTION ?

2. How many depth cues can you see in Figure 2.18, and what are they?

▲ Figure 2.18

Constructivist theory

The constructivist theory is about constructing meanings from what we already know. We have to use our brains to do this, so this theory is known as a top-down theory of processing. You can always remember this by thinking that our brains are at the top of our heads.

The constructivist theory of perception suggests that the images that fall on the back of the retina alone are meaningless, so we have to use our past experience and knowledge to do our best to interpret the retinal information and construct some kind of meaning from what we have seen. As a result, the experiences we have had and the knowledge we have gained will affect the way we interpret what we see.

This theory highlights the importance of nurture in our perceptual abilities. This theory is known as a top-down theory of processing. What this means is that we use stored information in order to help us understand what we see. Without this stored information we would find processing very difficult.

Perceptual set

Further your understanding

Some of the visual illusions can be explained by top-down processing – for example, the Ponzo illusion works because we think of parallel lines converging in the distance (linear perspective) and we compensate for the relative size of the horizontal lines.

When we see or experience something, we will store information about that event for future use. So the next time we experience something familiar, we will expect it to be the same as the last experience and are therefore likely to jump to the same conclusion. However, this process – known as perceptual set – is not a conscious process and at times can be incorrect.

Context

The two rows of images in Figure 2.19 will affect how you see the last image, so that in the first row, it looks like a man with glasses, and in the second row it looks like a mouse. The previous information has affected how you perceive the last item.

Motivation

Your motivation will also affect your perception of an object. If you are trying to avoid someone in a silver Volkswagen Golf, you suddenly realise just how many silver Volkswagen Golfs there are on the road. In fact, every third car seems to be a silver Volkswagen Golf!

Figure 2.19

Expectation

This is when you expect to see something and this influences what you actually see. Take, for example, the illustration of a face mask in Figure 2.20. If you see it from the outside it is obviously convex (projecting outwards). If you rotate it very slowly so you are looking at the inside of the mask, the concave inside will suddenly seem to 'spring out', so it looks convex again. This is because we know that faces are convex, not concave, so we perceive the image as it should be seen and not as it actually is.

▲ Figure 2.20 Different images of the rotating face mask

Psychologists have been interested in how people from different cultures and different environments see the world, because if they see things differently, it would suggest that the way they interpret things (such as visual illusions) is related to their experiences. Evidence from a number of studies has shown that people from non-Western cultures are not taken in by geometric visual illusions in the same way as people from Western cultures, probably because they do not live in an environment that is full of straight lines and 90-degree corners. This supports the constructivist theory that we learn these skills. However, there is some evidence to suggest that some of these skills are innate.

Further your understanding

If you type 'rotating face mask' into a search engine, you will be able to see the mask moving to get the full effect of this illusion. You could also look at www.richardgregory.org

HOMEWORK

If you have already searched for visual illusions on the internet, see if you can explain why they work using your new-found knowledge.

It is worth remembering a few examples as a way of illustrating your answer in the examination.

Innate skills are skills we are born with rather than things we have learned.

HOMEWORK

Look up the 'visual cliff experiment' on the internet to see the apparatus used to test whether babies are able to perceive depth.

Criticisms of the constructivist theory of perception

Depth perception

There is evidence to suggest that people from various cultures see some things in the same way – for example, even very young babies can see depth and are frightened of falling (shown by measuring their increased heart rate), and babies who have just started crawling will not crawl over an imaginary cliff. This shows that we are born with skills to perceive depth that are not dependent on learning.

Facial preference

Newborn babies will choose to look at faces over other objects. It has been suggested that this is an innate skill that exists to help them to bond with their caregiver, rather than something they learn as they grow up.

Visual illusions

We know about visual illusions, yet we keep being taken in by their appearance. This is especially well demonstrated by Figure 2.17 (page 57).

Nativist theory

Nativist theory provides an alternative explanation of our perceptual skills. This theory suggests that we are born with all our perceptual skills, which are ready to be used and do not have to rely on experience. We have already seen, by the criticisms of the constructivist theory, that babies are born with certain innate abilities, such as perceiving depth or preferring to look at a human face, and both these abilities serve a purpose – to help the baby to survive in the world.

The nativist theory also suggests that there is enough information in the objects we are looking at to allow us to interpret and identify them without needing any additional information, so the theory is known as a bottom-up theory of perception because it is data-driven – that is, it depends wholly on the external information that we experience through our senses and does not rely on stored knowledge or information coming from the brain to help us to interpret it.

The theory of direct perception was developed during the Second World War by J.J. Gibson, who was responsible for preparing training films for pilots in order to show them the difficulties they would face when landing an aeroplane. He identified what he called optic flow patterns, which he said were good examples of information from the environment that were readily available to us without us needing to process them in any way.

If you watch a film that gives you the impression that you are a passenger in a spaceship, travelling fast through space with the stars whizzing by either side of you, this was what Gibson meant by optic flow patterns. He explained that the place you are aiming for (which he called the pole) appears to be stationary, while everything else seems to be moving away from that point. The further away things are from the pole, the faster they seem to be moving. That is why the stars that are going past you become blurred into a streak the nearer they get. Gibson explained that these optic flow patterns provide information for pilots when they are judging direction, speed and altitude when coming in to land. It is the kind of sensory information that is available to us from birth and therefore does not need any sort of top-down processing for it to make sense.

It would seem likely that perception is really a mixture of both top-down and bottom-up processing. We use the information coming to us directly from the environment and also use our stored knowledge to inform us what to do or whether we should moderate our response. It does seem that we can process visual information really quickly without any obvious conscious awareness, which suggests that it may not always take place. However, because the brain is so amazing, it is likely that top-down processing does take place, but we are just unaware of it, and because of this, it is impossible to separate the two types of processing.

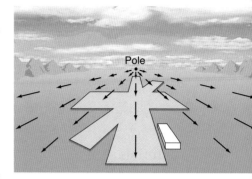

△ Figure 2.21 a and b These illustrations show the optic flow patterns available to pilots when they are coming in to land

CORE STUDY: R.N. Haber and C.A. Levin (2001)

R.N. Haber and C.A. Levin (2001) The independence of size perception and distance perception. Perception and Psychophysics 63(7), pp. 1140–52

Background

Previous research into perception focused on distance (how far away an object is from the observer), rather than a person's ability to judge the size of an object.

The authors were interested in finding out whether people use stored information (top-down processing) as a way of helping them to work out how big something is, and how this can help them work out how far away it is.

The aim of the study was to consider whether it is necessary for people to have stored knowledge of an object when making accurate judgements about the size of an object and how far away it is from them, or whether they are just good at estimating size and distance, regardless of the object.

> You need to be able to ... ✓
>
> - describe Haber and Levin's experiment into depth perception and familiarity of objects
> - outline the limitations of the study.

Describe the study

Haber and Levin conducted two laboratory experiments.

Experiment 1 – Sorting objects into different categories

Participants

One hundred and nine male undergraduate college students took part in the research as part of their course.

Materials

A questionnaire listing a number of familiar objects.

Procedure

At the end of a lesson, the students were asked to complete a questionnaire that asked them to rate the size of a list of familiar objects to the nearest inch. They later returned the questionnaire.

> This links to the work of Hudson on page 57, where our knowledge of the size of an elephant helps us to understand that it is further away.

Results

The results allowed Haber and Levin to categorise the objects on the list into objects that were a standard size and objects that could vary in size.

Conclusions

Because the students could not see the objects, they must have recalled the size of the objects from stored information from memory. This suggests that they used top-down processing.

▼ Table 2.3

Examples of objects that do not vary in size	Examples of objects that can vary in size
Baseball bat	Christmas tree
Basketball	Globe
Milk bottle	Teddy bear
Guitar	Table lamp

QUESTION ?

3. If the students had actually seen the objects when they were asked to estimate their size, rather than remembering from memory, what sort of processing would they have used (top-down or bottom-up)?
4. Write a brief description of the differences between top-down and bottom-up processing.
5. Give an example of a top-down process.

Experiment 2 – Do you have to have specific knowledge of an object to accurately estimate size and distance?

Participants

Nine male college students who all had normal eyesight.

Materials

A total of 45 objects divided into the following groups:

● 15 objects that may vary in size – for example, Christmas tree and teddy bear (Group A)

● 15 cardboard cut-out shapes (ovals, triangles and rectangles) painted different colours on hidden stands (Group B)

● 15 objects that do not vary in size – for example, milk bottle and baseball bat (Group C).

A large grassy field was divided into four quadrants, as shown in Figure 2.22. A, B and C contained different types of objects.

Procedure

Participants arrived at the field in a van and were divided into groups of three. One group at a time walked to the viewing position facing each area in turn. They had been given a checklist of all the objects in the field. As they looked at each area, they wrote down on the checklist their estimates of the height of each of the objects and how far away they were from them. They then returned to the van.

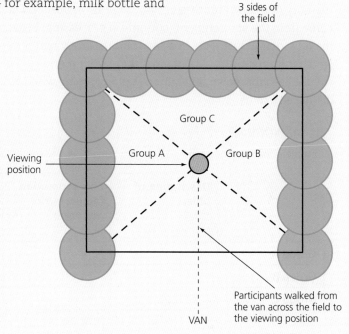

▲ Figure 2.22 How the field was laid out in four quadrants for the study

Results

Size:

● For the variable objects in Group A, the participants still made reasonably accurate estimates of size.

● For the cardboard objects in Group B, the participants were also reasonably accurate in estimating the sizes of the shapes, which surprised the authors, as they had not seen the shapes before, so had no stored knowledge to help them to estimate their size.

● For the more regular-sized objects in Group C, the participants estimated the sizes of the objects accurately and their estimations were quite similar (suggesting that they used stored knowledge to help them).

Distance:

● The participants were very accurate in estimating the distance they were from all the objects.

● The participants were more likely to underestimate distance if the object was of variable size or shape.

> *This is a repeated measures design because all the students completed each of the three parts of the experiment. See page 188 for more information.*

QUESTION ?

6. What sort of cues do you think the participants used to estimate the distance the objects were from them?

Conclusions

Haber and Levin could not explain how the participants accurately judged the size of the unfamiliar objects. They also concluded that they judged the sizes of the familiar objects accurately by using information stored in memory (top-down processing), but their estimates of distance must have come from the environment (bottom-up processing) because they were making their judgements in a situation that they had never been in before, so the information could not have come from memory. This suggests that we use both top-down and bottom-up processing when looking at size and distance from us.

HOMEWORK

Complete the following table to help you remember the results of the experiment.

	Description of object	Size estimation (accurate/not accurate)	Distance estimation (accurate/not accurate)	What kind of processing was used?
Group A				
Group B				
Group C				

Limitations

- The participants for both experiments were male students. There was an extremely small sample of students in the second experiment and we need to consider whether we can generalise the results from these students to the population as a whole.
- When the students were in the field looking at the objects, it is possible that they had a quick look at the other quadrants and the authors may have been unaware of this.
- Did the study have ecological validity? Was it true to life? After all, how many times do you go into a field to estimate the size of objects and how far away they are? Your answer may be occasionally, but is that also true for people who live in a city?
- Ethical concerns could be raised as the students were not given a free choice as to whether they wanted to take part (see the section on ethics in Chapter 6, page 192). They did not give informed consent and they were not debriefed. In fact, there are a number of ethical issues raised by this study.
- The students were asked to complete the questionnaires asking them to rate the sizes of objects and how familiar they were as part of a college course. Did the students take the process seriously?

HOMEWORK

Think of a list of as many objects as you can that do not vary in size and ask your family to guess how tall they are. Did their size estimations vary a great deal?

> ### Applications of research into perception:
> *advertising*
>
> Candidates should be able to:
> * explain how psychological research relates to advertising – for example, use of context in perceptual set, use of motivation in perceptual set, subliminal advertising and levels of perception.

Advertising

Retailers spend a tremendous amount of money on advertising each year. In order to make it effective, designers have to make the adverts as impressive as possible if they are to have any sort of impact on the public. For this reason, the advertiser will need to consider the following points.

* Stimulus magnitude: the larger the advert, the more likely it is to be noticed.
* Stimulus intensity: the more intense the advert is, the more likely it is to be noticed – for example, bright colours or loud noises.
* Stimulus changes: if the advert contains flashing lights or lots of different noises, it is more attention-grabbing than something that is monotonous.
* Stimulus repetition: if you see an advertisement regularly, this will affect your perceptual set or predisposition to notice it over other similar items. Therefore you will be more likely to notice the well-advertised brand of chocolate bar before you notice the others in a shop.
* Context: is the advertisement in the right context? If you are advertising wetsuits, it would not be very effective to put your advertisement in the foyer of a football stadium; a better location might be in the foyer of a hotel next to a beach.
* Motivation: are the people watching the advertisement likely to be motivated to look at it or ignore it? You may have noticed that a number of advertisers use the word 'SEX' to attract people's attention. When they come to read the small print, the text usually goes along the lines of, 'Now I have your attention, have you considered ...' Another technique is to advertise cool drinks on very hot days, or food at the end of a very long journey with no refreshments.

> **DISCUSS...**
>
> Make a list of some familiar advertisements. Think about how many of the listed criteria these advertisements meet – for example, have the advertisers made the advertisements large or used bright colours?

Subliminal advertising

Subliminal advertising is where we receive a very small piece of information that we may not be consciously aware of, but that might influence us to buy something. The first case of subliminal advertising occurred when two very short phrases, such as 'Hungry? Eat popcorn' and 'Drink Coca-Cola' were flashed for 1/3000th of a second during a film in the 1950s. As a result, sales of popcorn and Coca-Cola increased, although the audience did not realise they had seen the messages. The increase in sales may not have been completely due to the subliminal messages, however, as the film contained scenes of eating and drinking, which may also have affected the audience.

Choosing whether to view an advertisement or not is our free choice, but because we do not know about subliminal messages, we are deceived into watching them, which is unethical. As a result, the UK government has banned the use of subliminal advertising. The US government took longer to make that decision, finally banning it in 1992.

Exam-style question – Cognitive psychology: Perception

These questions are taken from the OCR B542 Psychology paper, from January 2011. For more past and sample papers plus answer exemplars visit the OCR website. OCR have not seen or commented on the quality of the sample answers.

1. There are a number of constancies in perception. Look at the following diagram. Draw a line between the two boxes to match the type of constancy to its example. [2]

CONSTANCY   **EXAMPLE**

colour constancy

shape constancy

Kim knows that the coin is always circular even though it looks different as she turns it between her fingers.

Rambir knows that the animals in the distance are not as small as they appear to be.

Jake knows that his shirt is still white even though it appears blue when he dances under the disco lights.

2. Look at the following picture.

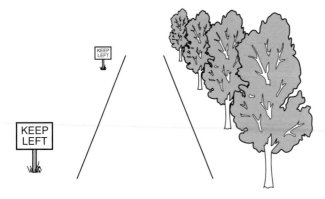

Explain how **two** depth cues have been used in the picture. [4]

The sign that is further away appears to be smaller – this is known as relative size. (2)
The trees that are nearer are overlapping the trees that are further away – this is known
as superimposition where we judge the nearer object to hide the objects that are further away
from us. (2)

The candidate has named both cues and explained how each of them apply to the stimulus picture
(2 marks for each cue).

3. Describe how top-down processing is different from bottom-up processing in perception. [4]

Top-down processing is when perception is based on what we expect to see rather than what's
actually there (1). Bottom-up processing is based on what enters the eyes in the first place (1).
Top-down processing is affected by what we know and is associated with the constructivist
theory (1) whereas bottom-up processing is supported by the nativist theory (1).

You can earn 1 mark each for a brief description of top-down and bottom-up processing. As the question
is a 4-mark question, you will need to elaborate a bit further on each to earn the 2 extra marks – you can
do this by identifying further differences between them. Any study of perception would be acceptable, for
example, cross cultural studies, as long as you feel you are able to provide a detailed enough answer.

4. Describe and evaluate **one** study into perception. [10]

Description:

Haber and Levin were interested in finding out if it was necessary for people to have stored
knowledge of objects in order to make accurate judgements about their size and how far away
the object was, or whether they could do it without stored knowledge. First of all they asked
students as part of their course, to estimate the size of a list of objects and then split the lists into
two - objects that had a standard size and objects that varied in size (using a questionnaire).
Haber and Levin concluded that the students must have remembered the size of the objects they
had seen in the past (using top-down processing) as they couldn't see the objects. In the second
part of the study, they put three lots of objects into a field which had been divided up.

The results showed that all the participants were able to accurately estimate the size of the objects,
even for the objects they had not seen before which Haber and Levin found hard to explain.

The objects were either variable-sized objects or objects that had a standard size (decided from
the first part of the study). There were also a group of cardboard cut out shapes (ovals, triangles
and rectangles) painted different colours. Nine students in groups of three, had to look at each of
the areas of the field in turn (not being allowed to look at the other parts of the field) and
estimate the size of the objects and the distance away they were on a questionnaire (this was a
repeated measures design because everyone did everything). The participants were very accurate
in estimating the distance they were from all the objects but were more likely to think objects
were nearer to them (underestimate distance) if the object was of variable size or a shape.

Haber and Levin concluded that people use top-down and bottom-up processing in estimating size and distance as they had never been in that situation before and therefore couldn't have stored information about how far objects were away from them. (5)

Evaluation:

The participants were all male students and were a small sample so were not representative of the population as a whole.

Perhaps the participants didn't take the study seriously as they were asked to take part as part of their college course. This might have affected the results.

The students may have looked at each other's estimates or have looked around the field at the other objects which may have affected their answers.

The students were not asked to give informed consent and were not debriefed so this broke ethical guidelines although they would not have been traumatised by the study. The study was not ecologically valid because this was not a real life situation. (5)

This answer would have gained the full 10 marks.

The study was well described including the method, the variables measured, the variables controlled, the design and the apparatus (for 5 marks), although a diagram could have been used, and there were five valid evaluations made (for the remaining 5 marks).

SECTION TOTAL [20]

3 Developmental psychology

Developmental psychology is the study of the changes we go through as humans from birth to maturity. Developmental psychologists consider the way thoughts, feelings and behaviours change during that time and how many of these changes are influenced by biology (nature) and by the child's experiences (nurture).

Unit B541: The first section in this chapter looks at the attachment that develops between a parent and a child, and considers Bowlby's theory that mothers and babies have an instinctive need for each other. The section also considers whether there is another explanation to the attachment relationship that forms between mother and baby, and what happens when that relationship goes wrong. The focus of the core study for this section is whether the kind of relationship a child has with its mother will influence the types of relationship it will have as an adult.

Unit B542: The second section looks at the development of cognition in children, focusing on Piaget's theory about how children's thinking develops. This section also considers Vygotsky's theory as an alternative explanation for the development of cognitive skills. The core study for this section is Piaget's experiment into the conservation of number.

Attachment

Overview

> *An attachment is a deep and enduring connection or bond formed between a child and their caregiver in the first years of the child's life.*

Unlike most animals, a newborn baby is utterly dependent on others for its survival for a long time. It needs others to provide food, warmth and protection. The baby will use innate behaviours, such as crying, making eye contact, reaching and grasping, all of which work as a means to influence carers to provide what it needs. Attachments or bonds between the baby and the carer form from these interactions.

For the first 3 months of life, most babies respond equally to anyone. After this they start to respond more to the people who are familiar to them. At this point a baby may wave its arms or smile when it sees its father's face and show little reaction to a stranger, but it will not mind being picked up by either. The baby continues to respond more to familiar people until it is about 6 or 7 months of age, when it will begin to show a special preference or attachment to certain people and distress when that person leaves.

Psychologists consider that infants have formed an attachment when they show two particular behaviours:

1. Separation protest – if the infant gets really upset and cries or calls out when its mother or caregiver leaves the room and tries to go after them, it is because that person is their security. If the infant has not formed an attachment they will not show any sign of distress.
2. Stranger anxiety – once the infant is about 6 or 7 months of age, if it is held by a stranger or a person it does not know well, the infant will do its best to get away from the stranger and go back to its attachment figure for security. If the child has not formed an attachment, it will not try to move away from the stranger and will show no distress at the stranger's presence.

▲ Figure 3.1

KEY CONCEPTS

The OCR examination requires candidates to be able to:

- describe separation protest and stranger anxiety as measures of attachment
- distinguish between different types of attachment – secure, insecure-avoidant, insecure-ambivalent.

QUESTION **?**

1. Fill in the following table for a securely attached child:

Age of child	Response to separation	Response to a stranger
2 months		
5 months		
7 months		

The security of attachments

Children need to feel confident that their caregiver will be able to meet their needs, both for food and for emotional security and warmth. As a way of assessing the type of attachments formed, an American psychologist called Mary Ainsworth developed a procedure called the 'strange situation'. This procedure involved controlled observations through a one-way mirror, through which observers watched the behaviour of children aged between 12 and 18 months when mothers and strangers came into and left the room. Ainsworth concluded that the type of attachment children showed could be classed into three different categories, secure, insecurely attached (avoidant) and insecurely attached (ambivalent).

HOMEWORK

List the kinds of behaviours you would expect to see in a securely attached child during each stage of the strange situation.

Further your understanding
Strange situation procedure

1. Parent and infant are on their own in the experimental room. Infant explores the room.
2. Stranger enters, and the parent leaves them alone.
3. Parent returns and stranger leaves quietly.
4. Parent leaves so infant is left alone.
5. Stranger re-enters and tries to interact with the child.
6. Parent enters, greets and picks up infant, and stranger leaves quietly.

The observers looked for the following:

- Did the child play with the toys or explore?
- How did the child respond to the parent leaving?
- How anxious was the child when it was on its own with the stranger?
- How did the child behave when the parent returned?

Type 'strange situation' into YouTube to watch the procedure.

Type of attachment	% of children	Attachment behaviours
Securely attached	70	Happy when mother present, distressed by her absence, went to her quickly when she returned; a stranger provided little comfort
Insecurely attached insecure-avoidant	15	Avoided the mother, indifferent to her presence or absence; greatest distress when child alone; a stranger could comfort just as well as the mother
Insecurely attached insecure-ambivalent	15	Seemed unsure of mother, more anxious about mother's presence, distressed by her absence, would go to her quickly when she returned, then struggle to get away; also resisted strangers

▲ Table 3.1 The results of Ainsworth's American research

Different types of attachment

Secure attachment (approximately 70 per cent of children)

- Securely attached children use their caregiver as a secure base and can explore because they feel confident that the caregiver is still around if they need her/him.
- This is because the caregiver has always been sensitive and responsive to the child's emotional needs and demands.
- The child feels loved and lovable, confident and competent.

Insecure-avoidant attachment (approximately 15 per cent of children)

- When a caregiver is aloof and cold and ignores or rejects the child's emotional needs and demands.
- The child becomes self-reliant in order not to upset the caregiver or provoke rejection.
- The child may appear to be really good, excessively helpful and compliant, which is a strategy they will use to protect themselves from rejection and to achieve some proximity to the caregiver.
- The child learns to avoid displaying feelings or asking for comfort, although inside they will feel angry and anxious and will doubt whether they are lovable.

Insecure-ambivalent attachment (approximately 15 per cent of children)

- When a caregiver responds inconsistently to the child's emotional needs and demands, the child will never know where they are with the caregiver. Sometimes the caregiver will be really loving and at other times cold and rejecting. Because of this, the child will love the caregiver one minute and hate them the next.

Further your understanding

Secure children are secure in the knowledge that they are loved.

Further your understanding

These children avoid being dependent. Instead they become self-reliant.

- In response to the caregiver's unpredictable availability, the child learns that a way of getting attention is to make frequent emotional demands, such as having tantrums or behaving badly.
- The child feels needy and anxious about how lovable they are, but they also feel angry with the caregiver, so will resist comfort when it is offered.

Ainsworth's study was carried out in the USA, but research using the same method has shown that the figures for the different types of attachment are very similar in the UK. Other cultures have different patterns of attachment and vary slightly in the proportions of attachment types, although research in Western Europe, Africa, China and Japan found the number of securely attached children are very similar to the American research.

Interestingly, a study conducted in northern Germany in 1985 found that at the time, a third of children were securely attached, a third were insecure-avoidant and a third were insecure-ambivalent. This may have been because independence was highly valued by northern German parents. A second study in southern Germany found the attachment classifications from this sample to be very similar to American studies. This shows how the values of a culture at certain times can influence parenting styles.

> ## Further your understanding
>
> These children are ambivalent, which means they have both positive and negative feelings towards the caregiver at the same time.

> *Ainsworth has been criticised for classifying children's attachments according to the child's responses to the mother in the strange situation. Perhaps these children had a different type of attachment to the father or grandmother.*

CORE THEORY: Bowlby's theory   IN THE EXAM

Candidates should be able to:
- explain the concept of monotropy
- explain the concept of a critical period in attachment
- describe the effects of attachment, deprivation and privation
- explain the criticisms of Bowlby's theory of attachment
- consider behaviourist theory as an alternative theory, with specific reference to reinforcement in attachment as opposed to instinct.

Bowlby's theory of attachment

John Bowlby's theory of attachment is one of the most well-known theories and still influences the work of many psychologists today. Bowlby worked as a psychoanalyst from the 1940s to the 1980s and his theory of attachment was based on his work. Mary Ainsworth was a student of John Bowlby, so it is not surprising that many of Ainsworth's ideas were similar to those of Bowlby. When Bowlby first started to work, mothers were the primary caregivers to most children, so he focused on mothers when talking about attachments.

Bowlby believed that attachments were instinctive and had a biological purpose, which was to make sure the baby survived and developed. He

HOMEWORK

Look up the following on the internet or in a psychology textbook:

- The work of Konrad Lorenz and his research with young geese, and how he identified a critical period for attachment.
- The work of Harry Harlow and his research with Rhesus monkeys, showing that young monkeys need a soft and cuddly figure to attach to, rather than one that simply provides food.

was influenced by the work of biologists such as Lorenz and Harlow, who realised the importance of a mother animal for the survival and well-being of their offspring.

Bowlby believed that the infant and the mother were biologically programmed to form an attachment. Babies cry, cling, make eye contact, smile and recognise human faces and sounds, and the mother is programmed to respond to these behaviours. This results in the formation of a mutual attachment or bond, and both the infant and the mother feel anxious if they are apart.

By 6 to 8 months of age, the child shows separation anxiety and stranger fear (as we saw in Ainsworth's research), which shows its special attachment to the mother; this is known as monotropy. Bowlby initially suggested that this attachment to the mother was the child's one main attachment and was different in quality from all other relationships, although he later suggested that the main attachment figure does not have to be the biological mother.

- *Attachment – a special relationship or bond with a significant person.*
- *Monotropy – the special attachment a child has with its mother or primary caregiver.*
- *Critical period – from 6 months to 3 years of age, when an infant is biologically programmed to form an attachment with its mother or primary caregiver, so needs to be exposed to that experience for the attachment to happen.*

Other critical periods exist during children's development. These are also limited periods, usually early in life, in which a child is required to be exposed to a particular skill or experience in order for it to be learned.

Bowlby believed that there was a critical period for attachments to form that was biologically programmed, during which time the baby can most easily form an attachment. This period was between about 6 months and 3 years of age. Bowlby argued that if an attachment had not formed during this time, the child would find it difficult to form attachments. He also suggested that if the child did not form an attachment, or if it was damaged in some way in the first 5 years of life (for example, by illness or the absence of mother figure), the child would have long-term and irreversible problems in their emotional and social development.

If a child has formed an attachment relationship with its mother or caregiver and this relationship is broken in the first few years of life, the child experiences maternal deprivation. This break in relationship may be due to illness, death or divorce. Children who experience maternal deprivation suffer from the loss of their secure attachment figure and may end up becoming withdrawn and insecure or angry and unhappy. Research has suggested that children who experience maternal deprivation in childhood are more likely to suffer with depression in adulthood.

The mother provides security and a safe base from which the child can explore their world. This unique relationship acts as a role model for all future relationships.

Bowlby said that attachment is as essential for the child's psychological well-being as food is for its physical well-being.

Mother/ caregiver relationship	Feelings about mother	Love experience	Self-worth	Feelings about others	Future relationships
My mother is attentive and there for me whenever I need her	My mother is reliable and trustworthy and this makes me feel safe	I know what it is like to receive unconditional love (good role model), so will be able to show it to others	I must be a worthwhile person and others will therefore trust and value me	I will trust and value other people because they are generally good	The relationships I have will be equal, as I will value other people and they will value me
My mother is not always there and I cannot depend on her	My mother is unreliable, although I still have a bond with her, but she does not make me feel safe	I do not know what it is like to have unconditional love or how to give it in return (to partner or children)	There must be something wrong with me and therefore others may not value or trust me	I will not value or trust others because they are all probably totally unreliable and inconsistent	The relationships I have with others may well end up being a power struggle as I cannot risk being vulnerable again

 Table 3.2 The kind of impact early relationships with a primary caregiver can have on future relationships

Some evidence for Bowlby's maternal deprivation theory came from his research with a group of 44 juvenile thieves and a control group who had emotional difficulties but had not been convicted of any crime. His results showed that more than half the thieves had been separated from their mothers for longer than 6 months during their first 5 years of life. He also found that several of the young thieves showed what he called affectionless psychopathy, which meant that they were not able to care about or feel affection for others. He concluded that the reason for the antisocial behaviour in the juvenile thieves was due to having been deprived of their mothers' love.

If a child never experiences the opportunity to form any sort of bond or attachment, this is when privation occurs. This may be because the child has a series of different carers, or perhaps family difficulties or neglect can stop the child from developing an attachment to anyone.

Research indicates that the effects of privation can be extreme and long-lasting. Children who have never formed an attachment to anyone experience difficulties such as poor language skills, behaviour problems and emotional difficulties, and may also grow very slowly. They frequently have great difficulty forming relationships with others through the course of their lives.

There have been a few case studies of children who have experienced extreme privation, being locked up by their carers, often deprived of food, light and exercise, as well as the company of other humans. For example,

QUESTIONS ?

2. Explain the difference between deprivation and privation.
3. Which has the more serious long-term consequences: privation or deprivation?

in the mid-1980s, the West became aware of the number of orphanages in areas of Eastern Europe such as Romania, where children were kept in horrific conditions.

Monica McDaid, a British teacher, explained her experience when she came across a Romanian orphanage in Siret: 'One thing I particularly remember was the basement. There were kids there who hadn't seen natural light for years. I remember when they were brought out for the first time. Most of them were clinging to the wall, putting their hands up to shield their eyes from the light' (BBC website 2005). How could children like these ever come to terms with their early experiences?

Many of these orphans were taken away from their surroundings and adopted in the USA and the UK. In a follow-up study 10 years later, Michael Rutter found that many of the children had not caught up and were still very affected by their experience. He wrote, 'Contrary to popular opinion at the time, we found there were definite long-term effects from being in an institution' (Rutter 2005).

Criticisms of Bowlby's theory of attachment

In spite of the fact that Bowlby's theory has generated a great deal of discussion and further research, there are a number of criticisms.

Relationships

It has been argued that children with a poor attachment to their mother always have poor relationships with others. In fact, some children form very good, strong relationships with other adults or peers, even though the relationship with their primary caregiver has been a difficult one.

Biological need

Bowlby suggested that children and their mothers have an instinctive biological need for each other, which does not take into account the nature of the relationship between them. If the mother is cold and unresponsive, the child will not form an attachment with the mother, which suggests that it is the nature of the relationship that is the key to attachment forming, rather than instinct.

Monotropy

Bowlby theorised about the special relationship between a child and the caregiver at a time when children were raised by mothers, as few mothers worked. Today things are very different, and children form a number of really strong relationships, not only with parents, but also with grandparents, childminders and some teachers. If these relationships are sensitive and caring, the child's bonds with these significant adults can be very strong.

> **DISCUSS...**
>
> If you were asked to take care of a child from an orphanage such as the one described above, what difficulties would they have? What could you do to try to help that child get over their early experiences?

Critical period

There is now a large body of evidence to show that children are able to form really strong attachment relationships, beyond the critical period described by Bowlby, up to and including their teenage years. In fact, a great deal of therapeutic work takes place with teenagers who have experienced maternal deprivation in the past. This is very good news for fostered and adopted children, who have had very damaging experiences in their early years.

Behaviourist theory of attachment

The early behaviourists argued that children are born with what is known as a 'tabula rasa', or a blank slate. This means that they have no sort of innate, pre-written format for development, so all that they learn and who they become are simply the result of experiences they have had in their lives. Therefore infants will learn about the world by the consequences or outcomes of their behaviours. If they do something that has a positive outcome, they will do it again; if the outcome is negative and unpleasant, they will not repeat their actions.

Behaviourists suggest that attachments also form as the result of their learning and experience. They suggest that attachments are formed as the result of the child receiving some sort of positive reinforcement for the first stages of their interactions with an adult. For example, a baby will initially gaze at the adult, or coo, or even cry, and the adult will respond positively by giving attention, changing nappies, feeding the baby or cuddling it. The baby will learn that by behaving in certain ways with the adult, that adult will provide it with what it wants. In return, the adult gets the positive behaviour of the baby – it smiles and coos and shows delight on seeing the adult, reinforcing a kind of feedback loop. On the other hand, if the adult does not respond to the baby's demands, the baby will stop demanding and will not see that caregiver as a potential provider. In cases like these, the attachment, which was in the first place a relationship based on necessity, will not develop.

This explanation helps to explain why the relationship between the primary carer and the infant is likely to be the strongest relationship, and why it does not matter whether the primary carer is male or female, biological parent or unrelated adult. It is the nature of the relationship that is of more importance, rather than Bowlby's suggestion that attachments are formed due to instinctive biological pre-programming.

> The reward that a child will get for an action is called a reinforcement. This can be a positive reinforcement, where the child will like the reward of a responsive and caring parent, or negative reinforcement, where the child will not repeat the action as the outcome of experiencing a kind of rejection is unpleasant.

DISCUSS...

How have your teachers used positive reinforcement to help you learn? Think about primary and secondary school situations.

> If you are asked in the exam to describe something, it may help to give examples of what you mean. For example, if you were to describe the behaviourist theory of attachment, you could explain that children learn by reinforcement, but it may help to give an example similar to the examples given here.

4. Complete the following table.

Type of attachment	Behaviour of caregiver	Behaviour of child
Securely attached		
Insecure-avoidant		
Insecure-ambivalent		

CORE STUDY: C. Hazan and S. Shaver (1987)

C. Hazan and S. Shaver (1987) Romantic love conceptualised as an attachment process. Journal of Personality and Social Psychology 52, pp. 511–24

Background

Bowlby believed that 'attachment behaviour' influences a person's behaviour throughout their life. The authors explain that they were interested in whether or not Bowlby's theory of attachment could help to explain the types of romantic relationships people have as adults.

Describe the study

Aim

The aim of the study was to consider whether people's adult love relationships may be affected by their attachment styles as a child (secure, insecure-avoidant, insecure-ambivalent).

Participants

A total of 1,200 people replied to a 'love quiz' questionnaire (a self-selecting sample). The authors analysed the first 620 replies: 205 responses were from men and 415 were from women. The average age of respondents was 36.

The questionnaire was also completed by 108 college students studying social psychology, who had an average age of 18. Thirty-eight were male and 70 were female.

Materials and procedure

Two questionnaires were used. The first was placed in a local newspaper and called a 'love quiz'. The second questionnaire was given to students as

> *You need to be able to …* ✓
> - describe Hazan and Shaver's survey of the relationship between attachment types and adult relationships
> - outline the limitations of Hazan and Shaver's study.

a class exercise during a lesson. The questionnaire asked them to describe their most important love relationships.

The authors were interested in measuring four variables:

- What sort of attachment relationship they had with their parents.
- What sort of love experiences they had as adults.
- Memories of their attachment figures.
- Their experience of loneliness.

Results

The results from the newspaper readers and the students were very similar, so the authors suggested that both groups of participants were representative of the population as a whole.

- Attachment relationships in childhood

The participants reported on their own attachment relationships in childhood. The largest group had experienced secure attachments as children.

- Differences in love experiences of participants

The following table shows the differences in love experiences of the participants. Because the students were very young, the lengths of their relationships (if any) were not recorded.

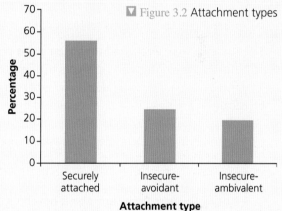

▼ Figure 3.2 Attachment types

Attachment type	Prediction	Newspaper readers	Students
Securely attached	Characterised by trust, friendship and positive emotions	Claimed their love experiences were especially happy, friendly and trusting (average length of relationship – 10.02 years; 6 per cent divorce rate)	Friendly, happy and trusting
Insecure-avoidant	Marked by fear of closeness and lack of trust	Love experiences were clouded by fear of intimacy, emotional highs and lows, and jealousy (average length of relationship – 5.97 years; 12 per cent divorce rate)	Marked by fear of closeness
Insecure-ambivalent	Experienced as a preoccupying struggle to become almost a part of the other person. This may be a way the person can ensure the romantic figure is consistent and predictable (unlike their attachment figure)	Characterised by obsession, emotional highs and lows, and extreme sexual attraction and jealousy; they wanted the other person to feel the same need to become part of them (average length of relationship – 4.86 years; 10 per cent divorce rate)	Marked by jealousy, emotional highs and lows, and a desire for the partner to return the same feelings of love

▲ Table 3.3 Differences in love experiences of the participants

The results show that the attachment types of the participants had influenced the feelings they had about their relationships as adults.

● Memories of their attachment relationships

The participants reported differences in the quality of the relationships they had with their parents.

Attachment type	Reports
Securely attached	Described warmer relationships with both parents and between both parents
Insecure-avoidant	Described their mothers as cold and rejecting
Insecure-ambivalent	Described their fathers as unfair

◀ Table 3.4

● Vulnerability to loneliness (only students completed this part)

The students were also asked to rate on a five-point scale (1 was the lowest score and 5 the highest) their answers to questions about 'state' and 'trait' loneliness. State loneliness refers to whether they have actually been physically alone. Trait loneliness relates to the whether they have felt lonely, because it is possible to feel lonely even if there are lots of people around.

The following are examples of questions used:

● During the past few years, have you lacked companionship?

[state loneliness]

● During the past few years, about how often have you felt lonely?

[trait loneliness]

The insecure-ambivalent students reported being the most lonely, and the secure students were the least lonely. The insecure-avoidant students said they were often distant from others, but did not feel lonely.

Conclusion

The authors concluded from their research that there is a relationship between the attachment relationships people have with their caregivers in infancy and the relationships they form as adults. They suggest that relationships all start with a romantic beginning, when the lovers are fascinated and preoccupied with each other. These relationships should then move into a type of secure attachment. However, the early relationship experiences people have with their parents seem to influence the nature and length

> **DISCUSS...** 💬
>
> Why do you think the insecure ambivalent students were the most isolated and felt the most lonely?

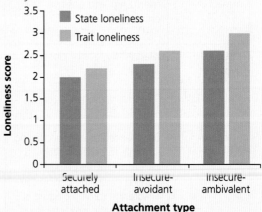

▲ Figure 3.3 The results showed that the insecure-ambivalent students felt the most lonely and were the most isolated

Attachment

of their relationships as adults. This provides strong evidence of the long-term effects of caregiver–infant attachments.

Limitations

Participants

The two groups of participants were not representative of the population as a whole.

- One group was a self-selecting sample of readers from one newspaper who chose to fill in the questionnaire. This may be because they were particularly interested in relationships – perhaps the quiz attracted people who had just broken up with a partner, or perhaps it attracted people who were particularly happy.
- The other group were students who were asked to fill in the questionnaire during a lesson, so perhaps they felt they had to do as they were asked but did not take the questionnaire seriously.
- There were about two-thirds women to one-third men. Would this have affected the results?

Ethics

Were all the participants told the purpose of the study and did they give informed consent? The newspaper readers were told the questionnaire was a love quiz.

Honesty of answers

In one question, participants were asked to put themselves in a category according to how they felt about their most important relationship. Did they feel securely attached, insecure-avoidant or insecure-ambivalent in their most important relationship (they were given descriptions of each category)? Did they categorise themselves accurately or did they feel that they ought to give the most socially desirable answer?

Accuracy of answers

Many of the questions asked participants to rate themselves or agree or disagree with statements. These questions force the participant to choose an answer (often called forced-choice questions), which may not have allowed them to say how they really felt.

HOMEWORK

Look at several questionnaires in different magazines or newspapers. Consider what sort of people might be interested in completing them and whether these would be representative of the population.

81

Applications of research into attachment:
care of children

Candidates should be able to:

- explain how psychological research relates to care of children – for example, dealing with separation in nurseries, encouraging secure attachments through parenting classes, dealing with stranger anxiety in hospitalised children.

Care of children

Research into attachment has influenced the way we now care for children. For example, we know from Bowlby's research that disruptions in early childhood relationships may have lasting effects on the child's ability to form good relationships and their emotional well-being. It is now generally understood that children do need to have one or more responsive and consistent attachment figures, although this does not have to the be the child's birth mother. This knowledge has affected the way that children are cared for in nurseries and hospitals.

Nurseries

Today both parents often work, so many more children attend nurseries than ever before, starting at a very young age until they go to school. Because of our knowledge of how important it is for children to have secure attachment relationships, concerns have been raised about the welfare of children going to nursery. Research has shown that if the nursery is staffed by adults who are sensitive and responsive to the children's needs, and are interested in stimulating and supporting the children, the experiences can actually be beneficial.

It is important that nursery staff:

- are well qualified and sensitive to the children's needs
- have a low staff turnover, to provide consistency in relationships and to allow attachments to develop
- have a high caregiver-to-child ratio (ideally no more than one to four)
- all develop a relationship with each child, so that if one staff member is absent, this does not disrupt continuity of care for the children
- use lots of language and play through conversation, games and songs.

When children enter nursery, if they are allowed to develop a relationship with the staff before the mother or caregiver leaves, this will reduce the separation anxiety.

Parenting classes

Parents who have had a difficult childhood themselves, and perhaps have not had the best role models, often benefit from support in managing their relationships with their own children. Also the high levels of divorce and reconstituted families (families where two partners have brought their own children from previous relationships), mean that there is sometimes little time to nurture secure and consistent relationships. Parenting classes are available to these parents. These often focus not only on managing children's behaviour, but also in helping parents to become sensitive and responsive to their children's needs, which in turn will lead to the development of secure attachments.

▲ Figure 3.4

   Classes focus on areas that are intended to help develop relationships in a firm but fair way, by supporting parents to:

- see things from the child's perspective
- be consistent in their relationship with the child
- care for the child, and understand and respond to the child's needs
- provide a safe and secure base for the child to use to explore the world
- be firm but fair when managing the child's behaviour.

This will help the child to feel safe and loved, and will help the child to develop an attachment to the parent, who, in return, will bond with the child.

Dealing with stranger anxiety in hospitals

Before hospitals understood how important bonding and attachments were to mothers and babies, the mothers who gave birth were separated from their newborn children to give the mother some rest before she took her newborn home. The baby would stay in the hospital nursery, which was clean and sterile, while the mothers remained on the wards, and they would only be together for small amounts of time during the day. Today mothers are handed the baby immediately after birth in order for the bonding process to start, and the baby remains with the mother at all times if possible. As a result, mother and baby have already begun to develop a relationship before they go home, and this early skin-to-skin contact has been shown to help the quality of the attachment between them.

   Parents of young children who had to go into hospital due to illness used to be restricted in their visiting, which left children, even those who had long-term illnesses, separated from their parents; this had a really negative effect on many of these children and disrupted their relationships with their parents.

We also know that children experience stranger anxiety at about the age of 7 months and use their safe and secure attachment figure to cling to when worried or frightened. A young child going into hospital will meet a large number of strangers – for example, they will meet doctors and nursing staff, but they might also see people like physiotherapists, occupational therapists and radiographers. In the past, children who were placed in hospitals due to illness were kept away from their parents, because it was believed that they would settle more quickly once they got into the routine of hospital life. Research in the late 1940s by James Robertson, a psychiatric social worker, and John Bowlby looked at the effects on children of staying in hospital away from their parents. They were shocked at the way children responded to this separation.

Robertson (1953) described three phases that the children went through when separated from their parents:

- Protest: The child is visibly upset and will cry and call for their mother, looking for her to come back.
- Despair: The child becomes withdrawn and miserable and seems to lose interest in everything.
- Detachment: The child becomes more interested in their surroundings and will interact with others in a superficial way, but if their mother appears, the child will appear disinterested and distant, and show no response when the mother leaves.

Robertson concluded that the last stage was extremely difficult to undo, as the child no longer seemed to need mothering at all and became emotionally switched off.

DISCUSS...

Below are the visiting times for the children's wards in London hospitals from a survey in the *Spectator* newspaper in 1949.

- Guy's Hospital: Sundays 2–4pm
- St Bartholomew's Hospital: Wednesdays 2–3.30pm
- Westminster Hospital: Wednesdays 2–3pm and Sundays 2–3 pm
- St Thomas's Hospital: no visits in the first month; parents could see children asleep between 7 and 8 pm
- West London Hospital: no visiting
- Charing Cross Hospital: Sundays 3–4pm
- London Hospital: under 3 years old, no visits, but parents could see children through partitions; over 3 years, twice weekly.

What impact would these visiting times have had on attachment relationships?

Today things are very different. Research has shown that the best way to help children cope with the fears they may have about going into hospital is to allow their secure attachment figure, who may be the mother or father or other caregiver, to remain in hospital with them. In fact, this practice is now common in all hospitals, with parent rooms being made available or parents remaining by the bedside of the child at all times. This has prevented the traumatic responses and damaged relationships that children experienced in previous generations.

DISCUSS...

Amy is 10 months old and her mother has returned to work. She has been placed in a nursery and Janet, her key person, has observed that she seems indifferent to the adults in the centre and shows no distress or worry when her mother leaves her every day. She does not seem to show any preference for any adult, be they familiar or complete strangers.

Janet is worried because Amy rarely smiles and does not take part with any enthusiasm in the play activities on offer. Janet has also noticed that there does not seem to be any closeness between Amy and her mother.

How do you think Janet could help to make sure that Amy's needs are met, both in the nursery and at home?

Exam-style question – Developmental psychology: Attachment

These questions are taken from the OCR B541 Psychology paper, from June 2010. For more past and sample papers plus answer exemplars visit the OCR website. OCR have not seen or commented on the quality of the sample answers.

1. The behaviourist theory states that attachments are learned through reinforcement. From the list below, identify two ways in which a carer would reinforce attachment in a baby. [2]

   If you tick more than two boxes, you will have one of your marks taken off.

   Show your answer by ticking the relevant boxes.

   comforting the baby ☑ *(1)*

   feeding the baby ☑ *(1)*

   frowning at the baby ☐

   ignoring the baby ☐

2. (a) Explain how a psychologist could measure separation protest. [2]

   Making the mother leave the baby and looking at how the baby behaves and whether it gets upset or not. (2)

   (b) Explain how a psychologist could measure stranger anxiety. [2]

   By leaving the baby alone with someone it doesn't know. (1)

   This answer is only worth 1 mark because the candidate did not actually talk about the measurement of stranger anxiety such as timing how long the child cries for.

3. Below are three statements which refer to Hazan & Shaver's (1987) study on attachment types. Identify whether the statements are true or false by circling either TRUE or FALSE. [3]

(a) Hazan & Shaver used a questionnaire to collect data for their study.

(TRUE)　　　　FALSE *(1)*

(b) Hazan & Shaver used a sample of children in their study.

TRUE　　(FALSE)　*(1)*

(c) Hazan & Shaver found that secure attachments were more common than insecure attachments.

(TRUE)　　　　FALSE *(1)*

4. Outline **one** limitation of the **procedure** used in Hazan & Shaver's study on attachment types. [2]

It was only carried out in America so the findings might only relate to people in America and not people in general. (2)

This answer is worth 2 marks as it has explained why doing the research in American is a limitation.

5. Describe Bowlby's theory of attachment. [4]

Bowlby said that children suffer if they experience maternal deprivation (1) which leads to irreversible effects (1). He said that people who experience maternal deprivation might develop affectionless psychopathy (1) where they will show no guilt or remorse for their deviant behaviour (1).

This is a well explained answer that has made 4 points for 4 marks because the candidate has explained the effects of maternal deprivation rather than just listing facts about Bowlby's theory.

SECTION TOTAL [15]

Cognitive development

Overview

In the past, people used to believe that children were really just small adults who thought about things in the same way as adults did. Thanks to our understanding of cognitive development, helped by people such as Jean Piaget and Lev Vygotsky, we now know that our understanding of the world changes as we grow up, and we think of things in a different way as adults to the way we thought about them as children.

Developmental psychologists consider the stages of development that a child goes through before they reach maturity. They have helped us to understand some of the changes that occur in a child's thinking or cognition. We are going to consider two of the most influential theories of cognitive development in this section, starting with the work of Jean Piaget and then moving on to the work of Lev Vygotsky.

How cognitive development occurs

Jean Piaget is probably the most famous developmental theorist, although he was not actually a psychologist. He was born in Switzerland and initially trained as a biologist and zoologist. He went to work in Paris in the 1920s, and helped to develop the first intelligence tests for the French Education Department, so that they could identify children who had learning difficulties.

Piaget worked with children and also spent time observing his own three children. He found that the children often gave the same kind of wrong answers to questions and tasks, according to their age. He concluded that the way children think is quite different from the thinking of adults, and he noticed that these changes in thinking go through different stages as they grow up. Because all children go through these stages, Piaget suggested that these stages must be biologically based.

Piaget claimed that once a child reached a certain stage, they could not go back to a previous stage. He said that each stage, or step, was like a building block, so all children had to go through each stage in turn. These stages are therefore invariant (do not vary from one child to the next) and were universal because all children, from any culture, went through every stage in the same order.

Piaget said that children actively try to make sense of the world and called them 'little scientists' because of the way they explore and test. They do this using whatever skills they have. For example, a baby's

This section still focuses on developmental psychology, looking specifically at the development of a child's thinking and reasoning, but it will be examined in the second examination paper you sit.

KEY CONCEPTS

The OCR examination requires candidates to be able to:
- describe how cognitive development occurs in invariant and universal stages
- outline the stages of cognitive development – sensorimotor, pre-operational, concrete operational and formal operational.

QUESTION ?

1. What did Piaget mean by universal and invariant stages?

grasping ability is inborn (or innate), and the baby will use this grasping ability to hold on to something such as fingers or clothes. The baby at this point has a mental structure, or schema, which contains all that it knows about holding on to something. If the baby is given a bottle of milk, it will use what it already knows to hold on to the bottle, but at this point it may find that its existing schema is not big enough because, for this action, it will have to change the shape of its hands and make them work together, which it has never done before. The baby has to assimilate the new information (bottle is a different shape, need two hands, and if I put the end of it in my mouth something nice comes out) and then adjust its existing schema to accommodate the new information. It will then use this new holding skill again and again in many situations.

> **DISCUSS...**
>
> Do you think you still assimilate and accommodate new information? Think of two examples.

> *Schemas*
> *When we experience something for the first time, we store the information about it in a kind of mental 'file'. As we get older, we may have the same experiences again and again, and each time our knowledge will increase about that experience. We store lots of different information in this mental 'file', including the way we should behave, and this knowledge is assimilated (taken in) and accommodated in the mental file.*

CORE THEORY: Piaget's theory

Candidates should be able to:
- describe the concept of object permanence
- describe the concept of egocentrism and the process of decentring
- describe the concept of conservation
- explain the criticisms of Piaget's theory of cognitive development
- consider Vygotsky's theory as an alternative theory, with specific reference to the zone of proximal development.

Piaget's stage theory of cognitive development

Piaget identified four stages of cognitive development and the skills that children have in each step of their progress. Piaget also said that children will learn as long as they grow up in an environment with lots of opportunities to learn by experimenting and exploring.

1. Sensorimotor stage
2. Pre-operational stage
3. Concrete operational stage
4. Formal operational stage.

Piaget's stages are like steps. Children go from one step to the next in the same order as they get older.

Stage 1: Sensorimotor (birth to 2 years)

This stage is called the sensorimotor stage because the baby explores the world through its senses (sight, sound, taste, touch and smell) and acts by moving its body in response to these. A major discovery for the child is realising that the things it does (the motor activity) will have an effect that will create sensations (sounds and sights and so on). It is the first stage of gaining mastery over the environment and also over their own actions.

Main features of this stage

Coordination

At first, the baby's movements are reflexes, like grasping and sucking, so the baby may watch a moving object and will reach out towards it to try to grasp it with no coordination. The baby will find it impossible to grasp the object at first, but after a few weeks the baby will finally be able to catch the object and will (probably) put it in its mouth, exploring the object using its sense of taste and smell.

Object permanence

When Piaget shook a toy in front of a 4-month-old baby, it reached out for it. Then a cover was placed over the toy, and the baby looked away and appeared to lose interest, as though the toy had never existed. He concluded that young babies do not realise that when an object is hidden from them, the object still exists, because they have not yet developed object permanence. When Piaget repeated the actions in front of an 8-month-old, the baby continued to reach for the toy, sometimes getting upset when it was covered.

Stranger fear

At first, young babies can be comforted by strangers, but at about 8 months of age, young children show a fear of strangers. Because they have developed object permanence, they have developed mental representations of the people they are attached to and no one else will do!

Self-recognition

Babies realise that they exist as a separate person when they start to recognise themselves in a mirror in the second year of their life. This is a further development of object permanence – realising that they continue to exist.

Stage 2: Pre-operational stage (2 to 7 years)

By 2 years of age the toddler starts to use symbols, signs or objects to represent things. This is an example of symbolic thinking, which is when we make something 'stand for' something else. For example, the 3-year-old will use a cardboard box as a house or a car.

Main features of this stage

Animism

Children up to about 4 years old think that inanimate objects have feelings in the same way as they have (this is animism). They might say that flowers are tired when they are actually wilting.

Egocentrism

Have you ever played hide and seek with a 3-year-old, who hides by standing in front of you, covering their eyes? Because the child cannot see you, they think you cannot see them; this is an example of egocentric thinking (or egocentrism). An egocentric child can see the world only from their own point of view, not understanding that other people may have different experiences or may see things differently to them. Egocentric children also focus, or centre, on one feature of a situation or problem (which helps to explain why young children have difficulty with conservation; see page 92).

Words are symbols. Children's language develops at a fast pace over this time. They understand that words stand for things that may not be present. This skill allows the child to develop thinking skills and to begin to solve problems.

The way to remember the meaning of egocentric is to think that the child is centred on their own ego.

Egocentric thinking

Piaget used his 'three mountains' task to test children's egocentric thinking.

The child sat in front of a large table on which was a model of three mountains. One mountain had a cross on top, one had snow and the last had a little house. The child had already seen the table from each side before sitting down. A doll was then put in various positions around the table and the child had to choose from a number of cards what the doll would be able to see from where it was placed. Children aged 4 and 5 years old thought the doll would be able to see the same view as them, which indicates egocentrism. However, most 7-year-olds could identify the doll's view correctly.

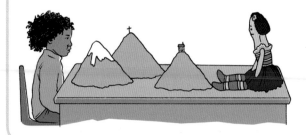

◀ Figure 3.5 The task for the child is to describe the view of the mountains that the doll has – for example, that the nearest mountain is the one with the house on top

Reversibility

Children in this stage cannot understand that things work backwards. For example, if you say to Masie, 'Do you have a brother?' she will say yes. Then if you ask her if her brother has a sister, she will say no.

Classification

People or objects can only belong to one category at a time in this stage. You can be a sister, but you cannot be a sister and a daughter.

Conservation

During this stage, children cannot conserve number, length, quantity, mass, weight and volume. They focus on what something looks like and do not understand that a quantity of something will remain the same even when it is presented in a different way. Piaget carried out a number of experiments to test the ability of children of different ages to conserve (described in detail in the core study for this chapter, page 96). Table 3.5 gives examples of his studies that have looked at the conservation of number, mass and volume.

Children's responses to each of these tests would have been focused on the appearance of the objects, so the answer to the second question in each conservation experiment would have been no.

Stage 3: Concrete operational stage (7 to 11 years)

During this time, children gain a better understanding of mental operations. They begin to think logically about concrete events, but they still struggle with understanding abstract concepts.

Main features of this stage

Can decentre

Early in the concrete operational stage, the child begins to understand that people see things differently from them. They are no longer egocentric, so they would be able to identify the doll's view in the three mountains task. They are decentring – not always looking at things from their own point of view.

Reversibility

Children realise that it is possible to reverse an operation. Take, for example, the sum of 4 + 4 = 8. If you then ask the child to solve the problem of 8 − 4, they will realise that the answer equals the original 4.

Classification

Children understand that objects can belong to more than one class – for example, they would be able to think of their brother as a brother and as a son to their parents.

QUESTIONS ?

2. Do you think that all children, once they reach a certain age, move into the next stage of development, or do some children progress faster than others?
3. What do you think it is that might affect their progress through the stages?

Conservation

Table 3.5 These methods are used to test children's ability to conserve. Pre-operational children would think that the materials had changed in quantity with a change in physical shape. Concrete operational children understand that the properties of certain objects are conserved (remain the same) even if the shape changes ▽

Children start to understand that the properties of certain objects can remain the same, even though their appearance changes (see below). Conservation develops slowly, but in the same order, with conservation of number appearing by about 7 years of age, then mass and length between 7 and 8 years, then weight between the ages of 8 and 10, and finally volume by 11 to 12 years. However, the children in this stage need to have the actual objects present in order to complete any tasks (which is why it is called the concrete operational stage). The core study in this section focuses on Piaget's experiments to look at the development of conservation of number.

Conservation	Method	Apparatus
Number	Two rows of equal numbers of counters, laid out in parallel with the items matching. The child is asked, 'Are there the same number of counters?' One row is stretched or rearranged, and again the child is asked, 'Are there the same number of counters?'	Child's row Adult's row Adult's row rearranged ▲ Figure 3.6a
Mass	Two identical pieces of clay are shown to the child (1). The child is asked, 'Is there the same amount of clay in each one?' One is rolled out into a sausage shape (2) and the child is asked again, 'Is there the same amount of clay in each one?'	1 2 ▲ Figure 3.6b
Volume	Two equal-sized glasses contain the same amount of liquid. The child is asked, 'Is there the same amount of liquid in each one?' The liquid from one is poured into a taller glass. The child is then asked again, 'Is there the same amount of liquid in each one?'	(a) (b) (c) ▲ Figure 3.6c

Stage 4: Formal operational stage (11 years and older)

HOMEWORK

What is meant by conservation? At what stage does a child learn about conservation? Use diagrams to illustrate your answer.

In this stage, the young person can manipulate mental ideas rather than having to have concrete examples. They can think abstractly, solve problems and manipulate ideas in their heads. A simple example is the ability to mentally consider size relationships, as in the following problem: *If Mark is taller than Ali, and Mark is smaller than Kerry, who is the tallest?*

In the previous stage, the child would have to draw a picture or use different-sized objects to solve this problem. Now the young person can manipulate the ideas in their head. They can do mathematical calculations, think creatively and imagine the outcome of particular actions. According to Piaget, once the young person has achieved formal operational thinking, there is no further change in the structure of thinking, only in how complicated, how flexible and how abstract these thoughts can be. In fact, this is the stage when young people develop adult thought.

Criticisms of Piaget's theory of cognitive development

Although Piaget's theory has had a tremendous impact on our understanding of children's development, there are a number of criticisms.

- Piaget did not actually explain how children go from one stage to the next; he only described the stages, so his theory is more a description than an actual theory.
- Children's development seems to be more continuous than the stages (or steps) Piaget identified. Children do not just go overnight from one stage to the next, whereas Piaget's ideas suggested that a child's new stage of reasoning is going to affect every area of the child's life.
- Children's development is dependent on input from parents and teachers, who facilitate or support children's learning. A child in a room on her/his own will not make much developmental progress.
- Children use different skills besides those tested by Piaget. Children can be very creative, but these skills were not assessed by the tests used by Piaget.
- Piaget's research methods were questioned. If he had used a different methodology, he may have obtained different results, so perhaps Piaget's results are questionable.
    - Samples: Many of Piaget's ideas are based on observing his own three children. Perhaps they were not representative of all children. At other times, the samples were very small and he did not explain how these were selected.

Consider how samples should be selected (see Chapter 6, page 189). Were Piaget's samples representative?

DISCUSS...

Do you think Piaget's children were representative of all children? If not, why not?

HOMEWORK

Looking at the criticisms of Piaget's methods, how could he have done things differently?

- Procedure: Piaget did not use a standardised procedure; he would repeat his questions in a different way if the child did not seem to understand what they were being asked. This may have given some children an advantage over others.
- Instructions: Piaget used instructions that might have been confusing to the children because he asked the same question twice in some of the interviews. If you ask a child a question and they answer, and then you ask them the same question again, they may think that the reason you asked the second question was because their answer to the first question was wrong. For example:

Piaget: Are there the same number of buttons in each row?
Child: Yes. [Piaget spreads out the buttons in the second row.]
Piaget: Are there the same number of buttons in each row?
Child [thinking perhaps I got the answer wrong the first time]: *No.*

Perhaps the children were able to conserve at a younger age than Piaget thought.

The study in this section explains the methodology used by Piaget when assessing conservation of number.

- Nature of the task: When Piaget investigated egocentrism, he used the three mountains task. Piaget said that children stopped being egocentric at about the age of 7, but later research suggested that they stop being egocentric at a younger age. One reason may have been the three mountains task that Piaget used when testing the children, which was criticised because it may have seemed strange to the children. Did the mountains look like mountains (they were made of wire covered with papier mâché)? It was also made more difficult because the child was asked to match the doll's view with a picture.

Piaget believed that an environment rich in opportunities would provide the basic canvas for children to develop cognitively. Piaget did not specify that social experiences were necessary for this development to take place. This is in total contrast to the view of Vygotsky, a Russian psychologist, who strongly believed that a child's cognitive development is dependent on social experiences. He saw the child not as a scientist, but as an apprentice who acquired knowledge and skills through interactions with others.

Vygotsky's theory

Piaget's approached to children's development was biological, suggesting that it is dependent purely on age. Vygotsky, on the other hand, believed that children are born with a whole range of cognitive abilities, which are accessed through socialisation and education. What he was suggesting was that children mature because of their social and cultural experiences, and that, without those experiences, children would remain immature in the way that they interact with the world.

Age/stage	Piaget	Vygotsky
Infancy 0–2 years	Sensorimotor	Affiliation (caregivers)
Early childhood 2–7 years	Pre-operational	Play (peers)
Middle childhood 7–12 years	Concrete operational	Learning (teachers)
Adolescence 12–19 years	Formal operational	Peer group
Adulthood 19–55 years		Work
Early old age		Theorising

Table 3.6 The differences in focus between Piaget and Vygotsky

As illustrated in Table 3.6, while Piaget focuses on stages, Vygotsky identifies important influences on children's development.

In order to compare the ideas of Piaget (biological maturity) and Vygotsky (social interaction), we could take the example of language, which we know Vygotsky felt plays a key part in development. We know that very young children cannot speak because their mouth is not yet the right sort of shape (their tongues are too big).

It is only by maturing physically that the young child is able to make meaningful sounds. However, if that child is totally isolated and is never spoken to, they will not develop the ability to use language, no matter how old they are.

Vygotsky also believed that culture plays a large part in children's development (this is why his approach is sometimes called a sociocultural approach). Piaget suggested that children learn through exploratory learning, and this is why it is necessary to make their environment full of opportunities to learn by trial and error. Vygotsky also explained that children can learn from others about various skills, such as how to mix colours in art, how to cook or how to behave in different situations, without having to find out for themselves.

Children who receive advice and guidance from an adult or more capable peer will store the information for use in the future. This cultural knowledge

Further your understanding

Vygotsky was born in Russia in 1896, the same year as Piaget. He studied at the Institute of Psychology in Moscow, where he developed his ideas about cognitive development. His work was available outside Russia only from the 1960s, although he actually died of tuberculosis in Moscow in 1928 when he was only 32 years of age.

Further your understanding

In order to learn language, children have to interact with others. Sitting in front of a television teaches children to mimic like parrots! They are unable to use language creatively, and this, in turn, prevents their cognitive skills from developing.

DISCUSS...

Describe the ideal day for an 8-year-old child, taking into account the theories of Piaget and Vygotsky.

can also be handed on without the child having to learn by trial and error. The child can later hand the same skills on to the next generation.

The zone of proximal development

Vygotsky believed that children are able to demonstrate some abilities on their own, but with help and guidance from others they can actually achieve more. This help and guidance, or scaffolding, may start off being really directive, but can slowly change as the child becomes more capable and manages to do things or reason out complex problems on their own.

Vygotsky described the difference between a child's achievements when working on their own and their potential achievements under the guidance of adults or other children who are more capable, and he called this difference the zone of proximal development. Vygotsky (1978, p. 86) explained: 'The zone of proximal development … is the distance between the actual developmental level as determined by independent problem solving and the level of potential development as determined through problem solving under adult guidance or in collaboration with more capable peers'.

We already identified how important social relationships are in other areas of children's development when we looked at attachment relationships in the earlier part of this chapter. Through his theory, Vygotsky highlights the importance of social relationships in learning. Because his theory focuses far more on the opportunities a child has to learn and experience, it is not an age-related theory in the same way as Piaget's is, although he believed that children do go through developmental stages in a uniform order. Vygotsky is therefore more flexible in the way that he looks at development.

QUESTIONS ?

4. Explain what is meant by the zone of proximal development.

5. Describe how a mother might be able to extend her child's knowledge and ability when sitting down with the child and playing with a box of wooden bricks.

CORE STUDY: J. Piaget (1952)

J. Piaget (1952) The Child's Conception of Number. *London: Routledge*

Further your understanding

The core study is taken from Piaget's book, *The Child's Conception of Number*, originally published in Switzerland in 1941. It contains 10 chapters, which consider how children learn about numbers. The core study comes from Chapter 4.

You need to be able to …

- describe Piaget's experiment into the conservation of number
- outline the limitations of Piaget's study.

Background

Chapters 1 and 2 in Piaget's book *The Child's Conception of Number* focus on a child's ability to conserve quantity. He investigated this using a number of different methods, including the conservation of liquid experiment (outlined earlier in this chapter, page 92).

Piaget believed that children between the ages of 2 and 7 years cannot understand that the quantity of something will remain the same when it is presented in a different way.

In Chapter 3 of his book, Piaget looks at the development of 'correspondence' – that is, the understanding that two quantities may be presented in a different way, but they are still the same in number. A simple example is shown in Figure 3.7.

As adults, we usually estimate quantity rather than actually counting, so we use the appearance of the objects to guide us. If a child can estimate quantity correctly, this is quite a mature skill.

Piaget tested this in two different ways. The first was to show a child a shape such as a diamond or circle, which used a certain number of counters. The child was then asked to take the right number of counters out of a box to copy the shape. If they took the right number of counters, this meant that they understood correspondence.

The second way was the focus of the core study.

Describe the study

In this part of the study, Piaget was interested in investigating correspondence further by looking at a child's ability to conserve number by putting counters, sweets or pennies into single rows rather than making shapes with them. He wanted to know whether they would be fooled into thinking that by changing the way a number of counters was presented, the counters had actually changed in number. If they were influenced by the outward appearance, it meant that they could not 'conserve' or remember the number of objects in their memory.

Participants

There were 17 children aged between 4 years 1 month and 6 years 2 months. Piaget did not say how these children were selected.

Materials

Counters, sweets and pennies were used to form rows.

Procedure

- First task:
  Piaget first laid out a row of counters (or other circular objects) on the table and asked the children to take some counters to make a row the same length as the one already there; he noted their responses. The children were asked to produce 1:1 correspondence.

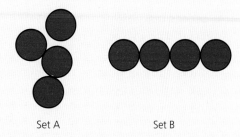

Set A   Set B

▲ Figure 3.7 Here you do not need to count the objects as you are able to see that the numbers correspond – that is, you are able to accurately estimate the quantity

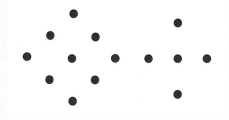

▲ Figure 3.8 These are the kind of shapes Piaget showed to children. They then had to choose the same number of counters as there were in each shape out of a box.

- Second task:
  Then, with two equal rows of counters in front of the child, Piaget changed the density of the rows, either by spreading out one row or pushing the counters closer together. He then asked the children if there was the same number of counters in each row.

△ Figure 3.9

> Piaget was interested in the following when trying to understand how children learn to conserve:
> - Density – how close the counters were together
> - Length – how long the rows were.

Results

The younger children were unable to conserve number. The older children in the sample, who were at the end of the concrete operational stage, were able to conserve number as they were able to choose the right number of counters, and to explain that the same number of counters were in the row, even when the appearance of the row changed.

△ Figure 3.10

Discussion

Piaget identified three stages that children go through before they are able to conserve number, all of which are related to length and density.

- Stage 1: Piaget found that the younger children had difficulty with both tasks. They found it hard to choose the right amount of counters and just looked at the length of the row, without noticing how close together the counters were. When Piaget changed the density of one of the rows (by pushing the counters together or spreading them out), the children either added more counters to the line to increase the length if Piaget's line was longer, or took counters away to make the line shorter (if Piaget's line was shorter).
- Stage 2: The children in the middle of the concrete operational stage were able to copy the length and density of a row. They could also say that there were the same number of counters in two rows that had been spaced in 1:1 correspondence (see above). But if Piaget changed one of the rows, the children would have to adjust the other row to correspond in order to say that there were still the same number of counters in each row. They were still unable to believe the relationship between the two lines as having the same number of counters, without proving it physically to themselves.

HOMEWORK

Design a piece of research to investigate children's ability to conserve volume.

DISCUSS...

Piaget suggested that children do not leave the pre-operational stage until they are 7, yet this experiment showed that children of 6 years 2 months were able to conserve. Can you explain this?

- Stage 3: The oldest children in the sample were able to conserve. They were able to copy the length and density of Piaget's model. They did not have to rely on the items being laid out to correspond with each other in order to know that there were the same number in each row.

Many people have challenged Piaget's theory over the years, but most of his ideas have stood the test of time. Piaget identified the fact that children's thinking is very different to the thinking of an adult. Today we generally accept that children go through a number of stages as they grow up, and Piaget's work continues to influence the methods used to help children to learn; it is difficult to think of many other psychologists who have had such a major effect on the way we see ourselves in the twenty-first century.

Limitations

Most of the limitations of Piaget's study are concerned with the methods he used to gain his evidence.

Standardisation

The core study comes from Piaget's book, *The Child's Conception of Number*. Piaget's research was taken from 'a set of investigations carried out over a number of years with a team of co-workers'. Because the information was gathered over a number of years by different people, we cannot be sure that they all used the same techniques of questioning, and this may have affected the results.

Sample and selection of participants

Piaget does not tell us about the children he worked with, so we cannot be sure of their level of ability; they may have all been very bright or might have had learning difficulties. Did they all have a good understanding of language generally, as this might have made a difference to their answers? We do know from other studies that most of Piaget's research was done in Switzerland, and he tended to work with white, middle-class children of professional parents, who were not representative of the population as a whole.

Because we have no information about the number of children Piaget worked with, we cannot be sure that he included the data from all the children.

Procedure

The procedure was not standardised. Piaget (or a colleague) asked children questions, and adjusted the questions to suit the child's responses. Perhaps the researchers gave some children better explanations and instructions, and this might have affected the results.

DISCUSS... 💬

Perhaps some of the researchers were very friendly to the children they worked with, while others might have been older and seemed quite scary to the young children. How do you think this might have affected the results?

99

Language

Piaget sometimes asked the child the same question twice, and on other occasions he used very similar questions. For example, he would say 'Are there the same number of counters in the row?' and the child would answer. Then he spread the counters out and asked the same question again. In normal circumstances, if we ask a child the same question twice, the child might think they are being asked again because they got the original answer wrong. Perhaps this was what happened with Piaget. The results suggested that when he only asked the question once, more children got the answer right.

Applications of research into cognitive development: *educating children*

Candidates should be able to:

- explain how psychological research relates to educating children – for example, key stages in relation to Piaget's stages, active/discovery learning, scaffolding in relation to Vygotsky's theory.

Educating children

Psychological research has had a significant effect on our understanding of how children learn, and education has taken this knowledge into account when planning the curriculum. Both Piaget and Vygotsky have been influential in this process, and their ideas have been incorporated in the way schools are organised and teachers teach.

Piaget

Key stages map onto Piaget's developmental stages

In the UK today, education is divided into different key stages, which have been designed to guide what pupils are expected to learn during that stage, and what knowledge they should have as they move into the next key stage. These key stages map onto the developmental stages described by Piaget, as you will see in the table below.

Table 3.7 Each key stage and the way children are taught, mapped on to Piagetian theory ▼

Age/stage	Key stage	
Infancy 0–2 years Sensorimotor	Key stage 0	Infants spend this time with their mothers or primary caregivers. If the infant goes to a private nursery, there will be a high number of adults, so the infants get a lot of attention, learning how to play and develop their social skills such as turn-taking. The environment should have lots of toys to help them develop their sensorimotor skills, such as toys that make noises, move and feel different.

Age/stage	Key stage	
Early childhood 2–7 years Pre-operational	Key stage 0	Children can start school between the ages of 3 and 5 years, depending on where they live. In some settings, opportunities are provided for play-based learning. A high number of staff are available to allow children to initiate activities, as well as providing adult-directed learning.
	Key stage 1	Children are provided with concrete props and visual aids whenever possible, to help them understand what they are being taught and to give them opportunities for hands-on learning. Because their language skills are still developing, teachers' instructions have to be clear and simple, and the children will need lots of opportunities to develop their language and vocabulary. Because they are still egocentric, turn-taking and sharing are important.
Middle childhood 7–12 years Concrete operational	Key stage 2	At the beginning of this stage teachers have to carry on using short instructions and giving concrete examples, allowing the children time to practise their skills. Physical props and visual aids are still necessary for the more complicated or abstract problems (e.g. in maths). Towards the end of this stage, the children are beginning to consider abstract concepts rather than having to revert to props. They are also given the chance to look at properties of materials (e.g. water) and learn to understand reversibility (water to ice and back to water). Children are no longer egocentric, so teachers encourage collaborative working by setting group projects that involve exploratory learning. Children are more cooperative during this stage and they are encouraged to negotiate.
Adolescence 12–19 years Formal operational	Key stage 3 (11–14 years) Key stage 4 (14–16 years)	During this key stage the adolescent is required to develop the ability to think in an abstract way without needing physical props. They learn to manage open-ended projects, where they can explore different solutions to problems. They will learn to think about possibilities, formulate hypotheses and consider alternatives. This means they become more able to evaluate theories and look at alternatives (especially through the teaching of subjects such as GCSE psychology).

Key stages guide the way that teachers teach

As we have seen, Piaget suggested that it was not worthwhile trying to teach children things that were beyond their stage of development and way of thinking, because they would be unable to do them. The key stages focus on providing opportunities for children in line with their stage of development.

Key stages take into consideration the way that children learn

In key stages 1 and 2, the focus is on active/discovery learning, with teachers supporting pupils to learn in this way. Children get the opportunity to use hands-on learning and exploration as a way of increasing their knowledge and understanding of the world.

In key stage 3, the focus is more on thinking and reasoning, which is in line with Piaget's formal operational stage.

Scaffolding in education

Vygotsky indicated the importance of providing 'scaffolding' as a way of helping children to understand the world. Scaffolding provides a kind of framework, like real scaffolding, in which a child can fit their new knowledge and experience.

Below is a good example of how scaffolding is used, which is adapted from Berk (2001).

If a child is given a task that is new to them, they may not be aware of the goal and will need to be shown what to do. If you take the example of a 9-month-old infant who has never before seen a jack-in-the-box, they would not have any knowledge of what the box contains. At first, the parent tries to get the child's attention by working the toy themselves, exclaiming 'Pop! What happened?' as the clown emerges.

▲ Figure 3.11 Here the adult is helping to scaffold the child's learning

HOMEWORK

Imagine you are a parent, teaching a child how to do a simple jigsaw puzzle. What sort of instructions would you give the child when they are 1 year old and then 2 years old?

Gradually, the adult shows the child how to use the jack-in-the-box. When the infant reaches for the toy, the adult guides the child's hand to turn the handle and to push the clown down in the box, knowing at that point that the child is not sufficiently able or coordinated to turn the handle to release the toy on their own.

As the child gets a little older and their motor, cognitive and language skills develop, they may try to turn the handle to make the jack-in-the-box work, and they will look towards the adult, asking for assistance. At this point, the adult can tell the child what to do, saying things like, 'Turn just a little more', and making hand gestures resembling a turning motion.

The adult is supporting the child's understanding and learning, first non-verbally and then verbally, according to the child's level of ability. This scaffolding framework allows the child to achieve their goal of working the jack-in-the-box. The parent is matching the amount of help they provide as a way of encouraging the child to move a little further on with their skills – within their zone of proximal development. How much longer would it have taken for the child to work it out on their own?

Teachers provide scaffolding by giving demonstrations, assistance and explanation when delivering new information, and offering feedback to students when necessary. They also focus on extending the student's learning in the zone of proximal development, but are careful not to pitch the information beyond 'the zone', as the students would be unable to understand what they were saying. Students are encouraged to get involved in group learning or peer mentoring (working with another pupil who may be more able or older, who will provide additional scaffolding to support learning). Teachers also focus on the need for developing a student's language, as Vygotsky believed that thought, language and reasoning are essential to cognitive development and learning.

Exam-style question – Developmental psychology: Cognitive development

These questions are taken from the OCR B542 Psychology paper, from January 2010. For more past and sample papers plus answer exemplars visit the OCR website. OCR have not seen or commented on the quality of the sample answers.

1. Describe **one** application of research into cognitive development. [3]

    Note this says one application. If you give two, only the best one will be given any marks.

    It can be used in education. (1 – this gives an area of application)

    Schools would be able to use their knowledge of cognitive development (1) so that they would realise what children should know at each key stage (1 – these two extra marks are because the candidate has elaborated on the answer using two points).

2.

> **A Family Affair**
> Nick has four children. According to Piaget's theory, each one of them is at a different stage of cognitive development.
>   Esther is the youngest child and has only just developed object permanence. Adam is the eldest child and is very good at solving abstract problems. Sophie is already very good at science and understands conservation. Luke's language development is very advanced but he is still very egocentric.

    Using the source;

    (a) give the name of the child who is at the sensori-motor stage of cognitive development; [1]

    Esther (1)

    (b) give the name of the child who is at the pre-operational stage of cognitive development; [1]

    Luke (1)

    (c) give the name of the child who is at the concrete operational stage of cognitive development. [1]

    Sophie (1)

3. Outline two criticisms of Piaget's theory of cognitive development. [4]

    This means 2 marks for each criticism.

    Children seem to be able to do things at a younger age than Piaget said. (1 mark as the candidate did not elaborate or explain their answer in any way.)

    Children's development does not jump over night from one of the stages to the next. Children can develop in one area but it takes a bit longer for them to be able to do something in a different area which is not what Piaget said happens. He said when they go from one step to the next, it will affect every area of their life. (2 marks as the candidate has explained their answer clearly.) (Total marks are 3/4 in this part of the question.)

4. Describe and evaluate one study into cognitive development. [10]

    Ten marks are available here. Remember you have been asked to describe AND evaluate so you can think of each part as being worth 5 marks.

Description: The study I am going to write about is Piaget's experiment into the conservation of numbers.

Aim: Piaget wanted to know how old children had to be to be able to conserve numbers. He wanted to see if they could still understand that there was the same number of counters in a row even when he changed what they looked like.

Method: 17 children who were aged between 4 and 6 were asked to put objects like pennies or counters in exactly the same layout as Piaget had done. If he put 6 counters in a row, the child had to do the same with the same number. Then Piaget spread his row out or pushed the counters closer together. The child was asked if there was still the same number of counters in each row. The younger children couldn't do it but the oldest children who were nearly concrete operations children, were able to say that there were the same number in each row. His conclusions were that the youngest children couldn't say there was the same number so they couldn't conserve. The middle children were able to say there were the same number if they spread their counters out to look like Piaget's. The oldest children were able to conserve numbers. (5)

Evaluation: The children were just the children of Piaget's friends. (O marks as we do not know who the children were or how they were selected.)

The children weren't given the same instructions and so the procedure was not standardised and this might have made the results inaccurate (1). Also there were different people working with the children and so some of them might have been more frightening to the children than others (1).

The children might have been nervous and not worked as well as they might have done at home (1).

Some children were asked the same question twice and this might have made them think they were wrong when they gave their first answer. (1) (Total marks are 9/10 in this part of the question.)

The candidate has described most of the features of the study and it is easy to understand what actually happened here. You could also draw an illustration if you think this will help to explain your answer.

SECTION TOTAL [20]

4 Social psychology

We are all social beings, and the relationships we have are one of the most important things in our lives. Research has shown how important others are to us because we have discovered that when humans are kept in solitary confinement for long periods of time, they often start to hallucinate or have vivid dreams about other people. Because our social relationships are so important to our well-being, this has resulted in a branch of psychology that focuses on understanding our social behaviour. Social psychologists have considered how our behaviour is influenced by the situation we find ourselves in, and also how good we are at communicating our feelings without using words.

Unit B541: The first section of this chapter gives some insight into the research that has been conducted to explain obedience, and the core study tries to find an explanation as to why we are more likely to carry out a task if we are asked by someone in a uniform.

Unit B542: The second section focuses on non-verbal communication, considering its function and how it develops. Non-verbal communication varies between cultures, and the core study focuses on the fact that some cultures view parts of the face as being more significant than others.

Obedience

Overview

Although most of us like to feel that we make our own decisions and are not pressurised by other people, we are more influenced by the things that others do and think than we would like to admit. It is really difficult to go against the majority and feel like the odd one out, even if we end up doing something we would rather not do. Similarly, if we are put in a situation where everyone is doing as they are told, we find it extremely difficult to go against the crowd and disobey, especially if the person giving the order is seen to be a person with legitimate authority.

Social psychologists have been interested in researching what makes people obedient, even when the orders given seem unreasonable. Is obedience a result of the situation, the person giving the orders or the nature of the individual who is being told what to do?

Definitions of obedience and defiance

Obedience can be defined as following a command, order or instruction that is given by someone in authority. We are often obedient, even when we do not want to be, because the person giving the order is someone who has some power over us. This could be a teacher or a policeman. It could also be someone we know who threatens to hurt us if we do not do as we are told.

Defiance is where we decide to defy or go against what is being asked of us. By resisting the command of another person, we are challenging or opposing their authority. By being defiant, we make active choices not to do something, but to do something else instead, although we understand what we have been told to do. The reasons we are defiant may be because we do not morally agree with what we have been ordered to do because it goes against our own values.

Defiance is sometimes considered to be more extreme that simply disobeying someone. We could argue that disobeying means just not doing as you have been told and trying to get away with it, whereas defying someone is openly standing up and saying, 'I'm not doing what you have told me to do'.

Denial of responsibility is what happens when people put the blame for their actions onto someone else. There have been a number of instances throughout history when people have done horrific things to others, but have claimed that they were not responsible for their actions because they

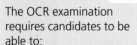

Obedience versus conformity

We sometimes get confused between the ideas of obedience and conformity. We conform by going along with the behaviour or opinions of others, but we are not instructed to conform – it is up to us. On the other hand, we obey when we are told to do something by someone else.

KEY CONCEPTS

The OCR examination requires candidates to be able to:
- distinguish between obedience and defiance
- explain what is meant by denial of responsibility.

DISCUSS...

Think of an example of when you may be obedient and then think of an example of when you might choose to be defiant. Which do you think would be easier?

were just following orders. This denial of responsibility happens when people act as 'agents' for someone else – they are in the agentic state. There are a number of very famous examples of how people, acting in an agentic state, have behaved in a different way to how they would if they were allowed free choice; we will consider these later in the chapter.

QUESTION

1. Define the following terms:

Word	Explanation (try not to use the word itself)	Example
Obedience		
Defiance		
Denial of responsibility		

CORE THEORY: theory of situational factors

Candidates should be able to:

* explain the effect on obedience of environment – i.e., setting, culture
* explain the effect on obedience of authority and the power to punish
* explain the effect on obedience of consensus
* explain the criticisms of situational factors as an explanation for obedience
* consider dispositional factors as an alternative theory, with specific reference to the role of the alternative personality in obedience.

Psychologists have tried to understand why people are obedient, even when they do not really agree with what they have been asked to do. Sometimes what people are told to do is relatively trivial, such as picking up litter from the ground; at other times it is quite horrific, like giving another human being electric shocks because they have not managed to learn something correctly.

As a result of their research, psychologists have come to the conclusion that there are a number of factors that influence why people are obedient, and they all seem to be linked in some way. We are going to consider each of these in turn.

* Environmental factors: Does the setting make the command seem more reasonable (a teacher asking a pupil to finish some work or a librarian telling someone to be quiet in a library)?
* Cultural factors: Some cultures expect obedience from the female members of the family.

- Possible punishments: Is the person who disobeys or defies a command likely to be punished?
- Consensus factors: Is everyone else being obedient?
- Personality factors: Is the person who obeys different to other people?

The effects of the environment on obedience

Setting

If you were standing in a coffee bar and someone came up to you and told you to get undressed, you would think they were very weird, and would either move away from them, get angry or feel really upset. On the other hand, if you were in a doctor's surgery, and the doctor asked you to get undressed, you would be far more likely to do exactly as you were asked. This should suggest to you that the environment or setting you are in will make a difference, because you will have a schema of the kind of things that will happen in each setting. You would not expect to be handed a cup of coffee in a doctor's surgery, just as you would not expect to be told to get undressed in a coffee bar!

When the things that you experience seem to be incompatible with the environment, you will feel very uncomfortable. If you think that what you have been told to do can be explained by the setting, you will feel more at ease and will be more likely to obey, even if what you are being asked is quite extreme.

Stanley Milgram's work on obedience

One piece of research that was influenced by the setting was the study into obedience conducted by Stanley Milgram in 1963. Milgram was interested in finding out whether people would be willing to give electric shocks to people as a punishment for getting the answers wrong during a memory test.

Milgram wanted to investigate whether Germans were particularly obedient to authority figures; this was a common explanation for the Nazi atrocities of the Second World War (1939–45). He planned to test obedience first in an American setting, before conducting the same research in Germany and seeing if there was a difference in the results.

He advertised for male participants between the ages of 20 and 50 years to take part in a study on learning at Yale University (one of the most distinguished universities in the USA). Participants were met by the experimenter, who was working for Milgram. They were told that the purpose of the study was to look at whether the threat of punishment would help someone to learn.

Milgram set up the experiment so that the roles of teacher and learner were drawn apparently at random, making the participant believe that it was purely down to chance that they had been assigned the role of teacher. The learner, who was introduced as Mr Wallace, explained that he had a mild heart condition. However, he was strapped into a chair and electrodes were attached to his arms.

The teacher, whose role was to help Mr Wallace learn word pairs, sat in an adjoining room containing a fake shock generator, with a row of switches marked from 15 volts ('slight shock'), through 375 volts ('danger: severe shock'), right up to 450 volts ('XXX'). The teacher was told that the way he was to help Mr Wallace learn was to give him an electric shock every time he got the answer wrong or said nothing. He was also told to increase the shocks by 15 volts each time.

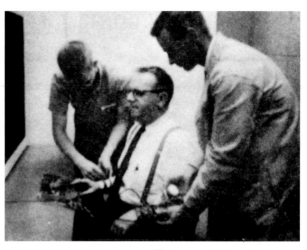

▲ Figure 4.1 Milgram's 'learner' having the electrodes strapped on, and the participant receiving a sample shock from the generator

Mr Wallace started off quite well, but as he made more and more mistakes, the teacher was prompted by the experimenter to continue to administer shocks: 'Please continue', 'Please go on', 'The experiment requires that you continue', 'It is absolutely essential that you continue' and 'You have no other choice, you must go on'. At 180 volts Mr Wallace shouted out that he could not stand the pain; at 300 volts he begged to be released; after 315 volts there was silence. (Of course, this was all artificial and he was fine in the next room.)

Before starting, Milgram explained the plans for his study to a number of psychiatrists and invited their comments. Both Milgram and the psychiatrists predicted that around 2 per cent would shock to the highest level, but that the majority of participants would refuse to continue at a very early stage. However, all participants shocked to 300 volts and 65 per cent of participants continued to 450 volts, which would have resulted in death for Mr Wallace.

Did the setting affect the results?

It was likely that the participants believed that research in a prestigious university must be very important and therefore quite safe. Even though they were told what was going to happen with the electric shocks, did they believe that Milgram would really expect them to kill someone?

Milgram repeated the study in a tatty, downtown office block, and here the obedience levels dropped a little, but were still 48 per cent. It appears that the setting had some influence on the results, although the setting could not be held responsible for these levels of obedience.

Further your understanding

Yale University is one of the Ivy League universities in the USA, similar to Oxford and Cambridge in the UK.

HOMEWORK

Look up Milgram's experiment on the internet. You will also find videos taken from the experiment on YouTube.

DISCUSS...

Imagine you drop some litter in the school playground. If the punishment was a telling-off, would you still drop it? What about missing your lunch break? And what if you were to lose your break time for a whole term? What if you were likely to be permanently excluded?

Culture

By culture, we mean a set of shared attitudes, values, practices and goals, which are found in different races, institutions, organisations and groups. If the majority of members of a culture share these 'norms and values', most people would find it very difficult not to conform to them.

Milgram's research was carried out in the USA as part of his research into whether Germans were more obedient than people from other cultures. He later conducted the same research in a number of other countries and achieved very similar results, which suggested that high levels of obedience were not only true of Americans. Other researchers repeated Milgram's study in the 1970s and they too obtained similar results. Australia had a 68 per cent obedience level, Jordan 63 per cent, Italy 80 per cent, and Austria and Germany had the highest obedience level of 85 per cent.

Perhaps we can explain levels of obedience by looking at the culture of the country. If people in a culture are encouraged to be individuals and to stand up for their rights, they will be more willing and confident to challenge and even openly defy authority. If, on the other hand, they are part of a collectivist culture, where harmony between groups is seen to be desirable, they will be less willing to go against what they see as an authority figure. China, Korea and Japan are examples of collectivist cultures, whereas Western European countries and the USA are individualist cultures.

The effect on obedience of authority and the power to punish

We are usually more likely to do as we are told if we think that we will be punished if we do not do so. This message is with us from an early age, with teachers giving detentions if pupils do not do their homework or break the classroom rules. As we grow up, we realise that on occasions we may choose to disobey or defy an authority figure because the punishment is not that extreme and it is our choice.

However, if the punishment is likely to be very serious or life-threatening, we are far more likely to obey.

- In the UK, the police hold a high level of power and can arrest people if they do not live by the law. People are far more likely to do what they are told by a policeman than a member of the public because of the level of coercive power held by the police.
- Soldiers obey their commanding officer because if they refuse to carry out an order, they are likely to be court-martialled and imprisoned.

Further your understanding

Coercive power comes from having the ability to punish the person if they disobey or are actively defiant.

Some countries are ruled by dictators, who are people with extreme levels of coercive power who rule by fear and threats to punish for disobedience. The populations of these countries rarely disobey, for fear of losing their lives.

The power of authority was demonstrated in study carried out in a real-life setting by Hofling *et al.* (1966). They were interested in finding out whether nurses would knowingly break hospital rules in order to obey a doctor. The authority and power that hospital doctors had in 1966 would have meant that it was extremely difficult for the nurse to challenge the doctor's authority, and she would fear being punished by losing her job should she refuse to obey his directions.

Hofling *et al.* set up the experiment in the following way:

A bottle of pills had been labelled 'Astroten' and placed in the ward medicine cabinet. The nurse on duty received a phone call from a Dr Smith from the Psychiatric Department, asking her to give his patient 20mg of Astroten straightaway. He explained that he was in a hurry and wanted the drug to have taken effect before he got to see the patient, and that he would sign the drug authorisation when he came on the ward in about 10 minutes' time. The label on the bottle in the ward medicine cabinet stated the usual dose as 5mg and the maximum daily dose as 10 mg.

These instructions broke the following hospital rules:

- nurses give drugs only after written authorisation
- nurses take instructions only from people they know
- maximum dosages should not be exceeded.

Nevertheless, 21 of the 22 nurses phoned by 'Dr Smith' obeyed the instructions, although someone stopped them from actually administering the drug (which was a harmless sugar pill). When interviewed afterwards, many nurses said that doctors often phoned them with instructions and would become very annoyed if the nurse protested. Here the nurses were denying that they were responsible for what they had done, blaming the doctors for their actions.

In a variation to his original study, Milgram followed the same procedure as before, but the experimenter gave up his grey laboratory coat and simply looked like a member of the public. The resulting level of obedience from participants fell to 20 per cent, which suggests that they did not believe that he had any power over them and that, as a result, the experiment was not legitimate.

QUESTION

2. Describe the factors that could help to explain why the nurses were so obedient.

Figure 4.2

ASTROTEN

5 mg capsules
Usual dose: 5 mg
Maximum daily
dose: 10 mg

Figure 4.3 This is the label the nurses saw in the ward medicine cabinet

QUESTION

3. What ethical guidelines were broken by Milgram's and Hofling *et al.*'s research? (See Chapter 6, page 192).

DISCUSS...

From what you have read so far, do you think that people's willingness to obey is due to the power of an authority figure to punish them if they disobey or defy a command, or do you think that the situation is more complicated? Work with a friend and try to think of the things that might have made Milgram's Yale participants obey.

DISCUSS...

Can you think of any situations you may have been in where you have gone along with the crowd, even though you would have preferred not to?

DISCUSS...

Recent events that resulted in rioting across the UK could be explained by consensus behaviour. How many of the people involved were law-abiding in other areas of their lives?

The effect of consensus on obedience

If you have been told to do something and you are not sure whether you should really obey, or even if it is the right thing to do, you will probably look and see what others are doing before you act.

Imagine the following situation. You have just started at a new school, and at break time the teacher tells you that now you have finished your work, you should go and get a toothbrush out of a pot on the side and go and clean your teeth. You are quite confused. You have not been told to bring a toothbrush. Which one is yours? Do you actually have one at all? In fact, do you actually want to clean your teeth? You look at the pot of toothbrushes on the side and notice that they are all the same colour and make. Should you take any toothbrush? Should you just refuse? The bell goes and all the other pupils come over to the pot and just take any random toothbrush. At this point, you make the decision to do what the others are doing, as they all seem to think that the teacher's direction was quite normal and acceptable. In fact, it would have been hard to go against the flow! Here, the consensus of opinion – that is, the widespread agreement among all members of the group – is to do as you have been told, and this consensus will affect your obedience.

The consensus of opinion can be very powerful in changing the behaviour of others who would, under different circumstances, act very differently. One example of a real-life situation that might be explained by this phenomenon was the massacre at My Lai during the Vietnam War. The commanding officer, Lieutenant William Calley, who had been told the enemy were hiding in the village of My Lai, ordered his soldiers to kill everyone (even though there were only women, old men and children).

Although individual soldiers felt very uncomfortable with the command, the consensus of opinion was that the commander is a legitimate authority figure and therefore must be obeyed. They consequently followed his commands. Calley was later court-martialled, and claimed that he too was 'only following orders'. One of the soldiers at Calley's trial explained:

> *Lieutenant Calley told me to start shooting. So I started shooting. I poured about four clips into the group ... They were begging and saying, 'No, No.' And the mothers were hugging their children and ... well, we kept right on firing. They were waving their arms and begging* (Life 67(23), 5 December 1969)

Because we human beings are social animals and want to be accepted by others as part of 'the gang', it makes us very unhappy if we are isolated, and it is this that makes us go along with others. Research has shown that when others refuse to obey, this gives individuals the confidence to say no to unreasonable requests. This was shown in a variation of the Milgram experiment when the participants were put with two other 'participants' who were actually confederates of Milgram. The fake participants were told to refuse to give Mr Wallace the fatal electric shocks during the experiment. In this situation, 90 per cent of real participants also refused to give Mr Wallace the fatal shocks.

Criticisms of situational factors as an explanation of obedience

There are some criticisms of the research evidence that have been used to support the idea that situational factors are an explanation of obedience. These criticisms focus not only on the research itself, but also suggest that there may be other reasons why we are obedient.

Setting

Were the results of Milgram's research influenced by the setting? Perhaps people would expect research into memory to take place in a university, so would be more willing to go along with the commands. This was why Milgram repeated his research in the downtown office block. Here there was still a high level of obedience, but not as high as the results from Yale University. This suggests that undertaking research into obedience in a university may not reflect accurately what happens in the real world.

Some of the research into obedience may have lacked ecological validity

Ecological validity is when the results of any research are actually valid in the real world. Research conducted in laboratories often lacks ecological validity because if it were carried out in a naturalistic setting, the results would be different. Sometimes part of the procedure is not realistic and this may have been the case in the original Hofling *et al.* study.

When Hofling *et al.*'s research was replicated, the researchers decided to use a real drug name rather than one made up, to increase the ecological validity. The drug used was Valium®, which was a familiar drug to all the nurses. Here only 2 of the 18 nurses obeyed the instructions. The conclusion was that the nurses defied the doctor because they felt confident that they knew the order they had been given was dangerous to the patient, whereas in the first study the drug was unknown to them.

Individuals do not always behave in the same way in different circumstances

When we cannot see the consequences of our actions directly, we are more likely to do something than when we are faced with the effects of our actions. For example, if a soldier is asked to shoot the enemy, this may be much easier from inside a tank than it would be if they were in the same room, face to face with the person they have been asked to shoot. This is because it is easier to be in the agentic state from a distance than it is when the outcome is seen first-hand.

This is what happened with the participants in the Milgram study, because when he gave his participants personal responsibility for the suffering of the learner, by making them put the learner's hand on the electric plate, their obedience levels dropped to 30 per cent. Originally they were in the next room to the learner and could only hear his cries over the intercom. Perhaps the fact that they were unable to deny what was going on meant that their personal values were more important than the pressures from the researcher in the university situation.

The effect of personality or motivation of participants on levels of obedience

Although Milgram's original research was carried out in a prestigious university, when he replicated the study in a downtown office block he found that people still obeyed the orders of the experimenter, to a much higher level than would be expected. Perhaps certain types of people were attracted to the task. Additionally, the participants were paid to take part in the research. They may have felt that they had to do as they were asked because they needed the money.

Dispositional factors as an alternative theory of obedience

Although most of the research suggests that the participants in Milgram's work, the nurses in Hofling *et al.*'s experiment and the soldiers at My Lai are really just ordinary people in extraordinary situations, we could ask ourselves if this really is the case. Perhaps the people who replied to Milgram's advertisement, or the nurses or the soldiers, were all a certain type of person. What if they specifically sought out those jobs, or sought out a murderous regiment in the US Army? Perhaps there was something about their disposition – factors associated with their personality – that made them want to get involved in these situations in the first place, rather than their behaviour being anything to do with the situation at all.

Adorno and his colleagues were trying to explain why anti-Semitism (prejudice towards Jewish people) had taken hold in Nazi Germany. Adorno was interested, as was Milgram, in whether there was something about the German population that was different from other nationalities. Adorno wondered why so many German people did not challenge the mass murder of the Jews. Adorno suggested that there might be a certain personality

QUESTION ?

4. Outline how dispositional factors can provide an alternative explanation of obedience (note: when explaining obedience, you need to describe what is meant by dispositional factors and then explain how they differ from situational factors).

type that would be more likely to obey orders and this was the basis of his research.

Adorno and his colleagues used various psychological scales to try to identify why some people are more likely to have fascist and authoritarian belief systems than others, thinking that this might be the explanation they were looking for.

Adorno gave questionnaires, other psychological tests and interviews to over 2,000 American adults. Once the data had been analysed, Adorno devised the F-scale, a scale for measuring fascism, which contained a list of statements that people would score on a six-point scale (see page 116 for examples).

According to Adorno, the authoritarian personality shows the following characteristics:

- They are very much more likely to conform than other people.
- They are subservient to people of higher status.
- They are intolerant of people they consider to be inferior.
- They generally dislike others who are different to them and are unwilling to tolerate them.
- They are quite insecure.
- They find it very difficult to think flexibly, have very rigid thought patterns and are unwilling to look for alternative opinions and views.

People who scored highly on his F-scale were classified as authoritarian personalities.

Perhaps these were the people who responded to Milgram's advertisement. Perhaps they were the kind of people who signed up to fight in the US Army.

Adorno claimed that the reason people develop an authoritarian personality might be due to early childhood experiences. In Chapter 1 we talked about psychoanalytic theory and gender roles. Freud's theory suggests that young boys take on their father's behaviour, speech and attitudes when they experience the Oedipus complex. According to Freud, if the father is very strict and highly authoritarian, the child may also become strict and authoritarian, and is likely to develop an authoritarian personality. Freud also suggested that most people hide their desires and drives that may not considered acceptable, but that these often surface in some way – as, for example, by projecting them onto minority groups such as the Jews.

Perhaps obedience is due in part to the nature of the person – if they have an authoritarian personality type – and in part to the situation. As with most psychological theory, there is rarely one answer to a question. More often than not, things can be explained both by the nature of the situation and the nature of the person.

Further your understanding

Fascism is a system where a dictator has complete power and suppresses any opposition. Fascist states are based on nationalism, discipline and political violence. When someone is called a fascist, it means they are oppressive, intolerant, dictatorial, racist and often aggressive.

Further your understanding

Prejudice is when we form a judgement or pre-judge something without knowing all the facts.

Discrimination is when we treat someone differently to another person on the basis of our prejudice.

Table 4.1 A sample of the statements from the F-test, together with the scoring system by Adorno *et al.* (1950) ▶

Obedience and respect for authority are the most important virtues children should learn.
A person who has bad manners, habits and breeding can hardly expect to get along with decent people.
The businessman and the manufacturer are much more important to society than the artist and the professor.
Every person should have complete faith in some supernatural power whose decisions he obeys without question.
What the youth needs most is strict discipline, rugged determination, and the will to work and fight for family and country.
An insult to our honour should always be punished.
Sex crimes, such as rape and attacks on children, deserve more than mere imprisonment; such criminals ought to be publicly whipped, or worse.
Most of our social problems would be solved if we could somehow get rid of the immoral, crooked and feeble-minded people.
Homosexuals are hardly better than criminals and ought to be severely punished.
Most people do not realise how much our lives are controlled by plots hatched in secret places.

Disagree strongly	Disagree mostly	Disagree somewhat	Agree somewhat	Agree mostly	Agree strongly
1	2	3	4	5	6

CORE STUDY: L. Bickman (1974)

L. Bickman (1974) *The social power of a uniform.* Journal of Applied Social Psychology 4, pp. 47–91

Background

So far, we have considered the effects of the situation on obedience by considering:

- the environment (setting and culture)
- authority and the power to punish
- consensus of opinion.

We have also considered whether the situation alone is a good enough explanation of obedience or whether there is something about a person's personality (disposition) that makes them more likely to obey.

The research by Bickman considers whether the appearance of a person will influence their ability to get others to obey them.

You need to be able to …

- describe Bickman's field experiment into the effects of uniform
- outline the limitations of Bickman's study.

People with uniforms are often considered to be more of an authority figure than people who wear their normal clothes, although some uniforms can suggest a higher level of authority (think about a policeman and a postman). In fact, wearing a uniform can affect the wearer themselves, making the wearer believe that she/he is more powerful.

Describe the study

The aim of this study is to measure the degree of social power that someone has if they are wearing a uniform, and to try to explain the nature of this power.

In order to look at all the aspects of power, Bickman conducted a field experiment, using white male students, aged between 18 and 20 years, to take the role of the authority figures, and one student to act as a 'stooge'. They all wore the same-sized suits and were of similar build.

The participants were an opportunity sample of pedestrians walking alone along a street in Brooklyn, New York, during weekdays.

> For more on field experiments, see Chapter 6, page 195.

Uniform	Clothes	Level of authority
Civilian	Sports jacket and tie	Lowest level of authority
Milkman	White coat, carrying a basket full of empty milk bottles	A little authority
Guard	Looked like a policeman, but with a different badge	Highest level of authority

◀ Table 4.2 Clothes worn by three of the experimenters

Procedure

Each experiment involved the experimenter (E) giving a pedestrian (P) orders to do a specific task.

- Paper bag: E stopped P and told them to 'Pick up this bag for me!' If P did not do it immediately, E would explain that he had a bad back. P was considered to have obeyed if they picked up the bag.
- Dime: E stopped P, pointed to a confederate standing beside a parked car at a parking meter, and said, 'This fellow is over-parked at the meter but doesn't have any change. Give him a dime!' If P did not do it immediately, E would explain that he had no change either. P was considered to have obeyed if they gave the confederate a dime or made an effort to find change by searching for it.
- Bus stop: If P was standing alone at a bus stop, E would approach and say, 'Don't you know you have to stand on the other side of the pole?' The sign says 'No Standing' (this actually meant that cars were not allowed to wait in the bus stop area). If P did not do it immediately, E would say, 'Then the bus won't stop here, it's a new law.'

QUESTIONS ?

5. Why do you think all the student experimenters were of similar size and build?
6. Why do you think the experimenters selected pedestrian participants who were walking along on their own?

If P did not do as they were asked, even after the explanation, E left.

Variations

The experimenters varied the experiment to see whether being observed by another person would affect obedience.

They also gave out questionnaires to college students, asking them if they thought they would be more likely to obey either a guard, a civilian or a milkman when being asked to do the above tasks.

Results

The results of the field experiments showed that the person wearing the guard's uniform had an effect on people's willingness to obey.

Uniform	% obeying in each of the following situations		
	Paper bag	Dime	Bus stop
Civilian	36	33	20
Milkman	64	57	21
Guard	82	89	56

◀ Table 4.3 Percentage of obedience over three situations

Overall, Bickman reported that there was no significant difference between obedience to the civilian and the milkman, and he suggested that any difference that did occur was due to chance (which could have been something as simple as the mood of the people on the day of the experiment).

Bickman also found that being observed (surveillance) had no effect on the obedience of the participants.

The results of the questionnaires given to the students showed that they did not think that the dress of the character (civilian, milkman or guard) made the request to help any more legitimate. They did think that the nature of the situation might influence the public to be more obedient. For example, in the bus stop condition, where you would think that it would be more reasonable for an authority figure to direct you where to stand, the guard received the highest rating for level of obedience.

Conclusions

Bickman suggests that how we judge an authority figure will be more important than the orders they give. (If we think the person is trustworthy, we are more likely to do what they ask than if we think they are untrustworthy.)

Bickman also suggests that someone wearing a guard's uniform is more likely to be taken seriously because people will think the person must have a responsible job. However, if people *always* believe that authority figures are legitimate, this can have important implications for society, because there have been cases where uniformed authority figures have asked people to do things that are unacceptable, such as the massacre at My Lai during the Vietnam War.

From this study the author managed to show that uniforms do provide a higher level of social power, but that the level of power does depend on the situation.

Limitations

Many of the limitations of Bickman's study relate to the methodology used.

Ethics

The participants who were involved in the field study on the streets of New York did not give their consent.

Methodology

Some data were collected from field experiments and some from student questionnaires. Do you feel that the questionnaires given to the students would provide accurate information?

Participants (field study)

The participants in the field study were an opportunity sample from a street in New York who were estimated to be between the ages of 18 and 61. Perhaps the researchers were mistaken about their ages, as they were never asked their actual age. Some may have been younger with less experience and this might have affected their responses.

The participants were selected if they were on their own. Were the participants representative of the population as a whole? Perhaps they were only representative of people in New York, which suggests that the research might be culturally biased.

Although the researchers suggested that those who took part had not seen any previous trials, they could not be sure that the participants had not walked past earlier and seen what was going on.

Participants (questionnaires)

College students completed the questionnaires. Were they representative of the population as a whole? Were they being rewarded to take part in the research? Would this have affected their motivation? It is worth remembering that American college students often get credits for their psychology courses if they take part in research during the period of their studies.

Experimenters

The experimenters were all young, white males. This may have affected the participants' responses, as gender may have played a part. Others

> **QUESTION ?**
>
> **7.** Would the results have been the same if the participants had been informed about the nature of the research?

might have felt intimidated or uncomfortable because of the characteristics of the young men.

Extraneous variables

Because this was a field study, the researchers would have been unable to control all the extraneous variables, such as crowds, time of day and other things happening on the street.

Applications of research into obedience:
keeping order in institutions and situations

Candidates should be able to:

• explain how psychological research relates to keeping order in institutions – for example, the use of punishment in schools, the use of authority in armed forces and the effect of a prison setting.

Keeping order in institutions and situations

Research into obedience has shown that the nature of the situation, the culture and the personality of the individual can all have an impact on how order is maintained in our institutions. We also know that wearing a uniform can affect behaviour, which may be one of the reasons why school children, the armed forces, prisoners and guards all wear uniforms.

● We can learn how to play the role that is required, either by experience or by instruction.

● Schools require pupils to maintain order, to attend lessons, to be polite, to be quiet in class and to study hard.

● Members of the armed forces also have roles that require compliance and obedience at all times in order to do their duty; if they do not follow orders, significant punishments are used.

● The role of the prisoner is to follow the instructions of the guards, to come and go as dictated by the prison regime, and to serve their time.

▲ Figure 4.4 Uniforms can affect behaviour

We also know that many people who have been very closely controlled rarely internalise these behaviours. When they are out of the control of the organisation or institution, they behave very differently. This suggests that people must be watched closely at all times to make sure that control is maintained.

Use of punishment in schools

Schools have expectations as to how the pupils should behave. In fact, if you speak to your grandparents, they may well remember when physical punishment was used in schools to keep order. The slipper, the ruler and the cane were all used as a form of punishment for bad behaviour. Today, such punishments are forbidden, so alternative punishments, such as removal from class, removal of privileges, detentions and exclusions, are used.

Behaviour theory suggests that punishment is not effective as a way of helping children to learn the correct way to behave. What happens if a child really does not know what the required behaviour is? How can they possibly know what they should be doing? Negative reinforcement is more effective as a way of shaping behaviour because ALL behaviour except the wanted behaviour should be punished. The trouble is that telling a child off for everything they do except the wanted behaviour seems really harsh, and very few teachers would be comfortable doing this.

Punishing children for doing wrong may simply teach them how to avoid punishment, so schools need to have clear rules, rewards and consequences as a way of helping students to know how to behave. We know from psychological research that rewarding behaviours is the most effective way of getting someone to do something again. The ultimate aim would be to help students to learn to internalise these behaviours rather than needing external controls.

Use of authority in the armed forces

One of the puzzles about Milgram's research when it was published was that it went against a lot of evidence from military historians. If it is so easy to get one person to give lethal electric shocks to another person, then it ought to be very easy to get a soldier to shoot at the enemy, especially when the enemy is firing at him. The history of warfare tells another story, however, and this makes the Milgram study even more remarkable.

Military historians studying past battles have suggested that, despite their training, many soldiers do not want to fire guns at other human beings. In the Second World War, a number of studies of US troops came to the same conclusion, suggesting that fewer than 20 per cent of soldiers would fire their guns even when they were under fire themselves. The reason was not fear, because these men often performed acts of great heroism.

Milgram's research stumbled on a way to break down the troops' unwillingness to kill. As a result, fire rates for troops have increased from 20 per cent in the Second World War, to 55 per cent in Korea (1950s) to 90 per cent in Vietnam (1960s and 1970s). Western forces are now much more efficient killing machines.

> *To internalise something means to make it part of the way you think rather than it being put on you by an outside force.*

DISCUSS...
How would you behave in school if there were no teachers?

DISCUSS...
Do you think school punishments are effective?

DISCUSS...
What rewards could schools use for good behaviour?

Members of the armed forces have to be trained to obey without question, because they will be going into dangerous situations under the command of someone with a much higher level of knowledge and experience than them. They are taught to obey immediately in order to keep themselves and each other safe. This starts from the beginning of training, with new recruits having their individuality removed by cutting their hair and putting them in uniform. This deindividuation makes them far more likely to adopt the roles they have taken on and to comply with the demands of their superiors. Senior officers are seen as having expert authority, and many of them will have had considerably longer in the forces than the new recruits. The hierarchy of leadership reinforces the status of the new recruits as being relatively powerless.

Recruits are also controlled by the fear of punishment if they were to go against the orders of their superior officers. Punishments such as withholding pay, additional physical exercise, withholding leave and courts martial for soldiers who go absent without leave are all made very obvious to recruits as a way of keeping them in order.

Personality screening could identify those soldiers who have an authoritarian personality. This could prevent the abuse of power over groups, and prevent blind compliance to unacceptable and irresponsible orders.

Prisons

When someone is caught following involvement in criminal activity, our society suggests that they should be punished. Prison could be a 'short, sharp shock', providing a harsh regime that will frighten the criminal away from a life of crime. We know that punishment alone is not effective, because it fails to help the prison inmate understand what they should be doing. In fact, rates of reoffending (recidivism) are high, ranging from 50 to 70 per cent, depending on the nature of the crime, the age of the criminal, and so on.

Prisoners have personal possessions taken away from them, and in the past have been given a kind of prison uniform in order to remove their individuality, as a way of making them conform to the prison regime. Guards also wear uniforms, and we can expect that this visual reminder of their authority may make the prisoners more likely to obey them. Wearing a uniform might make it easier for the guards to manage the prisoners, as they are simply 'following orders' rather than feeling personally responsible for the roles they have to play.

In order to prevent prisoners from getting together to gang up against the prison guards, the prisoners are separated for proportions of the day. When they are together, they need to be monitored closely; it is helpful to involve people who could provide a different view and challenge the thoughts and beliefs of the inmates. The aim is to stop the prisoner consensus being to overthrow the guards. If anything does go wrong, prison guards can punish prisoners by withdrawal of privileges or placing them in solitary confinement.

We know that rewards are the most effective way of changing behaviour; in addition to individual rewards, such as extra visits, telephone calls and television, group rewards could be used.

Exam-style question – Social psychology: Obedience

These questions are taken from the OCR B541 Psychology paper, from June 2010. For more past and sample papers plus answer exemplars visit the OCR website. OCR have not seen or commented on the quality of the sample answers.

1. Give one real-life example of obedience. [1]

   School pupils have to do as the teachers ask them to do in school. (1)

2. Give one real-life example of defiance. [1]

   Refusing to do as the teachers tell you. (1)

3.
   Investigating Obedience
   A psychologist used a confederate in an experiment to investigate obedience. However she told each participant that she was investigating sleep deprivation. The confederate pretended to be very tired.

   In the first condition the psychologist instructed each participant to stop the confederate going to sleep by prodding him.

   In the second condition, the participants were put in groups and had to decide together whether to follow the instruction to prod the confederate. This was a test of consensus.

   Using the source, explain how the participants may have behaved differently in the two conditions. [3]

   If one person in the group disobeys then the participant may disobey when he would not by himself (1) to fit in (1).

   This answer does not get three marks because the candidate has not explained why this happens by giving an answer based on the psychological theory they understand. This would be a better answer:

   They could be less likely to obey second time around (1) because if one person disobeys they act as a role model (1) and people may conform with this action (1).

4. Bickman (1974) carried out a field experiment into the power of uniforms.
    Identify **two** limitations of Bickman's study from the list below by ticking the relevant box. [2]

    If you tick more than two boxes, you will have one of your marks taken off.

    he only used male confederates ✓ *(1)*

    he only carried out his research in one area ✓ *(1)*

    he only got participants to obey one type of order ☐

    he only tested one type of uniform ☐

5. Describe how research into obedience can be used to help keep order in institutions. [4]

    By having to wear uniforms (1) prisoners lose their individuality (1) which means they are more likely to conform to group norms (1). If they don't obey, they could be punished (1).

    You get 1 mark for identifying a relevant institution, for example, army, school or prison. You get another mark for each statement which shows how obedience could be encouraged, for example, people wearing uniforms, having authority figures and punishing disobedience.

6. Explain the role of dispositional factors in obedience. [4]

    The theory is that an individual's personality will determine whether they are going to obey (1) not the situation they find themselves in (1).

    This answer is quite basic and not worth 4 marks. The candidate only makes two points in the answer. You can gain 1 mark for each brief statement made about the theory, for example, references to personality traits, upbringing and/or nature, authoritarian personality.

    This would be a better answer:

    Adorno suggested that people who are obedient have authoritarian personalities (1). This would be due to a strict upbringing (1) and means that they are more likely to conform than other people and are more willing to obey (1), but don't like people they think are inferior (1).

    SECTION TOTAL [15]

Non-verbal communication

Overview

When we think about communicating with each other, we usually think about communication using speech, but communication is far more complex than simply using words. In fact, the way we say these words can convey even more information than the words themselves. Aaronson, Wilson and Akert (1994) used the following exercise as an example of how even our tone of voice can change the meaning of words.

> Say the following words in as many different ways as you can:
> 'I don't know her.'
> Try it with an angry tone of voice, a loving voice, a sarcastic voice, a fearful tone and a surprised tone. Try emphasising the different words, first stressing the word 'I' and then the word 'her' (Aaronson et al. 1994, p. 159).

We can actually change the meaning of words by the way we say them and by the tone that we use. Among other things, we notice how a person looks, how they are standing, how loud they speak, their facial expression and the amount of eye contact they make. In fact, when we communicate with another person, research evidence has suggested that words provide only 7 per cent of the information, while 55 per cent of the information comes from the person's face and 38 per cent from their tone of voice.

Non-verbal communication

Non-verbal communication is the term used to describe literally how we communicate without using words. In fact, research has shown that non-verbal communication is four times more powerful and effective than verbal communication. If we have a conversation with a person, but what they say and the way they look do not match, we usually have a pretty good idea of what they really mean and will go with their appearance rather than their words.

Non-verbal communication serves a number of social purposes:

- to signal emotional states – putting your arm around someone's shoulders to show concern
- to signal attitudes – standing with your arms folded to show that you disagree with or are cross with the speaker

> *This section still focuses on social psychology, looking specifically at non-verbal communication, especially facial expressions, but it will be examined in the second examination paper you sit.*

KEY CONCEPTS

The OCR examination requires candidates to be able to:

- outline examples of body language as a form of non-verbal communication
- outline examples of facial expressions as a form of non-verbal communication.

- to help speech – by using tone or volume to emphasise meaning
- in place of speech – using gestures such as a sigh (to mean 'Oh, for goodness sake') or a shrug of the shoulders (to mean 'I don't know').

Because non-verbal communication varies between friends and acquaintances, males and females, old and young, and different cultural groups, it is impossible to provide any sort of non-verbal dictionary. Gestures or glances between friends can provide lots of information, but the same gesture towards a stranger could be misinterpreted, so it would be more helpful if we all shared the same understanding of non-verbal cues.

Body language as a form of non-verbal communication

Body language is a general term for any non-verbal signals using parts of our body – for example, posture, hand gestures, proxemics (how close we stand to someone) and touch.

- Posture involves the whole body and is a good signal of general attitude. We will stand with our legs apart and arms folded to show annoyance or aggression. A way of showing defeat is to slouch forward, with head bowed and arms hanging down by our sides.
- Hand gestures are actions made with our hands and arms. We may turn our palms upwards to signal 'I don't know', show a fist to signal anger or hostility, or hold a hand up in front of another person, palm facing their face, to signal 'stop'.
- Proxemics: We all need our own personal space, but the distance we stand from another person can vary according to the relationship we have with them. Hall (1968) identified four types of social distance, although these can vary in different cultures, which could result in embarrassment! For example, people from some Middle Eastern cultures stand much closer to each other than people from Western cultures. We can also use proximity to intimidate another person, because standing too close to them will make them feel very uncomfortable.

> Personal space is like a bubble that surrounds us, and when people invade our space bubble we feel really uncomfortable. It is personal and may vary from person to person.
>
> Social distance refers to the space requirements of a number of people and may vary according to culture.

Relationship	Distance
Intimate distance – special relationships, such as boy/girlfriend	0–0.5m
Personal distance – friend	0.5–1.2m
Social distance – people we do not know very well but are happy to communicate with	1.2–4.0m
Public distance – people we do not know	4.0–10.0m

Table 4.4 Four types of distance that are used to signify certain relationships (Hall 1968) ▶

- Touch can be used to show concern by putting a hand on someone's arm, but it can also be used as an indication of attraction – women often touch men on the arm to signal (sometimes unconsciously) that they find them attractive. The arm of someone with high status, placed around the shoulder of someone of lower status, can signal inclusion.

HOMEWORK

Look at the pictures in Figure 4.5 and see if you can identify what the body postures mean.
Ask friends if they agree with you. Does everyone interpret them in the same way?
Can you draw any more examples?

▲ Figure 4.5

Facial expressions as a form of non-verbal communication

Facial expressions are probably the most important part of non-verbal communication, especially as we tend to look at the face of another person when we are communicating with them. Because human faces have a large number of different muscles (more than 40), they are very mobile, so we can use the variations of facial expressions to communicate our emotional states and attitudes to others.

There are six facial expressions that are identified by all cultures. These are:

- happiness
- surprise
- fear
- sadness
- anger
- disgust.

Some of these are difficult to differentiate (surprise and fear look very similar), whereas others are much easier to identify (happiness).

Although some facial expressions are universal, others are culturally specific. One example of this is 'eyebrow flashing', which describes the

QUESTION

1. Two of your friends are being told off by the teacher. Christian realised he was wrong, but Bobby thought that the teacher was being unfair as he was not to blame.

- Describe Christian's facial expression.
- Describe Christian's body language.
- Describe Bobby's facial expression.
- Describe Bobby's body language.

DISCUSS...

Try this for yourself – why do you think surprise and fear look very similar?

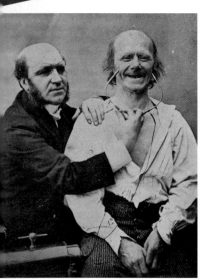

▲ Figure 4.6 Duchenne used electrical stimulation to make his participant produce a fake smile

Further your understanding

We are very good at recognising true emotions, and recent research has shown that children as young as 6 years old can tell the difference between a real smile and fake smile (http://bps-research-digest. blogspot.com/2010/06/ children-as-young-as-six-can-tell-when.html).

way we sometimes quickly raise and then lower our eyebrows, which happens when we recognise someone who is a distance away and cannot actually talk to them – for example, in a lesson or a meeting. Although eyebrow flashing has been found all over the world, it is actually considered indecent in Japan!

People are quite good at judging another person's emotional state from their face, which is very helpful because, as we said earlier, we are more likely to go with the non-verbal message than the words that are spoken. However, research into certain facial expressions has shown that some expressions can be false – for example, smiling. We can smile because we are happy and we can smile even when we are not happy – a false smile. This can be seen in Figure 4.6, which shows Duchenne, an experimental physiologist, using an electrical current to contort the facial muscles around his subject's mouth to make a false smile. A real smile, known as a Duchenne smile, involves a bigger range of muscles that affect the mouth and eyes, and raise the cheeks.

QUESTION ?

2. Complete the following table to show whether each feature of non-verbal communication is associated with facial expressions or body language.

(OCR January 2010)

Feature	Facial expressions	Body language
Arms folded		
Frown		
Crossed legs		
Eye contact		
Open palms		

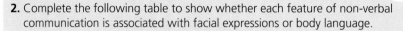

CORE THEORY: social learning theory

 IN THE EXAM

Candidates should be able to:

- explain the role of observation and imitation in learning non-verbal behaviour
- describe the role of reinforcement and punishment in learning non-verbal behaviour
- describe cultural variations in non-verbal communication
- explain the criticisms of the social learning theory of non-verbal behaviour
- consider evolutionary theory as an alternative theory, with specific reference to survival and reproduction.

Have you ever thought how we learn our non-verbal behaviours? Darwin has suggested that some are innate – that is, we are born with the ability to produce them – such as showing anger or fear, or showing pleasure by laughing. What about others, such as using the thumbs-up sign to signify that you are okay, or the arms-folded stance when you are in a huff?

In Chapter 1 you read about social learning theory and the work of Bandura, and how he discovered that children learned aggressive behaviour from observing the behaviour of an adult with a Bobo doll. In fact, both children and adults can learn any sort of behaviour by observation, not just aggressive behaviour. Think back through your life – did you ever see someone doing something else that you thought looked pretty good, so you copied their behaviour or actions perhaps? It would therefore seem quite likely that some of our non-verbal behaviours have been learned by observing others and then mimicking that behaviour, until, in the end, it may simply form part of our automatic responses.

> *Social learning theory proposes that we learn by observing other people and then imitating their behaviour (see Chapter 1, page 23).*

The role of observation and imitation in learning non-verbal behaviour

When you watch parents and babies interacting , their behaviour almost looks like a non-verbal conversation. Baby coos and the adult coos back or responds in some way. If the adult pokes their tongue out, the baby might copy the adult. Research has shown that very young babies can imitate some of the facial expressions they see, which suggests that children are almost pre-programmed to imitate the non-verbal behaviours of others. On the other hand, these are very basic facial expressions and actions, but non-verbal behaviour is much more complicated than simply poking your tongue out, so these behaviours must have been learned.

Children learn initially from parents and siblings, and later from other children. If their role models are positive, they will learn good non-verbal behaviours and social skills and have no difficulty interacting with others. On the other hand, if they see inappropriate, aggressive or even extremely passive behaviours, this will seem normal for them, but will make it difficult for them to get on with other people without having problems.

Once children have seen these behaviours, they may imitate them. If the behaviour is rewarded or reinforced in some way, by praise, by really good feedback or by increased friendships, the behaviour is more likely to be repeated. If it is ignored or punished, it will probably stop.

DISCUSS...

Think of the following gestures:

- a high-five
- the sign for victory
- it is perfect
- it is okay.

Can you remember where you learned them? Can you think of any more common gestures that you know – ones that are not rude!

The role of reinforcement and punishment in learning non-verbal behaviour

Learning theory, which we will talk about in more detail in the next chapter, shows that we are likely to repeat a behaviour if it is rewarded (or reinforced). On the other hand, behaviour that is punished, by which we mean behaviour that results in something unpleasant happening, is less likely to appear again (see Chapter 5, page 150). It would make sense to think of non-verbal behaviours being learned in the same way.

> *Positive reinforcement acts as a reward and increases the chance of the behaviour being repeated.*
>
> *Negative reinforcement punishes all behaviours except the wanted behaviour, so works to help shape what you want someone to do.*
>
> *Punishment punishes the unwanted behaviour, but does not give any idea or indication of what the right behaviour would be. (See behaviourist theory in Chapter 5, page 150.)*

- Imagine a young child watching a couple of adults shaking hands with each other. The child who imitates this behaviour by offering their hand would receive a warm response from the adult, who is likely to be delighted by the behaviour and will smile and react positively to the child. This response will act as a positive reinforcement, so the child will have learned that shaking hands as a greeting is a good behaviour to repeat.
- Imagine you are delivering mail to a house where they have a large Rottweiler dog. The dog will jump up at you and cover you with mud unless you walk in a certain way. You have been delivering mail there for a number of weeks and have been knocked over or covered in mud many times, but the dog is not nasty so you are still persevering with the mail delivery! One day you find the dog does not leap all over you. On this day you have walked really slowly, with your arms down by your sides, smiling as you go. The next day you do the same and the dog leaves you alone. The next day you might need to check whether it is this that has made the difference so you go in with your arms bent at the elbows. Sure enough the dog leaps up again, so you have learned how to behave for this particular dog. This is an example of negative reinforcement where all behaviour except the wanted behaviour has worked to teach you Rottweiler dog-appropriate non-verbal behaviour.
- Imagine the experience of being with someone you do not know very well who keeps touching you or wanting to stroke you or play with your hair; this behaviour would not be appropriate and you will probably avoid them in the future. They would probably get the same response from others, and this response to their behaviour would act as a kind of punishment. It does not tell them what you want them to do, but it may make them realise what you do not want them to do!

Learning by observation has a number of stages, which can be mapped as follows:

1. Observation of role model. If the role model is rewarded in some way, this makes the observer more likely to copy them.

2. Imitation of role model.

3. Reinforcement or punishment. Depending on the response to the behaviour, it will either continue (reinforcement) or stop (punishment).

4. Behaviour has been learned and may become automatic.

One piece of research evidence illustrated how the responses of adults help to shape young people's understanding of personal space. Fry and Willis (1971) surveyed adults and found that they expected children to have learned appropriate personal distance by the age of 10 years. They organised for children aged 5, 8 and 10 years to stand 15cm behind adults in theatre queues and looked at the adult's responses. The results showed that the 5-year-olds received a positive response, the 8-year-olds were ignored and the 10-year-old children were given a cold reaction. It is responses like this that help to teach us non-verbal behaviour.

Cultural variations in non-verbal communication

We mentioned on page 126 that personal space varies between cultures and that this can affect the way we respond to people from different cultures. Because there are so many cultural variations in non-verbal communication, this supports the idea that we learn culture-specific behaviour rather than it being innate; otherwise we would all behave in exactly the same way.

Table 4.5 shows some of the non-verbal behaviours that vary according to culture.

▼ Table 4.5 Non-verbal behaviours that vary according to culture

Non-verbal behaviour	Cultural variations
Eye contact	Western cultures encourage eye contact because it indicates that we are interested. It is considered intimidating and rude in some Asian and African countries.
Winking	In North America and Europe, winking suggests sharing secrets, but in most other cultures it is seen as flirtatious.
Closed eyes	In North America or Europe, closed eyes indicate boredom or sleepiness. In Japan, Thailand, China and other Asian countries it shows you are listening.

Non-verbal behaviour	Cultural variations
Raising eyebrows	In North America and Europe, raising eyebrows suggests either shock or disbelief. In most Asian countries, it means 'yes'. In the Philippines, it means 'hello', and it is used as a sign of disagreement for Greeks.
Kissing cheek	In southern Europe, the Mediterranean and Latin America it usually means 'goodbye'. In Asia, kissing is considered an intimate sexual act and is not permissible in public.
Tapping the side of the nose	In England, it means 'It's a secret'. In Italy, it means 'Watch out' or 'Be careful', but in Japan, it means 'It's me'.
Facial expressions	Facial expressions are usual in North America and Europe, although smiles are often used to conceal embarrassment, pain or anguish. It is common for people from Asian cultures to try to remain expressionless, as they consider it rude to express emotions in public.
Arms	Some cultures, such as the Italians, use arms freely to gesticulate. Other cultures, like the Japanese, consider it impolite to gesticulate with the arms.
Handshakes	Handshakes signify greeting and are used to confirm an agreement or deal. In the Middle East, handshakes are supposed to be with a gentle grip. In Asia, the handshake uses a gentle grip and avoidance of eye contact. The left hand is considered unclean in much of the Middle East and parts of Asia, so is rarely used.
Finger communications	The okay sign (holding the thumb and index finger in a circle) means 'okay' or 'good job' in most cultures; it means 'zero' or 'worthless' in France and many European countries; in other countries, like Greece, Brazil, Italy, Turkey and Russia, it is considered an insult.
	The thumbs-up sign is considered an insult in some Middle Eastern countries, West Africa and most parts of South America.
	Pointing with an index finger is considered impolite by the Japanese and Chinese, who prefer to use the whole open hand to point; people from Malaysia prefer to point with their thumbs.
Personal space	Non-contact cultures (Asian) prefer to have little or no physical contact, so are comfortable with a personal space of 4m and over.
	Low-contact cultures (North American, northern European) favour little, if any, physical contact, so prefer 1m to 4m.
	High-contact cultures (Mediterranean, Arab and Latin cultures) prefer the intimate and personal zones, and mutual contact, so feel quite comfortable with touching and maintaining a space of just over 1m.

Exam hint

You do not need to know all these facts for your exam, but they are good examples of cross-cultural differences. If you are explaining that some non-verbal communications must be learned because they are not the same across all cultures, you could give a couple of examples from this list to support your argument.

Criticisms of the social learning theory of non-verbal behaviour

Some of our non-verbal behaviours seem to be spontaneous, while some are under our cognitive control

We can make ourselves smile; we can shake someone's hand; we can choose to stare at someone. On the other hand, some of our behaviours seem to be beyond our control, such as looking scared or crying. This suggests that social learning theory cannot explain all behaviours – some are just innate responses that have not been learned and therefore cannot be controlled.

DISCUSS...

Discuss the types of behaviours that you have been taught by your parents or by school.

Sometimes our non-verbal behaviour is not reinforced or rewarded, but we still go on doing it

Social learning theory suggests that we observe the behaviour of others and then copy, and if we get a positive response, we will go on doing that behaviour. This is not the whole story, because there are some behaviours that are not reinforced, yet we still go on doing them. For example, when we scowl or frown we do not look particularly beautiful, but we cannot help making those facial expressions in certain situations.

There are occasions when we might try to behave in one way, but our non-verbal behaviour will say something completely different

Take lying, for example. When we tell an untruth, our non-verbal signals might give us away. When people lie, especially over something serious, they often shake, sweat and talk in a shaky voice, or end up with a really red face, having no control over this form of non-verbal response. Even if they are able to control these obvious signs, they sometimes give themselves away with a small but noticeable action, like tapping their foot very quickly.

Sometimes people learn non-verbal behaviours by direct instruction rather than by observation

Children are actually taught to behave in certain ways. Do you remember your parents telling you not to laugh in certain situations and not to poke your tongue out at people, not to talk in a certain tone of voice and not to shout. Similarly, your teachers may have told you to look at them when they were talking to you or to take your hands out of your pockets, to stand up straight and to stop slouching. The same applies when teaching prisoners how to behave in a less aggressive and more socially acceptable way.

> ### QUESTION   ?
>
> **3.** Choose a word from the following list for each gap in the paragraph below.
> **developed, imitates, observes, punished, reinforced**
> Social learning theory states that non-verbal communication starts when a child _____ other people using non-verbal signals. The child then _____ these signals by performing them themselves. If the signals help them to communicate, these are _____ and they use them again. However, if the signals do not work or the children are _____ for inappropriate use they are less likely to use them again. (OCR Jan 2010)

Evolutionary theory

We know that a number of non-verbal behaviours are learned by observation, but in the evaluation of social learning theory, we have noted that occasionally our bodily responses override the behaviour we would like to produce. We have also discussed the way that certain non-verbal communication is demonstrated across all cultures, and evolutionary theorists suggest that this is because they were not learned, but have been passed down from our ancestors through their genes.

Evolutionary theory suggests that we inherit behaviours and traits that have the function of helping us to survive, so that we can reproduce and pass our genes down to the next generation. These inherited behaviours and traits need to be understood by everyone in order for this to happen. In order to survive, we need to protect our territory and our food. If we are to reproduce, we need to somehow communicate to our possible mate that we are interested in them in a sexual way.

> *In 1872, Charles Darwin suggested that facial expressions can convey the most important emotions, which are understood by all humans from all over the world. He gave the example of how we will wrinkle our noses if we smell something horrid, or smile to show that we want to be friendly. He believed that facial expressions are significant for survival (nose-wrinkling means something is unpleasant and should be avoided; smiling means 'I am not hostile').*
>
> *Ekman and Friesen (1971) provided evidence to show that the six main emotional expressions (anger, sadness, happiness, surprise, fear, disgust/ contempt) are universally understood. They carried out research with a remote tribe of people in New Guinea. Members of the tribe were told short stories with emotional content. They showed the tribe members photographs of American men and women showing these six emotions and asked them to pick the photograph that went with each story. They were very accurate in picking the right photographs.*
>
> *Go to Paul Ekman's website for more information (www.paulekman.com).*

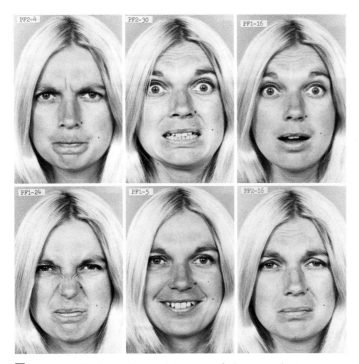

▲ Figure 4.7 Photographs used in some of Ekman and Friesen's research, showing anger, fear, surprise, disgust/contempt, happiness and sadness

Survival

In the animal world, animals often need to warn off others in order to survive. Animals show their aggression by baring their teeth, curling their noses or squaring up to an opponent, but they rarely fight to the death. What they do is show their hostility by using ritualised non-verbal behaviours to pass the message on to their potential opponent that they are not to be messed with. Human beings act in a very similar way. They might square up to a possible opponent and stare at them, flaring their nostrils and possibly even invading their personal space. This is usually enough to warn another human being not to come any closer and that they mean business. The other person will often leave at that point and neither is hurt in any way. Therefore both survive and live to tell the tale!

Reproduction

If an animal wants to reproduce, first of all they have to attract a mate. In the animal kingdom, mating displays are often very complex and colourful, with the males doing their best to attract an available passing female. Humans may not be quite so impressive in their efforts to attract the attention of a member of the opposite sex, but they still do their bit! Humans may dress in a certain way, use body postures, tone of voice, prolonged eye contact, pouting lips, walking with a swaying motion and so

Further your understanding

Evolutionary theorists believe that human beings are animals that have evolved the most. When they explain behaviour, they often refer to lower-order animals to explain the genetically inherited survival and reproductive behaviours that animals and humans have in common.

on. By using non-verbal communication, it is possible to indicate interest without actually saying anything, so if the other person is not keen, they can simply move on without either of them becoming embarrassed.

 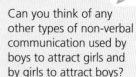

 Figure 4.8 This peacock is displaying his splendid tail to a passing peahen, to attract her attention

CORE STUDY: M. Yuki, W.W. Maddux and T. Masuda (2007)

M. Yuki, W.W. Maddux and T. Masuda (2007) Are the windows to the soul the same in the East and West? Cultural differences in using the eyes and mouth as cues to recognise emotions in Japan and the United States. Journal of Experimental Social Psychology 43, pp. 303–11

You need to be able to …
- describe Yuki *et al.*'s experiment into cross-cultural differences in interpreting facial expressions
- outline the limitations of the study.

Background

Because facial expressions are our main way of showing how we feel, it is really important that we can interpret other people's facial expressions. Recent research has shown that people from different cultures interpret facial expressions in a different way and that we are better at judging the facial expressions of our own culture than those of other cultures.

It was thought that this might be because different cultures have different facial 'accents' that are more easily understood by the people who belong to that particular group. This idea comes from the fact that people from different areas have different vocal accents – for example, people from Liverpool, Newcastle and the south of England all have very different accents. Although someone who has learned English will understand the basic language, they might find it hard to understand and interpret the local accents.

Past research had not managed to identify these 'accents' in facial expressions, so the authors suggested that facial cues from different parts of the face might be more significant in interpreting emotions for different cultures – for example, that the eyes would carry more meaning for one culture and the mouth for another.

Their idea was based on the fact that in the West, people are encouraged to be independent and to express their emotions openly. In contrast, in East Asian countries, such as Japan, China and Korea, where the people have a more collectivist culture, it is really important to make sure that you get on with other members of your society. By hiding emotions, this harmony is more likely to be maintained, as you would not be imposing your feelings on others.

The authors speculated that because the Japanese, as a culture, hide their feelings, the best way to do this would be to control their facial expressions. How then would they know how someone feels? They would have to focus on the parts of the face that are hard to control (the eyes) as their only way of interpreting the emotions of others. Americans, on the other hand, would not have to worry so much whether others see how they feel, so they would not have to be as good at interpreting emotions and would just focus on people's mouths.

Further your understanding

A true smile, or Duchenne smile (see page 128), involves the contraction of a group of muscles around the eyes, while other types of 'fake smiles' involve a different group of muscles around the mouth. This suggests that, when we smile, our eyes are a more accurate cue to what we feel than the mouth. This is not to say that the mouth is not important, however, as it is the most muscular and therefore most expressive part of the face, but it is also the part that can be controlled most easily.

Further your understanding

You will know probably know all about emoticons – they are combinations of punctuation marks that people use in text messages and emails to indicate facial expressions.

Japanese and American emoticons are different – American emoticons focus on the mouth, while Japanese emoticons focus on the eyes:

- In the UK and USA the emoticons :) and :-) denote a happy face, while :(and :-(denote a sad face.
- In Japan, the emoticon (^_^) denotes a happy face, while (;_;) denotes a sad (or crying) face.

Aims

The authors intended to investigate their beliefs using two studies.

- Study 1: to look at how American and Japanese participants interpreted the happiness/sadness of emoticons.

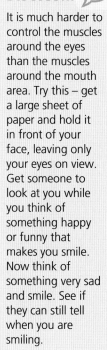

DISCUSS...

How do you think people from different cultures might feel about seeing a man cry?

DISCUSS...

It is much harder to control the muscles around the eyes than the muscles around the mouth area. Try this – get a large sheet of paper and hold it in front of your face, leaving only your eyes on view. Get someone to look at you while you think of something happy or funny that makes you smile. Now think of something very sad and smile. See if they can still tell when you are smiling.

Because Japanese and Americans use different types of emoticons, Yuki *et al.* wondered if the Americans were not familiar with the 'happy eye' expression (^_^). They decided to carry out a further study using photos of the eyes and mouths of real people as a way of getting over this cultural difference.

● Study 2: to look at how American and Japanese participants interpreted combinations of eyes and mouths taken from the happy and sad faces of real individuals.

Method

Questionnaires were used for both studies.

Study 1

Materials

Questionnaires were designed to show participants six emoticons, with combinations of happy, neutral and sad eyes and mouths.

Participants

A total of 118 American students and 95 Japanese students volunteered to take part in the experiment to earn partial course credits in an introductory psychology class.

Procedure

Participants were asked to rate the emoticons on a rating scale of 1 (very sad) to 9 (very happy).

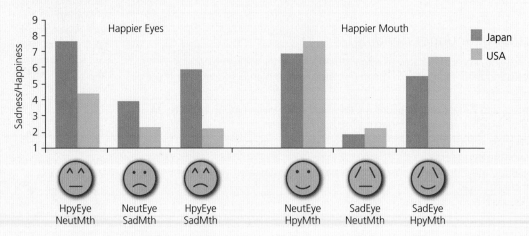

▲ Figure 4.9 The results showing participants' rating of happiness for each of the emoticons. The Japanese rate the eyes as more indicative of happiness, whereas the Americans rate the mouth as more relevant

(This Figure and Figure 4.10 are reprinted from *Journal of Experimental Social Psychology*, 43, 303–11, Yuki *et al.*, 'Are the windows to the soul the same in the East and West?', copyright 2007, with permission from Elsevier)

Results

● The Japanese rated the happy-eye emoticons more happy than the Americans.

● The Americans rated the happy-mouth emoticons more happy than the Japanese.

HOMEWORK

Carry out your own research looking at whether different cultures, genders or ages see these emoticons differently.

When you have chosen your focus (culture/gender/age), decide on a hypothesis or prediction as to what you would expect to see.

Photocopy these emoticons and then ask your selected participants to rate them for happiness/sadness on a nine-point scale.

When you have your results, decide what they have told you about your prediction.

How could you display your results?

Discussion

Results from Study 1 supported the authors' predictions. The Japanese participants focused more on the eye expressions, while the Americans gave more interpretive weight to the mouth when rating emotions.

Study 2

Materials

Photographs were selected from the collection of 110 photographs of facial expressions that have been widely used in cross-cultural studies because they are universally recognisable expressions of various emotions.

  The photographs were 'taken apart' (using a computer) and their mouths and eyes were used to create the same combinations of mouths and eyes that were used for the emoticons in Study 1.

Participants

A total of 87 American students and 89 Japanese students volunteered to take part in the experiment to earn course credits in an introductory psychology class.

Procedure

Participants saw 60 faces projected one at a time on a screen and were asked to rate the faces in the same way as the participants in the first study.

Results

The results indicated that the Japanese again focused more on the eyes when judging emotions, whereas the Americans focused more on the mouth.

HOMEWORK

Type 'pictures of facial affect' into a search engine and you will find information about Ekman's photographs used in the second study. If you use the same search term and look under Google images, you will find lots of photos of facial expressions. Choose a couple of sets of photos and ask people to say what emotion is showing on their faces. See if people suggest the same emotion for each face.

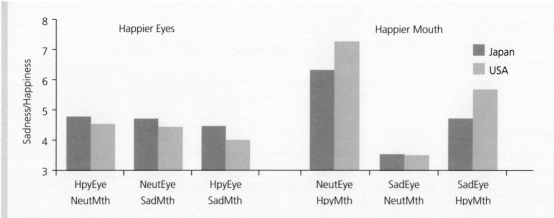

▲ Figure 4.10
The results of the research (Study 2) (Yuki *et al.*, 2007, reproduced with permission)

Discussion

The results from both studies supported the prediction that the Japanese participants used eyes as a major cue to judge emotions, while the Americans focused more on the mouth. The emoticon that had competing emotions (e.g. happy eyes/sad mouth) provided the strongest support for their predictions.

Yuki *et al.* believe that this is the first research to show that people from different cultures focus on different areas of the face to interpret and express different emotions.

HOMEWORK

Imagine you are trying to teach a robot how to be more like a person. Create your own body language guide. You could use websites like www.bodylanguageexpert.co.uk to give you some ideas. There are also a number of video clips on the internet from companies selling guides to body language.

Limitations

Ecological validity

The first part of the study used emoticons, which are not the same as human faces. The second part of the study used real photographs, which had been broken down into parts. When they were reassembled, Yuki *et al.* said they looked quite bizarre – for example, the photograph with happy eyes and a neutral mouth looked like a kind of scowl. Perhaps using whole faces might have been a more realistic study.

Rating scales

The way the authors measured the responses of the students may have affected the results. For example, if you were asked to say whether a face looked happy or sad, you may say it did not look happy or sad, but actually looked confused or annoyed. Because that option is not available to you, the results would not really indicate what you believe.

Reliable results

If you were shown 60 faces, would you lose interest towards the end? Would your responses be a reliable measure of what you really felt? If the students completed the questionnaires in groups, they may have copied each other's answers or come to some sort of joint agreement that did not express what they felt as individuals.

Participants

The sample, which consisted of students who were gaining points towards a first-year course, is not representative of the population as a whole. They were a self-selecting sample who may have lacked motivation to take the whole study seriously.

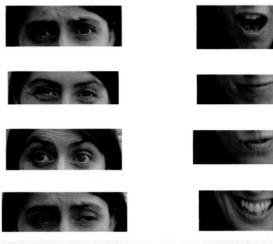

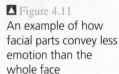 Figure 4.11
An example of how facial parts convey less emotion than the whole face

> **Applications of research into non-verbal communication:**
> *social skills training*
>
> ---
>
> Candidates should be able to:
> - explain how psychological research relates to social skills training –
>   for example, rehabilitation of criminals, customer service training and
>   managing conflict by managing body language.

Social skills training

Psychological research has identified the social skills that are necessary to help us get on with each other. We have considered a number of these skills in this chapter – for example, facial expressions, tone of voice, body postures, social distance and so on. Most of us learn our social skills without any awareness of the process, and we learn what is effective and what does not work by the feedback we get from other people (reinforcement). Other people either do not develop these skills or need to have them fine-tuned so that they can improve the kinds of relationships they have with others.

The story of Dave, a man who had great difficulty getting on with women and had never had a girlfriend, explains what happens when things go wrong. Dave decided he needed to have some sort of social skills training, which would, he hoped, help him get on better with women in the future. During their conversations, Dave remembered that there was one occasion when he did have a very interesting and longer-than-normal conversation with a woman; this took place in a lift. The social skills trainer had noticed that Dave had no idea of personal space and stood too close to everyone he talked to. Of course, the woman in the lift had no way of escaping, so she was in a position where she had to talk to him and could not try to make the interpersonal space between them enough so she would feel comfortable. The trainer reflected that unless he wanted to spend his life in a lift, he needed to look at where he stood in relation to other people!

It seems strange to imagine having to learn how to look at someone or how far away we should stand. There are some people who have to be taught these skills, either because they have a condition such as autism, or because they have difficulty with social skills because they have been brought up with poor role models. Other groups whose work requires that they finely tune their social skills, such as salesmen, attend courses to help them develop these skills even further.

Further your understanding

Some children with autism find it impossible to learn and understand non-verbal behaviours. They often misread social cues, and are often either overpowering and over-directing, or become socially isolated. These children find it extremely difficult, if not impossible, to see things from the perspective of others, so they are unaware of how others feel, and what they like and do not like. This means that things like social distance, eye contact, gestures and so on, are either not used or are used incorrectly. They cannot read body language, so they often misjudge and misinterpret situations. They may stand too close or keep talking when the other person is trying to signal that they have something to say.

Evidence to support the idea that social skills can be learned comes from the way autistic children are supported to learn appropriate behaviour. They are actually taught where to stand and how to maintain eye contact, usually by the adult teacher modelling the behaviour for the child. When they do produce the correct behaviour, even though they do not necessarily understand the reason behind it, they will find that the outcome is positive, so they will probably go on doing it.

Rehabilitation of criminals

You may have heard someone say 'What are you looking at?' when they think another person is looking at them in a way that they consider threatening. Often this is due to the misinterpretation of a simple glance.

Many criminals have poor social skills, often as a result of their early experiences, and it is these that may get them into trouble. For example, they may appear to be aggressive and hostile when this is not what they actually feel, and this can lead to unwanted attention or responses from others who think they are 'up for a fight'. They may also misinterpret the non-verbal communication of others, perhaps thinking someone is looking at them in a hostile way and in turn responding aggressively.

As part of any rehabilitation programme, offenders are given social skills training (SST) to help them manage future situations in a different way. SST involves teaching more effective ways of acting and also how to interpret the behaviour of others.

The trainers go through a number of steps, as follows:

- modelling or demonstrating the required behaviour, and instructions on when that behaviour should be used
- practice of the new skills, sometimes recording the offenders during role plays so that they can see themselves and can then discuss how things are going
- feedback on their performance and praise for using the skills properly
- encouragement to practise the new skills between sessions to reinforce learning.

The effectiveness of SST programmes has been investigated by a number of researchers. The research suggests that young offenders who attend short courses in SST find it much harder to use the skills in real life, while longer training has had much better outcomes. This would suggest that the skills need to be practised over time in order that they become automatic. We know that in times of stress, we often go back to the behaviours we are familiar with, rather than having the time to stop and think 'How should I behave now?'

Customer service training

Have you ever been into a shop where the salesperson is too pushy when you just want to browse, or is totally indifferent to you when you are standing looking towards them needing some help? On either occasion, you will probably walk out of the shop and go somewhere else. Shops lose trade because of this kind of behaviour from sales staff, so it is really important that they understand non-verbal communication in order to get it right! As a result, a number of companies offer customer service training for their staff, to help them develop and maintain good relationships with their customers. These training courses are based on the information provided by psychological research into non-verbal communication skills.

Customer service training covers the following areas:

- non-verbal communication – tone of voice, posture, interpersonal space
- confident voice, expressive tone and professional language
- building a relationship with the customer
- active listening skills and eye contact – hearing what they are saying, not what you want to hear!
- keeping calm under pressure, and managing conflict with aggressive or awkward customers.

DISCUSS...

Do you think most of the elements of customer service training apply to telephone sales?

Which, if any, are not important for telephone sales?

HOMEWORK

Imagine that it is your job to teach SST to your employees in a clothes shop.

Write a little sketch describing the worst case of customer/salesperson conflict you can think of, and then offer your staff guidance at each point on how they could have improved the situation between the salesperson and the customer, using the list of customer service training elements as a guideline.

Managing conflict by managing body language

We mentioned above how a number of offenders often find it difficult to manage conflict, and their body language often makes the situation worse. Think for a moment how you might feel if you found yourself in the following situations:

- A person stands in front of you with their chest puffed out and their arms folded, legs slightly apart, staring at you with a fixed gaze.
- A person starts to shout at you, pointing their finger at you and staring into your eyes.
- Someone comes up to you and pushes you backwards as they start to talk to you in a loud, aggressive way.
- Someone starts to try to explain something to you in a loud and hostile voice, and as they speak they bang their fist down on the table in front of them.

The likelihood is that, for each of these situations, you will feel that the other person is being intimidating and hostile towards you. You have two options; you can stay and fight it out or you can just walk away. You probably will not listen to what they have to say because the way they have behaved will have made you feel anxious and aroused, and feelings like these act as obstacles to any sort of compromise. If, on the other hand, the person were sitting down or standing with their arms by their sides, possibly speaking in a quiet, calm voice, with a neutral facial expression or even a smile, maintaining the appropriate social distance, you would immediately be more willing to listen.

These are the kinds of conflict resolution strategies that might be taught in any sort of social skills programme.

Exam-style question – Social psychology: Non-verbal communication

These questions are taken from the OCR B542 Psychology Paper, from January 2011. For more past and sample papers plus answer exemplars visit the OCR website. OCR have not seen or commented on the quality of the sample answers.

1.
> **A good telling off?**
> *A teacher was telling off Neil and Kristina. Neil recognised he was wrong. He showed he felt sorry by holding his hands up and raising his eyebrows in an apologetic way. Meanwhile, Kristina thought it was unfair that she was being told off. She stood there with her arms folded and her mouth turned downwards.*

Using the source:

(a) Identify the facial expression used by Neil. [1]

raised eyebrows (1)

(b) Identify the facial expression used by Kristina. [1]

mouth turned downwards (1)

(c) Identify the example of body language used by Neil. [1]

holding his hands up (1)

(d) Identify the example of body language used by Kristina. [1]

arms folded (1)

The candidate has not confused body language and facial expression.

2. Answer the following questions about Yuki *et al*'s (2007) study of facial expressions.

   For each question, choose one answer by ticking the relevant box.

   (a) What type of study did Yuki *et al* use? [1]

   (i) correlational ☐   (ii) longitudinal ☐   (iii) cross-cultural ☑   *(1)*

   (b) Who did they compare American students with? [1]

   (i) Chinese students ☐   (ii) Japanese students ☑   (iii) Russian students ☐   *(1)*

   (c) Which feature did American students focus on the most? [1]

   (i) eyes ☐   (ii) mouths ☑   (iii) noses ☐   *(1)*

   (d) Which of the following is a criticism of the study? [1]

   (i) they only tested two dimensional (2D) faces ☑   (ii) they only tested children's faces ☐
   (iii) they only tested faces from one culture ☐   *(1)*

3. Social learning theory is one explanation of non-verbal communication.

   Draw a line to match each social learning term with its correct example. [2]

   TERM   **EXAMPLE**

   ┌─────────────┐   ┌──┐
   │ Imitation   │ ───→ │ A child copies the gestures that his parents use. │
   └─────────────┘   └──┘
                        ┌──┐
                        │ An individual is punished for using a rude hand signal. │
   ┌─────────────┐   └──┘
   │ Reinforcement│ ───→ ┌──┐
   └─────────────┘   │ An infant is given positive feedback when she smiles. │
                        └──┘

4. Outline **one** criticism of the social learning theory of non-verbal communication. [2]

   You might expect children brought up in the same family to use similar gestures because they
   have the same role models (1) but evidence suggests that this is not necessarily the case (1).

5. Describe how social skills training is used in real life. [3]

   Social skills training involves teaching people how to communicate better (1)

   To get all the marks for this question, you need to explain where the social skills training would be
   found, the reason for the training and the purpose it would serve.

   SECTION TOTAL [15]

5 Individual differences

Most psychological research focuses on what most people do – that is, it focuses on the 'average'. Although psychologists acknowledge that we are all different, with different experiences and different abilities, they provide theories to help us to understand the way that the majority of us function. However, it is important for psychologists to help identify not only the similarities but also the differences, as a way of continuing to explain how we live and operate in our world.

Unit B541: The first section of this chapter focuses on atypical behaviour, by which we mean behaviour that is not typical of the average. We will focus on how we learn, and how, for some of us, that learning can become distorted and develop into a kind of mental disorder known as a phobia. The study for this section looks at how it is possible to create a phobia in a child.

Unit B542: The second section considers the self, by which we mean who we are. Different psychologists hold different beliefs about the self, some saying that because we are all unique we cannot be measured and compared with each other. Others suggest that we do actually have lots of aspects of our personality in common, so can be compared. The core study focuses on how pet ownership can affect the way young people feel about themselves and uses methods that allowed the researchers to compare one young person with others.

Atypical behaviour

Overview

Every one of us has different life experiences, and these will have affected the way we think and feel. These life experiences can be as basic as growing up in a family with lots of brothers and sisters, few or none, having both parents or only one, having grandparents or not, moving around the country or staying in one place, and so on. Therefore, when we consider human behaviour, it is always necessary to bear in mind that we can generalise about what the majority might do, but there are always going to be exceptions to every rule.

Typical and atypical behaviour in relation to fear

As we learned in the last chapter, fear is one of the primary emotions, together with anger, surprise, disgust/contempt, happiness and sadness. Fear is experienced by all animals (including humans) as the result of a real, possible or imagined danger.

It is quite normal, or typical, to feel frightened of certain things. Fear actually has the function of keeping us safe, because if we did not feel fear, we would not avoid dangerous situations and would probably come to some sort of sticky end!

The typical way that we would respond to feelings of fear might be to think about how likely we are to be hurt and then to act accordingly. Take, for example, parachute jumping. We know that parachuting has a small degree of danger attached to it, so being afraid of jumping out of an aeroplane with a parachute attached does make some sense. What we would do as a way of managing that fear would be to note that the number of parachuting accidents is extremely low, and the probability of being involved in an accident is minimal. We could then hold that fear, but would still be able to parachute because we have rationalised to ourselves that it will be okay. On the other hand, if we were told that the likelihood of having an accident was very high, it would be atypical, or very unusual, to choose parachuting as a sport because the risk would be too great.

> *Fear is a distressing emotion that we experience as a result of what we believe to be an approaching danger. The danger can be real or imagined.*

DISCUSS...

Work with a friend and try to find out what you have in common in your lives and what things are different.

Then choose three topics, such as working parents or the importance of education, and see if you can work out whether your early experiences have influenced the way you feel about these things.

KEY CONCEPTS

The OCR examination requires candidates to be able to:

- distinguish between typical and atypical behaviour in relation to fear
- outline common types of phobia – agoraphobia, social phobia, school phobia, acrophobia and arachnophobia.

> *Typical behaviours are behaviours that we would expect to see from the majority of the population and which would be considered normal.*
>
> *Atypical behaviours are behaviours that we would not expect to see from the majority of the population and which would be considered abnormal.*

QUESTION ?

1. Think of typical and atypical behaviours in relation to the following (an example has been given for the first subject):

Subject	Typical	Atypical
Crossing the road	Looking both ways and listening as you cross	Walking out without looking for any oncoming traffic
Sitting an examination		
Meeting someone new		
Finding a spider in the bath		

Phobias

A phobia is an intense, persistent and irrational fear of something, which is accompanied by an overwhelming desire to avoid and escape it.

There are some people who experience extreme fears of an object or situation, even though they may know that these fears are totally irrational. The way they respond to these fears is atypical (not typical of normal fear responses), and they may experience panic attacks as a result. They will do anything they can to avoid the feared objects or situations and can have a panic attack just thinking about them. These people have what is known as a phobia.

People can develop all sorts of phobias. They can be of a particular object (such as a spider), a situation (heights), a place (school) or an activity (flying). The fear may be so powerful that it stops the person's normal everyday functioning.

Although there are thought to be over 500 phobias, some of the more common phobias are listed in Table 5.1. Remember that a phobia is an irrational type of fear.

Further your understanding

When someone has a panic attack in response to their phobia, they may experience the following symptoms:

- shortness of breath, resulting in over-breathing or hyperventilating
- increased heart rate
- feeling sick
- dizziness or feeling shaky
- sweating.

Type of phobia	Description
Agoraphobia	Fear of being in an open space or a place from which the person is afraid they will be unable to escape. The word *agora* means marketplace in Greek; if you think about it, a marketplace is often very busy, crowded and can feel quite uncomfortable. Many people who have agoraphobia will not go out, preferring to stay in their own homes because they feel safe there.
Social phobia	Fear of social situations where the person feels concerned that others are looking at them, criticising what they are doing or even judging what they are thinking. They get very concerned that they will do something embarrassing or foolish, so they will avoid any sort of social situation and often become quite isolated, even finding the company of familiar people difficult to manage at times. They find authority figures especially frightening.
School phobia	Fear of attending school. Young people who have school phobia are also known as school refusers. They become very anxious about leaving their home, where it is safe, and going into busy school buildings. Fear of reading in class, being isolated in the playground, being bullied by their peers and getting changed for sports activities are all reasons young people give for school phobia.
Acrophobia	Fear of heights. A typical response is being wary of being at a great height, especially when we look over the edge of a cliff without a barrier to stop us falling. However, some people are as frightened of being at the top of a tall building as they are of climbing up a ladder. It is thought that between 2 and 5 per cent of the population suffer with acrophobia and it affects twice as many women as men.
Arachnophobia	Fear of spiders. This is the most common specific phobia and is more common in women than men (although perhaps men are less willing to admit to being afraid of spiders!). People with arachnophobia go to great lengths to make sure they do not encounter a spider. This may include getting people to check rooms, shoes and even beds to make sure there is no spider present. Some people experience such an extreme fear of spiders that they cannot even deal with pictures, cartoons or toys in the shape of a spider.

Remember, the word agora is Greek for marketplace – imagine a busy marketplace.

Think of an acrobat on a tightrope as a way of remembering the word 'acrophobia', meaning fear of heights.

◀ Table 5.1 Types of phobia

For the examination, you must know about the five phobias in Table 5.1 because they are the ones you may be asked about. However, read the question carefully. If the question asks you to talk about 'any' phobia, you can use another example, but you need to know the name of the phobia you are describing.

A case of agoraphobia described by a sufferer:

> *I remember the first time it happened, walking near my home suddenly everything seemed unfamiliar. I felt panic rising. I felt unreal, as though I didn't exist. I was sweating, my heart was pounding and my legs turned to jelly. I felt that if I took another step I would go over the edge into a dark pit. My only thought was that I must get home. Holding on to fences for support, I struggled home and collapsed crying.*
>
> *I couldn't go out for several days, but then I went out with my mother to visit my aunt, but again I felt panicky. I had shooting pains through my body and was sure I was going to die. My panic was uncontrollable. Since then I can't go out alone. I live in constant fear of getting another attack.*

HOMEWORK

Ask family members if they have any irrational fears and then go to a website such as http://phobialist.com to find out what they are called.

Choose four phobias (either from Table 5.1 or you may choose different phobias) and describe what people who suffer from these phobias might do to avoid the feared object or situation.

Most phobics know that the thing they are frightened of is really quite harmless, although they still experience the fear. Take, for example, the phobia known as octophobia, which is an irrational fear of the figure eight. Phobics will do anything to avoid their feared object or situation and plan in advance how they can avoid it. Because they know the fear is irrational, they may also try to hide their fear from other people and may feel ashamed of their fear.

CORE THEORY: behaviourist theory

Candidates should be able to:

- distinguish between an unconditioned stimulus, a neutral stimulus and a conditioned stimulus
- distinguish between an unconditioned response and a conditioned response
- use the process of classical conditioning to explain the onset of phobias
- explain the criticisms of the behaviourist theory of atypical behaviour
- consider evolutionary theory as an alternative theory, with specific reference to preparedness.

Behaviourist theory

Behaviourist theory is sometimes referred to as stimulus-response theory, because it suggests that all behaviours are a response to some kind of stimulus.

Behaviourists believe that most of our behaviour is learned rather than the result of our innate biological responses, and they also believe that we learn to be phobic towards certain things. However, behaviourists do accept that we also have instinctive reflex behaviours that function to help us survive. Our fear responses, such as flinching from pain or withdrawing our hands if we touch something hot, are actually reflex behaviours that are innate and are used as a way of protecting ourselves in order to survive.

Behaviourist theory is used to explain two different methods of learning: classical conditioning, where your response is a reflex response, and operant conditioning, where you learn a new (and not reflex) behaviour. Behaviourists suggest that we probably learn most phobias through the process of classical conditioning, although we can also use operant conditioning to explain some phobic behaviours.

> Responses such as flinching from pain or running away from danger are survival responses. When we experience the same things again, we feel fear.

Classical conditioning

Sometimes we seem to learn an association between an object and an instinctive response unconsciously; as a result, we may come to believe that it is the object that causes the instinctive response rather than the instinctive response being there due to another cause. This process is called classical conditioning.

If you heard a loud, unexpected noise, you would probably jump, your heart rate would increase and you might experience other physiological fear responses. Your 'jump' is an automatic response because you have no control over it. This automatic or reflex response is called an unconditioned response (UCR) because it does not have to be learned. The cause of this response (the loud noise) is called the unconditioned stimulus (UCS).

According to the principles of classical conditioning, you can learn to 'jump' in response to an entirely different stimulus, such as a spider, that you had no fear of before the classical conditioning process.

How does this learning occur? When the stimulus that made you jump (the loud noise) is presented at the same time as a different stimulus (spider), which is known as the neutral stimulus (NS), you associate the two. Once you have learned this association unconsciously, showing you the spider on its own will produce the automatic response of fear.

The principles of classical conditioning were first identified by Ivan Pavlov, a Russian physiologist who was studying digestion in dogs in the 1890s. While he was measuring how much saliva the dogs produced in different circumstances, he noticed that they began dribbling (salivating) when they heard the researcher's footsteps approaching. Pavlov deduced that the dogs in his study had learned to associate the sound of footsteps with the arrival of food because the two stimuli (footsteps and food) had occurred together so many times.

Figure 5.1 shows how the dogs learned to make the association between the sound of the boots (unconditioned stimulus) and food.

DISCUSS...

Think about the instinctive reflex responses we have to the following:

- loud noises
- hot surfaces
- pin pricks
- the smell of freshly baked bread
- rotten food
- having the area just below your knee cap tapped with a rubber hammer
- someone throwing a ball of screwed-up paper at your face.

Salivation is an automatic response that all animals have when they smell food (salivation is an unconditioned or reflex response). Have you ever noticed that your mouth waters when you smell chocolate or something you really want to eat?

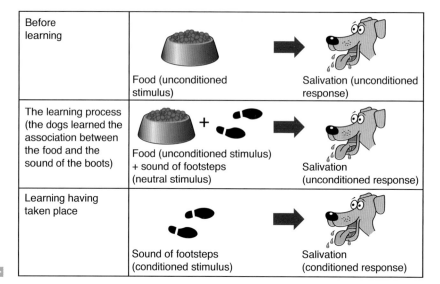

Before learning	Food (unconditioned stimulus)	Salivation (unconditioned response)
The learning process (the dogs learned the association between the food and the sound of the boots)	Food (unconditioned stimulus) + sound of footsteps (neutral stimulus)	Salivation (unconditioned response)
Learning having taken place	Sound of footsteps (conditioned stimulus)	Salivation (conditioned response)

Figure 5.1 ▶

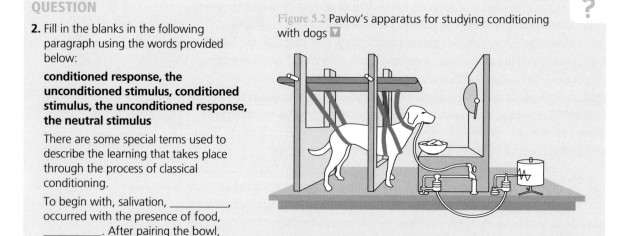

QUESTION

2. Fill in the blanks in the following paragraph using the words provided below:

conditioned response, the unconditioned stimulus, conditioned stimulus, the unconditioned response, the neutral stimulus

There are some special terms used to describe the learning that takes place through the process of classical conditioning.

To begin with, salivation, _____, occurred with the presence of food, _____. After pairing the bowl, _____ and the food together many times, the dogs had become conditioned to salivate to the empty bowl. This empty bowl is therefore the _____, and salivation is now called the _____ because it occurs with the conditioned stimulus.

Figure 5.2 Pavlov's apparatus for studying conditioning with dogs ▼

How can classical conditioning be used to explain phobias?

In the earlier examples, we talked about how Pavlov's dogs learned to associate the sound of footsteps with the arrival of dinner, and how someone might learn to associate the sight of a spider with fear. This is the process by which we start to develop a phobia. In fact, the example above may well be the way we could learn to fear a spider. You might not remember learning to associate fear of spiders with the sound of a bell because we do not often learn associations by repeatedly pairing the UCS and the NS. In fact, if our reflex response to the UCS is extreme, and the first time we hear it we also experience the NS, then once is enough for us to develop an extreme and irrational fear (phobia). At this point, the phobic will do all they can to avoid the feared object!

Figure 5.3 demonstrates another example.

People who develop phobias often cannot remember their first experience of fear, but this may be because they were very young at the time. For example, if a young child were to see a parent show terror at the sight of a spider, the child might also become very frightened because their parent was behaving in a frightening (and abnormal) way. This terror might then become associated with the sight of any spider in any context. At this point, we would say that the fear has been generalised, meaning it has been generalised to all spiders, and the person could then be described as having arachnophobia.

School phobia can develop if the child has a really frightening experience at school and makes the association between the event and school itself, even though the event could have happened anywhere. The child may then feel the same about any school as they will have generalised their fear response, so even if the child's parents suggest a different school, this will not help a school phobic as their fear is irrational.

> *This is also known as one-trial learning and depends on us being extremely frightened.*

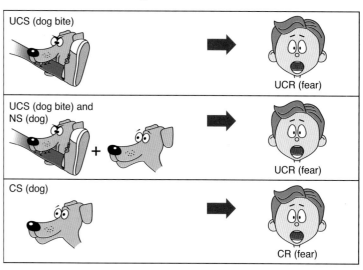

▲ Figure 5.3 Dog phobia (cynophobia)

> *Stimulus generalisation means that the conditioned response is generalised to all spiders, and, in extreme cases, pictures of the feared object or even similar objects, such as ants or other creepy crawlies.*

Operant conditioning

Before we move on, it might be useful to understand that classical conditioning and operant conditioning are both learning processes, but one involves reflex responses and the other involves learned responses (and they can both be related to phobic behaviour).

▼ Table 5.2

Classical conditioning	Involves a reflex response to reduce fear or anxiety	Person unconsciously learns an association between an unconditioned stimulus and a neutral stimulus
Operant conditioning	Involves a learned response (not a reflex), which gains some kind of outcome (either positive or negative)	Person learns that a behaviour results in some kind of reward: if the consequences are positive, they will repeat the behaviour; if the consequences are negative, they will be unlikely to do the same thing again

DISCUSS...

See if you can work out how these phobias may have developed:

- frogs (batrachophobia)
- hospitals (nosocomephobia)
- old people (gerontophobia)
- sharks (selachophobia)
- wasps (spheksophobia).

153

We have already mentioned in Chapter 3 that children's behaviour is likely to continue if it is reinforced. The idea of reinforcements or rewards to help shape behaviour comes from the theory of operant conditioning.

Operant conditioning and phobias

Operant conditioning can be used to explain the continuation of phobic behaviour because if a person develops a phobia as the result of classical conditioning, they will use different behaviours to avoid the feared object. As some of these behaviours will have a positive outcome, in so far as they prevent the person from finding themselves in a situation that they find really frightening, they are more likely to repeat these behaviours in the future.

Can a conditioned response be removed?

- Classical conditioning: Imagine that, over time, Pavlov's dogs were no longer fed by a human being, but instead were fed by a machine that silently dispensed food down a chute at random times. The dogs would start to realise that the approach of human footsteps no longer meant food was on its way and, over time, they would stop salivating. At this point, we could say that the salivation response has been removed over time and is now extinct.
- Operant conditioning: It is also possible to remove an operantly conditioned response by removing the reward. For example, if you give a dog a biscuit every time it begs, the dog will come to you and beg on a regular basis. If you stop giving the dog treats, over time, it will stop begging.

Criticisms of the behaviourist theory of atypical behaviour

We will begin by looking at the weakness of the behaviourist theory of atypical behaviour and then consider an alternative explanation.

- Behaviourist theory looks only at the stimulus and the behavioural response and does not take into account any of the cognitive or thinking processes that take place in between. The theory does not take into account the fact that we have different emotions, different levels of ability and also that we can learn by observing others. These differences between us are why we do not all react in the same way to things. Take the example of the person with no previous experience of pets, who has become cynophobic (dog phobic) as the result of being bitten by her grandmother's dog when visiting her. Another person, who has a pet dog, may have had the same experience at his grandmother's house, but would realise that on that occasion, the dog was protecting its home and it did not mean that all dogs are vicious. The second person might become more wary of dogs in the future, but would not become cynophobic as a result. The thought processes between the two people were very different and led to different outcomes.

We discussed the behaviourist theory of attachment in Chapter 3, page 77, when we talked about how babies learn that by behaving in certain ways with an adult, that adult will provide the baby with what it wants. This increases the chance that the child will repeat the behaviours because they have learned what pleases adults. For example, when the baby feels hungry (stimulus) it has learned that by crying (behaviour) it will get food (response).

- Behaviourist theory suggests that in order to develop a phobia, people will have had a terrifying experience of the object or situation about which they are phobic, although this is not always the case. Sometimes people learn by observing the behaviour of others towards a feared object or situation. We considered social learning theory in Chapter 1, page 23, when we talked about how children imitate adult role models. Not surprisingly, children who are frightened of spiders often have a parent who also fears spiders. They may learn this 'fear' from observing the way their parent behaves, so the next time they see a spider, they may imitate their parent's behaviour and the reinforcement will be that the parent comes to console them.

- Behaviourist theory cannot explain why some phobias are really common, even though people who have these phobias may never have encountered the feared item. If you look on the internet at various lists of the most common phobias, they all include a fear of snakes or spiders. Although most of us will have experienced a spider at some point, we know that spiders in the UK are not harmful, so the likelihood of having a direct experience of a dangerous spider is very unlikely. On the other hand, there are people who have never encountered a snake at first hand and may only have seen a live snake in a zoo. However, they have an irrational fear of snakes and will do anything to avoid them. Evolutionary theory can provide an explanation for this irrational fear, as it suggests we have an innate readiness to fear things that look very different to us.

Evolutionary theory as an alternative theory to explain phobias

Why are people more likely to develop a phobia of spiders than, for example, cars (which are much more dangerous)? Is there an innate element to such fears?

HOMEWORK

Test evolutionary theory for yourself by making a list of ten animals (including both domestic and wild animals), ten different insects and ten different birds. Try to choose creatures that vary in size and appearance as much as possible. Put the creatures in random order and ask five to ten people to rate them on a five-point rating scale – where 1 is not frightening and 5 is very frightening. Total the scores for each creature and see which ones gain the highest fear scores.

> *Biological preparedness means having an innate biological predisposition (being 'hard-wired') to notice something – for example, things that are dangerous.*

Further your understanding

Another example of biological preparedness can be seen with what are known as taste aversions. Have you ever eaten or drunk something that has made you ill? How have you felt when being faced with the same item again? Often, when we are sick as a result of eating something, we find that we cannot bear the taste of it and will avoid it or anything like it in the future. This is also thought to be a survival mechanism that helps us to avoid potentially poisonous foods in the future before they can do us harm.

Because our ancestors were threatened by many dangers, they needed to become extra sensitive to things that were extremely dangerous in order to increase their likelihood of surviving. Evolutionary theory suggests that the people who learned more quickly about what was threatening were more likely to survive and go on and reproduce. As a result, humans seem to have evolved the ability to associate certain things with danger, and this ability (or preparedness) explains some of the more common phobias to things (spiders and snakes) or situations (heights) that are dangerous to humans. It seems that this preparedness may have been passed on through our genes from one generation to the next, which might explain why we are more likely to be frightened of some things than others.

Research has shown that humans find living creatures that look like us are the least frightening, while creatures that are very different in appearance, such as snakes and spiders, are always rated as the most frightening. Perhaps this is because if the creature looks like us, we feel we are more able to predict its behaviour. On the other hand, spiders and snakes do not look like us, so appear much less predictable and may, in the past, have posed a greater threat.

Some of the best human laboratory evidence for biological preparedness has come from manufacturing fear using classical conditioning techniques. Researchers compared how easy it was to condition their participants to fear 'natural' items, such as spiders and snakes, rather than man-made but potentially dangerous items, such as weapons and electricity outlets. This was done by wiring up (willing) participants to receive an electric shock every time they saw certain photographs, as a way of developing their association between specific items and pain. They tried to condition them to fear both 'natural' items and man-made objects, but found that the participants were more likely to develop a fear of the 'natural' items and the effects were much more long-lasting (Davey 1995).

CORE STUDY: J.B. Watson and R. Rayner (1920)

J.B. Watson and R. Rayner (1920) Conditioned emotional reactions. Journal of Experimental Psychology 3(1), pp. 1–14

Background

Infants are born with a number of reflex actions – fright, anger and love. These innate responses only appear to a very limited number of stimuli. Babies get frightened of things that startle them, such as loud noises; they get angry if they are hungry or wet and uncomfortable; and they show love if they are treated affectionately. On the other hand, adults are frightened of lots of things, such as spiders and heights, and Watson wondered how this occurred.

You need to be able to …

- describe Watson and Rayner's experiment to induce a phobia in a young child
- outline the limitations of the study.

Describe the study

Aims

The aim of the study was to find out if it was possible to teach a young child to be frightened of something that had not previously frightened him. In order to do this, Watson intended to use the process of classical conditioning.

Method

The method used by John Watson and Rosalie Rayner was an experiment, but it was written up as a case study.

Participant

The subject of this study was 'Little Albert', who was described as healthy and well-developed, stolid and unemotional. He had never shown fear or rage and hardly ever cried. Because he was so stable, the authors felt the experiment would do him no harm.

Procedure

- Session 1: When Albert was about 9 months old, he was tested to see what he was frightened of. They recorded and filmed his reactions to a white rat, a rabbit, a dog, a monkey, people with masks, people with and without hair, cotton wool, burning newspapers, and so on. Albert was not frightened of any of the objects and just wanted to touch them. However, he was frightened of the noise of a suspended steel bar (measuring 120cm in length by 2cm diameter) being hit with a hammer.

  > *The child started violently, his breathing was checked and the arms were raised in a characteristic manner. On the second stimulation the same thing occurred, and in addition the lips began to pucker and tremble. On the third stimulation the child broke into a sudden crying fit.*
  > (Watson and Rayner 1920, p. 3)

- Session 2: When Albert was 11 months old, he was brought back to the laboratory and Watson and Rayner started the classical conditioning process. They showed Albert a white rat. As he reached out and touched it, Watson struck the bar directly behind Albert's head. Albert jumped violently, fell forward and began to whimper.
- Session 3: Seven days later, Albert saw the rat and showed some fear. Watson repeated the bar-hitting procedure five more times during that session, and by the end of the session Albert cried the minute he saw the rat. This was the last time Albert heard the iron bar being hit by the hammer.
- Session 4: Five days later, Albert was shown the rat, then a rabbit, a dog, a fur coat, cotton wool, Watson's hair and a Santa Claus beard. He showed fear when presented with each of them.

Albert was shown the rat and some of the other feared objects twice more. He continued to be afraid of them, although his fear was not so extreme. Watson and Rayner were not able to find out how long Little Albert's fear remained, as his mother took him away from the laboratory.

Results

Little Albert was conditioned to be afraid of something he was not initially afraid of. This fear was generalised to other objects that were similar (furry or hairy objects).

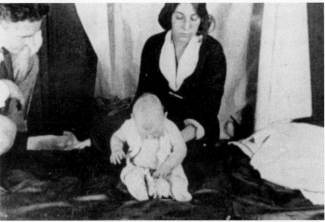

▲ Figure 5.4
Little Albert with John Watson and Rosalie Rayner (1920)

Conclusions

Watson and Rayner explained that it is possible to condition a fear response (by the process of classical conditioning) and suggested that this was probably how people develop different phobias.

Limitations

- The results may not be generalisable. Watson and Rayner's study investigated the development of a phobia in one child, and, by their own admission, this child was particularly placid.
- The experiment lacked ecological validity. Any research in a laboratory is well controlled, whereas in the real world there are lots of other things going on. When people develop phobic responses, they usually have no idea where these have come from, but it would certainly not be from a laboratory setting. Therefore the study lacks ecological validity because it showed how you can create a phobia in a small child in a laboratory, but not how phobias develop in the real world.
- There were ethical difficulties. At the time of this research, ethical guidelines as we know them today did not exist. If you read the description of poor Albert and his growing fear of fur and hair, it is hard to imagine how his mother could have agreed to let him go through this level of discomfort. Were Watson and Rayner honest about the nature and process of their research? Did Albert's mother give informed consent to her son taking part? Researchers are also supposed to make sure that the participant leaves the experiment in the same state that they entered, but Albert was not deconditioned as his mother removed him. (Perhaps, somewhere in the world, there is a very old man called Albert who is terrified of anything with hair or fur.)

QUESTION ?

3. List the ethical guidelines broken by this study. What could Watson and Rayner have done to make the study ethical? (See Chapter 6, page 192.)

> **Applications of research into atypical behaviour:**
> *behaviour therapy for phobias*
>
> Candidates should be able to:
> - explain how research relates to psychological behaviour therapy for phobias – for example, use of stimuli, systematic desensitisation, use of classical conditioning in flooding and implosion therapy, cognitive therapy for going beyond behaviour modification.

Behaviour therapy for phobias

Watson and Rayner's research showed that phobias may be the result of maladaptive learning. Therefore the idea behind the treatment for phobias is for the person to relearn that the thing they are frightened of is actually not scary after all. If they realise that the object is not really scary, and that nothing is going to happen to them if they come into contact with the feared object, the association they have made between the feared object and danger will eventually become extinct.

We are going to use the example of a spider phobia for this section.

Use of a stimulus

The stimulus – the feared object – is used both for treatment and to check a person's responses to find out whether the person is cured. The stimulus may be the actual object, such as a spider, or it may be a photograph or film of a spider or a model spider. Sometimes people cannot cope with the actual object, so a photograph or model might be less terrifying.

Systematic desensitisation

If someone has developed an irrational fear to an object, the idea behind systematic desensitisation is to replace feelings of fear with feelings of relaxation. The way this is done is by going through a process known as counter-conditioning, which involves going through a new process of conditioning to counteract the previous one.
The process goes something like this:

- Think of the most frightening things you can in relation to your phobia and then put them in a hierarchy, with the most frightening at the top and the least frightening at the bottom. The most frightening might be to be shut in a coffin with hundreds of spiders, and the least frightening might be to find a picture of a spider in a children's book.
- Now I am going to teach you to relax so you can imagine every muscle in your body losing any sort of tension. Once you have done this, the process of desensitisation can begin.

HOMEWORK

Look up on the internet methods of relaxation and make a list of the relaxation techniques that could be used to help someone with a phobia to relax.

HOMEWORK

Pretend you have a fear of heights. Describe the process a therapist might use to systematically desensitise you.

The therapist then gets the person to relax and asks them to think about the least frightening thing in their hierarchy. This may have to be done several times before the person automatically relaxes, as they make the association between the spider in the children's book and a feeling of calm (just as Little Albert associated the white rat with a feeling of fear). Then they are asked to think of the next thing in the hierarchy, and so on. This process happens over a series of sessions, until the person is able to imagine the most frightening situation without any fear or anxiety. Finally, this relaxation technique is used in real-life situations.

Flooding and implosion therapy

People who have phobias will do anything they can to avoid the feared object. In fact, some people go to extraordinary lengths to avoid any sort of situation where the object might be present, to the extent that they will never go into a certain room in their house and will seal up the door with tape because they once saw a spider in that room. This means they will never challenge their fear. Flooding and implosion therapy make them challenge this fear by exposing them to the feared object, as quickly and extremely as necessary.

The difference between flooding and implosion is as follows.

- Flooding means actually exposing someone to the object head-on. With a spider phobic this might involve throwing a bucket of spiders all over them; with someone with agoraphobia, it might be to deposit them in the middle of a desert. The idea is that they will be very frightened, but the body cannot maintain that level of arousal for any length of time because it becomes exhausted. The level of fear cannot go any higher, so it will have to come down; with this, the person will realise that the feared object is not so scary after all.
- Implosion uses the same technique, but instead of the person being exposed to the actual object, they will be told to imagine the most horrific situation (the item that came top of the list in the process of systematic desensitisation) and the therapist will describe it and exaggerate it, to make sure that the person experiences a really high level of fear.

Cognitive therapy

As you will have realised, people are actually quite complex, with complex thoughts and feelings that are sometimes disordered and therefore incorrect. It would make sense that some people with strange phobias may have disordered thoughts and feelings – after all, why should anyone be afraid of the number eight (octophobia), since there is no obviously logical reason for this fear.

The way we think affects how we feel and our feelings affect the way we behave.

We think spiders are really horrible and may bite us, which makes us feel frightened, which makes us avoid spiders or anything to do with spiders at all costs. Although this is an incorrect belief (certainly in the UK), it can affect our behaviour, and because we do not face our fears by having any contact with spiders, this makes the thoughts stronger. Figure 5.5 shows the cycle of behaviour that keeps a phobia in place, as we continue to avoid spiders.

Cognitive therapy, which is also known as cognitive behavioural therapy (CBT), relies on challenging negative, automatic thoughts and replacing them with different thoughts. If we take the example of a fear of spiders, the following conversation shows how, by challenging these thoughts, the person will come to reassess their beliefs.

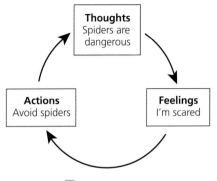

▲ Figure 5.5

Negative automatic thought: Spiders are horrible scary things that will bite me and I might die.

> *Question:* What is your evidence?
> *Answer:* Well, people do get bitten by spiders.
> *Question:* How many people do you know about who have been bitten by a spider and then died?
> *Answer:* Lots of people in Australia have been bitten by spiders and I expect lots of them have died.
> *Question:* What is your evidence?
> *Answer:* Well, er, um …
> *Question:* According to the BBC Health News in 2004, only 26 deaths from spiders have been recorded in Australia in the past century. No deaths have been recorded from spider bites in the UK. How likely do you think it is that you will die from a spider bite?
> *Answer:* Not very likely.
> *Question:* What is your evidence?
> *Answer:* No one in the UK has ever died of a spider bite.
> *Question:* Do you know anyone who has ever been bitten by a spider?
> *Answer:* No.
> *Question:* What is your evidence?
> *Answer:* If they had they would have told me.
> *Question:* How many times have you been bitten by a spider?
> *Answer:* Never.
> *Question:* How likely do you think it is that you will be bitten by a spider?
> *Answer:* Not very likely.
> *Question:* What is your evidence?
> *Answer:* Because neither I nor any of my friends has ever been bitten by a spider.

The therapist is challenging the negative automatic thought and making the person think about their beliefs. By asking for evidence to support the disordered or incorrect train of thought, the person begins to see how their arguments are not based on facts. This will make them feel very different about things, and this should then affect the way they behave.

We will look again at CBT in the second part of this chapter, page 179.

Exam-style question – Individual differences: Atypical behaviour

These questions are taken from the OCR B541 Psychology paper, from June 2010. For more past and sample papers plus answer exemplars visit the OCR website. OCR have not seen or commented on the quality of the sample answers.

1. State what is meant by 'atypical behaviour'. [1]

   Behaviour which is not typical behaviour. (1)

2.

   > **Treating Phobias**
   > A behaviour therapist was treating a new group of clients for their phobias. His youngest client, Shaun, had a fear of spiders. His other clients had more complex problems. Gemma had a fear of going to school. Sally had a fear of being around other people. John's phobia was even worse; he refused to leave his house because of his fear of open spaces.

   Using the source:

   (a) name the person who was suffering from agoraphobia; [1]

   John (1)

   (b) name the person who was suffering from social phobia; [1]

   Sally (1)

   (c) name the person who was suffering from arachnophobia. [1]

   Shaun (1)

3. Gavin has a fear of heights. Explain how Gavin's fear of heights could be treated using behaviour therapy. [3]

   Implosion therapy (1) would involve Gavin imagining his most feared situation such as being on a rope bridge in a canyon (1) until he forms a new association with it (1).

   You can earn 1 mark for identifying a behavioural technique, either by name or by describing the technique, for example, 'you could make Gavin face his worst fear'. Then you get additional marks for elaborating the technique and looking at the outcome.

4. Watson & Rayner (1920) carried out a study to show how classical conditioning could be used to explain phobias.

   Outline **two** limitations of Watson & Rayner's study. [4]

   Because it was a case study with only one child, you can't generalise from a sample of one. (2)

   Albert didn't leave the experiment in the same state as he entered which goes against ethical guidelines. (2)

   You can earn 2 marks for each limitation if you can provide more information than just 'one boy was tested' or 'it broke ethical guidelines' which are only worth one mark each.

5. Describe how classical conditioning can be used to explain a school phobia. [4]

   You can learn a school phobia by association (1). If something bad happens at school, like being threatened by another pupil, this causes a unconditioned response (1) of fear. This fear becomes associated with the neutral stimulus of school (1). In the end, the school becomes the fearful place rather than the bully. The person has now got a conditioned response to fear school. (1)

   If you wanted to, you could answer this question by drawing a diagram to help you to explain your answer. The diagram on its own would only be worth three marks.

   SECTION TOTAL [15]

The self

Overview

In the first part of this chapter, we talked about how a person's learning experiences can influence the way they react to different situations. You will have realised that because we do not all have the same experiences as each other, we do not always act in the same way and are not always predictable. In this part of the chapter we are going to consider what it is that makes us unique, and also look at the methods psychologists use when they want to compare us to each other.

This section still focuses on individual differences, but will be examined in the second examination paper you sit.

The self – how each of us is unique

KEY CONCEPTS

The OCR examination requires candidates to be able to:

- understand the idea that individuals are unique
- explain the concept of free will.

Some psychologists do not feel that we should group people into categories and say that we should always remember that each person is unique, with their own set of hopes and fears for the future. Because no two people have the same experiences, this does make sense.

Even children from the same family will not have the same life experiences. They may share genes and be part of the same family structure, but they will still vary considerably in ways that, at first glance, might seem relatively unimportant. They will have a different family position, with the eldest child having had the experience of being an 'only child' before the birth of the next one, while younger children will not have that experience. They may be different genders, have different school experiences, different teachers and different friendships. They may have seen different things or have been reinforced for certain behaviours. Even experiences that we tend not to think of as being that important may have a significant effect and help to explain the uniqueness of each individual child.

All these experiences contribute to making us unique and having a very different inner being (or self) to each other. Our self is who we are in every aspect: our physical, emotional and spiritual being is our self; the way we think and feel is our self; the way we are individual is our self.

QUESTION ?

1. Think of as many factors as you can that are likely to vary between one person and the next, which might, in turn, affect the way they think, feel and behave.

The concept of free will

Most people believe they have free will to make their own choices in life. The question is whether we really have absolutely free choice, because the factors that make us different from each other often influence and sometimes restrict the life choices we make. This suggests that our wills

Having free will suggests that you can choose to think and act as you wish, and make your own decisions.

are not really free after all! After all, our life experiences and knowledge will probably affect what we think about.

Consider how you would the following questions:

- Could you be an astronaut?
- Could you be a model?
- Could you own a helicopter?
- Could you be a jockey?
- Could you win the lottery?
- Could you be a brain surgeon?
- Could you travel the world?
- Could you be a university lecturer?
- Could you have your own family?
- Could you live happily ever after?
- Could you do whatever you want, whenever you want?

The answers you will probably give to these questions will be mixed. To some you will answer no, whereas others are possible through a mixture of hard work, luck or opportunity. Among other things, physical appearance, life chances and ability will all affect our achievements and may actually limit the choices available to us.

Psychologists and philosophers have often debated whether or not we have free will, explaining that there are so many factors that might influence us. Freud, for example, believed that our behaviour was determined by the experiences of our early childhood, while behaviourists suggest that our behaviour is shaped by the rewards we received in the past. The answer probably lies somewhere between the two – some of our behaviours are determined, but we still have a certain degree of free will, and our ability to think about our life chances actually makes us different from other species. Remember, anyone could own a helicopter if they worked hard enough and saved enough money, and anyone could be a jockey, even if they are really tall or really heavy – they would just find it difficult to get someone to employ them and they would be very unlikely to win any races!

DISCUSS…

There are also external constraints that restrict our freedom (laws, rules and regulations). These are intended to be for the good of the majority over the minority.

Discuss with your classmates who should decide what is best for the majority.

Discuss with your classmates whether you think that laws, rules and regulations take away our free will.

CORE THEORY: humanistic theory

IN THE EXAM

Candidates should be able to:

- distinguish between self-concept and ideal self in relation to self-esteem
- explain the idea of unconditional positive regard
- explain the idea of self-actualisation
- explain the criticisms of humanism as an explanation of the self
- consider trait theory as an alternative theory, with specific reference to extraversion and neuroticism.

Humanistic theory

The humanistic approach to psychology was developed by the psychologists Carl Rogers and Abraham Maslow in America during the 1950s, in response to the Freudian and behaviourist approaches to behaviour. It is called humanistic psychology because it has the core belief that humans are basically good and that, because of this, humanity should be respected.

- You may agree with Freudian theory and feel that you are driven by unconscious forces that have been shaped by your early experiences.
- You may accept the theory of behaviourism and believe that your life has been shaped by the reinforcement you have received from others.
- You may instead take the humanistic view, which suggests that, although you have had some restricted life opportunities and may have been pressurised to behave in certain ways, at the end of the day you do have the ability to choose how to act – that is, you do have free will.

DISCUSS...

Sometimes you hear teachers in school saying, 'The behaviour is behaviour, not the child.' What do you think this means?

Further your understanding

Imagine you have been raised in an environment where crime is the norm. You may feel pressurised to conform to a criminal way of life by your parents and friends, and you may have seen people rewarded for their criminal activities by having lots of material possessions. You still have the choice of whether to go along with a criminal way of life because you can actually say, 'No, I don't want to.' So you can choose whether to become a model citizen or a criminal, a leader or a follower. It is just that some life choices are easier than others!

This example shows how, despite external pressures, it is still possible to choose which way to respond – because we have free will.

Humanists hold the following beliefs:

- We are individual and unique and each of us has our own thoughts, feelings and values, so we can only make sense of others by understanding how each individual perceives and understands the world.
- We are born with free will, which gives us the ability to make choices (although humanists accept that we have some limitations due to external factors).
- We must take responsibility for both our positive and our negative actions in order to be mentally healthy.
- We each have great value, so even if we have acted in a negative way, it does not take away our value as a person.
- We should focus on the present because what has happened in the past cannot be changed and we cannot predict the future.
- We aim to self-actualise. We have an innate wish to grow and develop and fulfil our ultimate potential in order to achieve true happiness.

● We should not be categorised. The only way people can be categorised is by using tests and having the answers scored as an easy way to make predictions about their future behaviour. But these tests are man-made, so we cannot be sure that they are really accurate, and people may be affected by demand characteristics, so may not answer accurately.

> *Demand characteristics occur when people behave in the way they think the questioner wants them to behave. (See Chapter 6, page 196.)*

Self-concept, ideal self and self-esteem

Self-concept

Our self-concept is the concept (or theory) that we have about ourselves, and what and who we are. We develop our self-concept in early childhood, focusing, at first, on external things like the way we look or what we own. As we get older, we think more about what we are like as people; whether we are confident or shy, kind or cruel, and whether others like us or not.

Our self-concept is made up not only of factual information, but also by how we evaluate ourselves in comparison with others. We might think that we are wonderful, but we might feel that we are worthless compared with the people we know. What other people say about us will also affect our self-concept. If someone keeps saying that we are stupid, we may come to believe that we really are stupid. The most important thing to remember is that we find it very difficult to see ourselves as others see us, and our self-evaluations are rarely accurate.

Self-concept is important because it will affect the way we behave. If we believe we are strong and capable, we are more likely to take on challenges and push ourselves further than if we think we are weak and ineffective.

HOMEWORK

If you have younger brothers or sisters, or family members between the ages of 6 and 10 years, ask them to tell you at least eight things about themselves. They should start with, 'I am …' Then do the same thing with the same number of teenagers (but it is probably best not to choose people who are studying psychology).

Divide the descriptions into external descriptors (things about their looks or what they own) and internal descriptors (what they are like as a person), and then add them up for each age group in a table like the one below.

Age group	Internal descriptors	External descriptors
Below 10		
Above 10		

Look at the data and see if there is a difference in the number of internal and external descriptors according to age.

Ideal self

This is how we would like to be – for example, physically we might want to be tall and good-looking, or we might want to be rich and famous. However, you would probably agree that you might be rich and famous and very beautiful, but you may be very unhappy inside and surely that is not ideal. Therefore, your ideal self should include other things besides external factors. It should also take into account how happy and contented we are and how satisfied and fulfilled we feel.

Self-esteem

Our self-esteem comes from comparing our actual self with our ideal self. If your self-concept is positive and you think you are a good and worthwhile human being, who is clever and popular, this is quite likely to be close to your ideal self, so you will have high self-esteem. If there is a huge gap between what you think you are like and what you want to be like, your self-esteem will be low.

HOMEWORK

See if you can work out your self-esteem using the following method. (Remember, this is just a bit of fun, not a serious exercise.) For the purpose of this exercise, imagine that really high self-esteem (when you feel really good about yourself) would give you a score of 1. Anything less than 1 would suggest that your self-esteem could always improve!

First of all, using a ten-point scale, with 1 being the lowest score you could give yourself and 10 being the highest, rate how you feel about yourself (which would include how you look, how nice you are, and so on). It will not necessarily be accurate, but it will give you an idea of how you feel about yourself at any one point.

Do the same for your ideal self, on a ten-point rating scale where 10 is pretty much perfect and 1 is the opposite. Most people may be happy to rate their ideal self at 10, although others may rate it slightly lower because they may feel that by being a 10 (or being perfect) might be quite boring!

Divide your rating for self-concept (how you see yourself) by your rating for ideal self (how you would like to be) in order to get a score for self-esteem. For example, if you rated your self-concept as 4, and your ideal self as 8, you would divide 4 by 8, which gives you a score of 0.5. This would be self-esteem that is about midway. This technique shows that the bigger the gap between self-concept and ideal self, the lower a person's self-esteem will be.

QUESTION ?

2. The humanistic theory is one explanation of the self. Complete the following passage, on humanistic theory, by filling in the gaps with the terms listed below:

**ideal self,
self-concept,
self-esteem**

Humanistic theory says that everyone has a _____, which is how they see themselves. We also have an idea of who we would like to be, which is known as the _____. The difference between the two is a measure of our _____.

(OCR GCSE paper Jan 2011)

Unconditional positive regard

Why do some people have high self-esteem and others seem to have low self-esteem and very little self-confidence? According to Rogers (1959), parents can have a significant influence on their children's self-esteem. He suggested that some parents (and other significant adults) give their children unconditional positive regard by providing genuine praise, pleasure in sharing their company, support and care. This will make the child feel really good about themselves, because they know, no matter what they do, that their parents genuinely love them for who they are and their care is not conditional on them behaving in certain ways. On the other hand, some parents place conditions on the love and attention they give to their children – for example, saying things like, 'I will only love you if you get all your spellings right in the next test.' The trouble is, this might set the child an unrealistic target – a target that they would ideally like to achieve, but perhaps never can. Therefore the gap between their actual self (poor at spelling and unloved) and their ideal self (brilliant at spelling and loved) will be huge and will lead to the child having very low self-esteem.

Self-actualisation

Everyone has an ideal self – the image of what we would really like to be. As we said, our ideal self covers how we feel about ourselves, including whether we feel a sense of inner calm and fulfilment.

Self-actualisation is the process whereby we reach the utmost pinnacle of success and satisfaction. It is not to do with material possessions, but more to do with achieving the sense of self-fulfilment and contentment when all is right with the world. In fact, if we managed to become like our idea selves, we would probably have achieved self-actualisation. We all strive for self-actualisation, but the majority of us do not manage to achieve this state because we are too busy dealing with day-to-day events.

The idea of self-actualisation came from Abraham Maslow (1954). Maslow explained that there is a hierarchy of human needs and that we must achieve the lower levels before we can finally reach the top level, which is self-actualisation or fulfilment. Figure 5.6 illustrates this hierarchy and shows how basic physiological needs, such as food and drink, come at the bottom of the hierarchy and need to be fulfilled in order for us to climb to the next step of the ladder, which is the need for safety (we could not find safety if we were weak through lack of food and water!). Towards the top of the hierarchy you will see the more complex needs, such as achievement,

Figure 5.6 **Maslow's hierarchy of needs** ▽

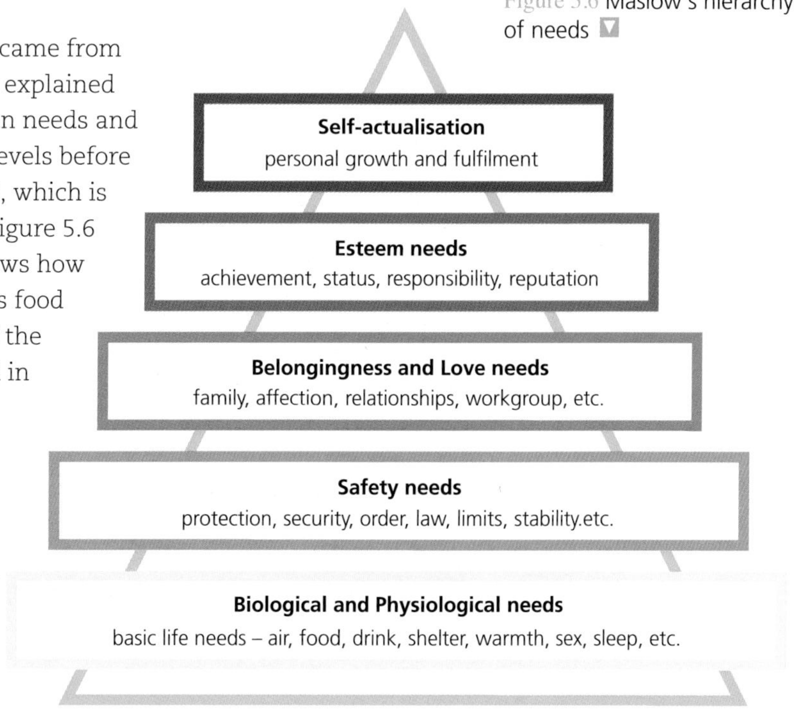

Self-actualisation
personal growth and fulfilment

Esteem needs
achievement, status, responsibility, reputation

Belongingness and Love needs
family, affection, relationships, workgroup, etc.

Safety needs
protection, security, order, law, limits, stability.etc.

Biological and Physiological needs
basic life needs – air, food, drink, shelter, warmth, sex, sleep, etc.

status and reputation; finally, the top level of self-actualisation can only be reached when all the other component parts have been satisfied.

Criticisms of humanism as an explanation of the self

Different areas of psychology look to explore and measure the 'average' behaviour or cognitive skill as a way of understanding how things generally work with human beings. If you have an average, then you can look at how individual people compare. You can also look at a change in someone following therapy to see if the measures on which they have been assessed have changed in any way.

- Humanistic theory makes the generalisation that all people are basically good and are striving for self-actualisation. However, many people make poor life choices, even though they could have chosen a much more positive outcome. An example would be someone who decides to drink excessively or take drugs to escape from what they consider to be life's difficulties, even though they know that by taking drugs they are likely to shorten their lives and cause themselves pain and suffering – hardly a step towards self-actualisation!

- Humanistic theory focuses on individual experiences, and this makes it very difficult to study and evaluate. With humanistic theory, there are no averages, as people are valued for their uniqueness, but this, in turn, makes it impossible to evaluate objectively. An example would be the assessment of whether someone has actually managed to self-actualise. How would we know? Self-actualisation will vary from person to person. What one person might consider to be self-actualisation is likely to be very different to the next person's view, so how can we ever know if someone has achieved this ultimate state?

- Humanism ignores some of the really important genetically inherited factors that can affect a person. There is evidence to suggest that we inherit certain characteristics from our parents – for example, our physical characteristics, some personality traits and predispositions to illness. These factors may also affect the way we develop, as you will realise from the nature/nurture arguments.

- Humanistic theory suggests that we need to fulfil our basic needs before we can self-actualise, but this may not always be the case. Artists have been known to go without food in order to continue to paint, while others put themselves in positions of extreme danger in order to achieve some sort of extraordinary goal.

Further your understanding

Michael Reardon, one of the most famous free climbers, who climbed without any sort of ropes or safety gear, found his fulfilment in climbing some of the world's most challenging rock faces. He would be missing out on the lower-level needs such as safety and security in order to put himself at great risk, although perhaps this was his personal 'self-actualisation'. To find out more about Michael Reardon type his name in to a search engine.

Trait theory – extroversion and neuroticism

Unlike the humanists, traits theorists are interested in looking at the things that people do have in common, so they focus on identifying and measuring these personality characteristics or traits that we each have in lesser or greater quantities.

Trait theorists believe that personality traits are relatively stable over time, so measuring them might prove helpful to compare people with each other. Traits are also continuous dimensions. This means that we can be measured to have less or more of each particular trait. For example, if we take a measurement of aggression, each of us could be measured for aggressive characteristics. Some people would have high scores, while others would have very low scores. If we mark where we are on a line, from very aggressive to not at all aggressive, we could provide a label for the non-aggressive end of the continuum, and that would be passive.

Some people are very sociable, while others are antisocial – so this might give you a sociability measure.

Some people are very anxious, while others are really confident and self-assured – so this might give you a rating for anxiety.

Trait theorists do not dismiss individuality, but they say that we may all gain different measures on each of the traits we all have, and it is these different scores that give us our individuality.

> We mentioned personality in Chapter 1, page 17, when talking about criminals.

> Traits are not to be confused with types. Types are an all-or-none measure (such as male/ female). For example, you are not either sociable or antisocial; you are more likely to be somewhere in between, which puts you somewhere on a continuum

> Traits are habitual patterns of behaviours, thoughts and emotions, which are relatively stable over time and influence our behaviour.

HOMEWORK

How many different traits can you think of? When you have done this, go online to see how many character traits you can find (type 'character traits' into a search engine).

Choose ten reasonably common traits. Then choose a name for the other end of the dimension (as in the aggressive/passive example above) and see how difficult it is to rate yourself on the ones you have chosen. You could ask an adult who knows you well to rate you separately and see if your scores agree!

One of the first trait theories was that of Hans Eysenck, whom we mentioned in Chapter 1, page 18, when talking about criminal personalities. Eysenck suggested that we have two main traits, which are measured on a continuum, just like the idea of aggressive/passive; one of these in extroversion versus introversion and the other is neuroticism versus stability.

- Extroversion: how outgoing, talkative and sociable you are. Extroverts prefer to be with others, tend to enjoy parties and other social events, and get bored easily.
- Introversion: How shy and reserved you are. Introverts do not mind being on their own or with small groups.

● Neuroticism: how likely you are to be nervous or upset, and become anxious or even depressed.
● Stability: how likely you are to remain emotionally calm and constant, even under pressure.

These traits are assessed by people completing the Eysenck Personality Inventory (EPI). This gives a measure on these two continuums and your scores can tell you a great deal about your personality because they will place you somewhere on Eysenck's map of personality.

HOMEWORK

If you type 'Eysenck Personality Inventory test' into a search engine, you will find a copy of the EPI to complete online.

Further your understanding

Eysenck suggested that our personalities are inherited in part from our parents. He also believed that personalities are biologically based. He suggested that we all have an ideal level of arousal. This means that if we are highly aroused we become very anxious, and if we are under-aroused we may feel bored. Ideally we want to be stimulated, but not over-stimulated, and this is known as our optimal level of arousal. Eysenck suggested that people with extrovert personalities are under-aroused and bored, and need lots of external stimulation to bring them up to the optimum level. On the other hand, introverts are over-aroused and need a quiet life in order to lower their levels of arousal.

If you look at Figure 5.7 you can see the two dimensions of introversion/extroversion and neuroticism/stability. If you achieved a high score of extroversion and you were emotionally stable (low score on neuroticism) you would fit into the pink area. This would then give you a description of other personality traits you are likely to have.

Figure 5.7

Source: H.J. Eysenck and M.W. Eysenck (1985) *Personality and Individual Differences: A natural science approach*, New York, Plenum Press. Reproduced with kind permission from Springer Science & Business Media B.V.

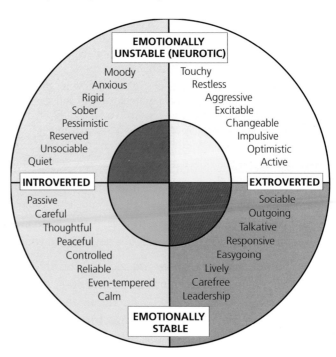

CORE STUDY: B.A. Van Houtte and P.A. Jarvis (1995)

B.A. Van Houtte and P.A. Jarvis (1995) The role of pets in preadolescent psychosocial development. Journal of Applied Developmental Psychology 16, pp. 463–79

You need to be able to …

- describe Van Houtte and Jarvis's interviews about pet ownership among pre-adolescents
- outline the limitations of Van Houtte and Jarvis's study.

Background

Animals are often very important family members and it has been shown that they often have a very positive impact on people's well-being. The authors were interested in whether the same was true for pre-adolescents.

Young people between the ages of 9 and 12 years are known as pre-adolescents because they have not yet reached adolescence. During this time, pre-adolescents experience a number of changes, including changes in their physical appearance, their relationships with parents and the way they think and feel about themselves and others, all of which may affect their self-esteem.

Previous studies into pet ownership by young children had found that pets were considered to be like special friends to young people. They were also rated above other people (but not above parents) in making them feel good or satisfied with themselves, and the loss of a pet was considered to be important enough to affect their pre-adolescent development.

The authors noticed that most of what has been written about the importance of pets in children's lives was either descriptive or anecdotal, and they felt it was important to carry out some scientific research to see if pet ownership really did have a positive effect on pre-adolescent development.

Self-esteem is the term used describe a person's sense of self-worth or personal value.

Anecdotal evidence is evidence from recalled stories or anecdotes, so its accuracy is likely to have been affected by the passage of time

Describe the study

Aims

The aim of this study was to investigate whether pet ownership was linked to high levels of autonomy, self-concept and self-esteem.

Method

Researchers used an interview and questionnaires to gather background information about the children, such as age, gender and family size, and also pet ownership. The children also completed a number of psychometric tests, which covered the following:

- autonomy (how independent they were)
- self-concept (the mental picture the children had of themselves, and whether this was positive or negative)
- self-esteem (whether the children had a feeling of self-worth and pride in themselves)
- attachment to pets (how meaningful the relationships with pets were to the children).

Procedure

The authors were given permission by an American primary school to carry out the study. They explained the purpose of the study to the children and asked them if they were willing to take part; those who agreed were told they could withdraw from the study at any time, although none of them chose to withdraw.

The children then took part in the interviews, and completed the questionnaires and the psychometric tests. This involved the children rating whether they agreed or disagreed with a number of statements, such as 'I am happy', using different ratings, from 1 to 4 (self-esteem and autonomy), 1 to 5 (self-concept) and 1 to 7 (attachment), where 1 was 'strongly agree' and the highest number represented 'strongly disagree'. They were also asked questions about their types of pets and how long they had owned them. Letters were sent to parents to confirm the children's responses.

The data gathered from the children were used to divide them into two groups – pet owners and non-pet owners. The children were then matched on three measures:

- parental marital status (whether their parents married, separated or divorced)
- socio-economic status (decided by their parents' income and occupation)
- number of brothers and sisters.

> The children were not physically put into different groups. The researchers used the data they had provided to put them into the different groups and to match them. When this had been done, the data were analysed to look for differences.

Participants

From 152 possible participants, the data from 130 school children was used in the study (71 boys and 59 girls), giving 65 in each group. They ranged from 8 to 13 years of age and came from four different year grades, with average ages for each grade as follows:

- Third-graders: 8 years 7 months
- Fourth-graders: 9 years 6 months
- Fifth-graders: 10 years 7 months
- Sixth-graders: 11 years 6 months.

Results

- **Autonomy** (how independent the children were): All the pet owners reported more autonomy than the non-pet owners, with the fifth-graders having higher autonomy (independence) scores than children from the other three grades. Pet owners were also more likely than non-pet owners to perceive their parents as people (rather than just 'parents').
- **Self-concept** (the mental picture the children had of themselves, and whether this was positive (happy) or negative (sad)): Among the pet-owning groups, the sixth grade had the highest scores for self-concept,

and their scores were significantly higher than the scores for the non-pet-owning sixth-graders. However, the pet-owning fourth- and fifth-grade children had slightly lower self-concept scores, although the researchers said they were not significantly different and this difference may have been due to chance.

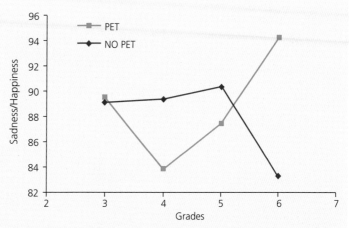

- **Self-esteem** (whether the children had a feeling of self-worth and pride in themselves): For self-esteem, pet owners on average reported higher self-esteem than non-pet owners. The only exception was the fourth grade, where the non-pet owners reported higher self-esteem.

▲ Figure 5.8 Average self-concept scores for pet owners and non-pet owners in each school grade (This Figure and Figure 5.9 have been reprinted from *Journal of Applied Developmental Psychology*, 16, 463–79, Van Houtte and Jarvis, 'The role of pets in preadolescent psychosocial development', copyright 1995, with permission from Elsevier.)

- **Attachment** (how meaningful the relationships with pets were to the children): The results for attachment did not seem to depend completely on pet ownership, as some of the younger children who did not own pets rated the relationships as more meaningful than some of the younger pet owners.

Conclusions

The findings of this study support past research, which suggested that pets generate feelings of being loved and that a pet's behaviour may be viewed by its owner as reinforcing. Pets may also be viewed as displaying unconditional positive regard to their owners, which means that they do not put conditions on the affection they show and will love their owners no matter what happens. This in

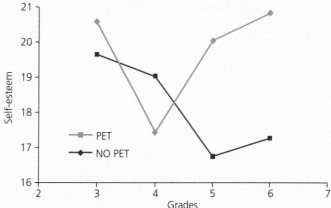

▲ Figure 5.9 Average self-esteem scores for pet owners and non-pet owners in each school grade

turn makes people feel more positive about themselves. Because pets were found to influence increased self-concept and self-esteem in pre-adolescents, they could be used as a source of support in times of stress, for people who were experiencing lowered self-concept and self-esteem.

The results for attachment did not seem to depend on pet ownership, especially in the younger children. This might have been because the younger pet-owning children had less to do with looking after the pets

QUESTION ?

3. What is meant by the term 'unconditional positive regard'?

(OCR GCSE paper June 2010)

than the older children. On the other hand, it might have been because the younger non-pet owning children saw pets in an idealised way and did not realise that they often chew things or leave muddy footprints about the place or cover things with hair!

The pet owners also reported greater autonomy, which means that pets could be used to help children develop more autonomous characteristics, such as responsibility and self-reliance.

The authors suggested that pets may have their greatest impact on children's lives as they enter adolescence, and could be used as substitutes for human support when this is not available. The authors also explained that children who did not actually own a pet also felt that relationships with animals could be very meaningful.

Limitations

- The study included only cats and dogs, although the non-pet-owning participants may have owned another kind of pet, such as a gerbil or a rabbit, which might have influenced their reports of their relationship with their pets. The questionnaire did not ask them about other pets.
- This research was intended to look at measures of various parts of our personality and whether they are affected by pet ownership. This involved measuring one person's personality and comparing it to someone else's by using their scores on personality tests. We need to consider whether personality tests really do measure personality and whether this was a good way of comparing the different children.
- The authors did not specify who completed the questionnaires, although it would seem likely that it was the children themselves. Perhaps the children were not honest in the answers they gave, or perhaps they said what they thought the researchers wanted to hear.
- The total number of pupils who took part was only 130, from one school in America, and these children were divided into eight groups (four grades and pet owners/non-pet owners). Therefore each group was quite small. Were these children representative of all children?
- Although the authors said they carefully matched the groups, there may have been other factors that had not been taken into consideration, such as ethnicity or level of ability. This may have affected the results.

QUESTION **?**

4. Outline the procedure used in Van Houtte and Jarvis's study into self-esteem in pet owners.

(OCR GCSE paper June 2010)

DISCUSS... 💬

Do you think the relationship you have with a gerbil or a rabbit would be the same sort of relationship that you would have with a cat or a dog? How might it be different? Do you think this might have affected the children's feelings about pets?

When someone answers in the way they think the researchers want them to, this is called answering according to demand characteristics. (See Chapter 6, page 206.)

Applications of research into the self: *counselling*

Candidates should be able to:

- explain how psychological research relates to counselling – for example, raising self-esteem in depressed people, individual choice in careers counselling, humanistic principles of relationship counselling.

What is counselling?

Counselling is a process where a person (usually known as the client) who is experiencing some kind of emotional or mental difficulty will share this with a counsellor, who is a person trained to listen and support them. Some of the reasons people go to counsellors are because they are suffering from emotional pain, which could be due to depression, grief or relationship difficulties.

The sessions take place in a private and confidential setting, where counsellor will listen carefully, clarifying what the client is saying if necessary. A counsellor does not judge their clients. This relationship between counsellor and client involves a very high level of trust and confidentiality.

Psychological research relates to counselling because counsellors learn about different psychological perspectives. The perspective that they favour will affect the way they look at the client's difficulties and will guide the way they work with their clients.

Depression

We all feel 'low' or miserable at odd times in our lives, often, but not always, as a result of some experience or event. However, when the feelings of sadness and misery are completely out of proportion to the event itself, or when they go on for a very long period of time and stop a person from functioning properly (eating, sleeping and socialising), this is known as depression.

Research evidence has shown that people with low self-esteem are more likely to suffer from depression. If people feel that they are worthless and believe that things are not going to get better, this will affect their attitude to the whole of their life.

If you remember, the way we evaluate our self-worth comes from comparing our actual self with our ideal self. If we feel that we are worthless and very different to our ideal self, we will have low self-esteem. Sometimes we set our goals too high and expect too much of ourselves, and if we cannot live up to our own expectations we feel pretty useless.

We also mentioned that our self-evaluations are not always accurate and we think we are 'worse' than we really are. How often have you looked in the mirror, thinking you look awful, and then someone comes along and says how nice you look?

Using counselling to raise self-esteem in depressed people

There are different counselling therapies based on different psychological perspectives, that can be used to support people with low-self esteem and depression. Below we have outlined the three main therapies used.

Freudian therapy

We talked about Freud when we considered gender development in Chapter 1. Freudian therapists are interested in the negative past experiences the client may have had, which they believe will have been pushed into the client's unconscious mind. The client will not be aware of these forces, so it is the psychoanalytic therapist's job to help them gain some kind of insight or understanding of the forces that are affecting their current emotions and behaviours and making them feel that they have little self-worth.

This is an intensive form of counselling therapy, and the client will probably meet with the therapist weekly over a period of months or even years. During this time the client should begin to realise that their poor self-esteem comes from past experiences, probably from childhood. By working through these past feelings, the client should begin to realise that they are actually better than they thought they were. This, in turn, will raise their self-esteem, which will change the way they behave, which in turn will reduce their level of depression.

Humanistic therapy

Humanistic therapists believe that the client, not the therapist, holds the answers to their problems. Through counselling, the therapist aims to understand the client and help them to grow in confidence and self-esteem by showing them the following:

- Congruence: this means that the relationship between the therapist and the client will be more genuine and open than, for example, a doctor–patient relationship, where there is a kind of unequal power. In a congruent relationship, people do not try to appear to be anything other than what they are. Although this does not mean that the therapist talks about their own problems to clients in therapy sessions!
- Unconditional positive regard: this means that the therapist will accept the client for who they are, without judging them or disapproving. This provides a safe context for the client to explore how they feel, without fear of rejection.

● Empathy: this is where the therapist tries to understand the client's situation from their point of view.

The therapist actively listens to the client and reflects (or repeats) back to them the things they have said. This allows the therapist to make sure they really understand what the client is saying and, at the same time, allows the client to think about what they have just said. The therapist does not try to change the client's thinking in any way, but simply allows the client to explore their feelings and beliefs through talking. By doing this, the client may start to look at things in different ways until they decide on the right solution for them.

Cognitive therapy

Earlier in this chapter (page 160) we mentioned cognitive behavioural therapy (CBT) as a way of treating phobias. This kind of therapy aims to change what we think (cognitions), because the way we think affects the way we act (behaviours), and the same techniques can be used to treat depression.

One way to help people who are suffering from low self-esteem is for the counsellor to help them to think differently about themselves, because their thinking may be distorted in some way by their negative automatic thoughts. If we feel we are clever or attractive or funny, we will have more confidence and this will make us behave differently; in return, people will respond to us in different ways. This response is the reinforcement for more positive behaviours.

CBT is now considered one of the most effective forms of treatment, not only for phobias, but also for depression.

Situation	You are walking down the corridor at school/work and someone you know completely ignores you	
	Normal depressed thoughts (unhelpful)	**New way of thinking (helpful)**
Thoughts	They ignored me because I am not worth talking to and they cannot be bothered with me	Perhaps the person has had some bad news and was too preoccupied to notice me
Emotional feelings	Miserable and rejected	Concerned
Physical feelings	Sick feeling in the stomach	No physical symptoms – feel fine
Action	Try to avoid the person in the future	Try to contact the person to make sure they are okay

◀ Table 5.3 How CBT helps the client to think about a sample situation in a different way

Individual choice in careers counselling

Careers counsellors are qualified professionals who usually work with schools or colleges in order to help young people with careers guidance. They ask questions about an individual's skills and interests and what they would like to do with their lives. They may even use personality tests as a way of gathering more information.

Humanistic principles focus on allowing the client to explore individually what is important to them, in order to come to their own conclusions and make their own choices, and careers counsellors' work is often based on these principles. Through listening to the client and through discussion with the client, counsellors will help them to identify the most appropriate career decisions, because the client will not pursue a career if they do not feel it is the right one for them. A careers counsellor will also ensure that the client sets realistic targets for themselves rather than having unrealistic goals.

Humanistic principles of relationship counselling

Because human beings are social creatures, they often become very distressed when their relationships fall into difficulties. Sometimes these difficulties are the result of one person somehow blocking the potential of the other, which in turn will set up tensions between the two. This may be by preventing them from doing something that is very important to them, or by criticising their efforts.

Humanistic principles focus on the fact that each individual aims for self-actualisation, so the way relationship counsellors will work is to try to help the partners to be aware of their underlying emotions and motives, and to see the situation from the perspective of the other person. As a result, the partners should decide on their own agreed solutions about how to save the relationship.

Exam-style questions – Individual difference: The self

These questions are taken from the OCR B542 Psychology paper, from January 2011. For more past and sample papers plus answer exemplars visit the OCR website. OCR have not seen or commented on the quality of the sample answers.

1. The humanistic theory is one explanation of the self.

   Complete the passage below, on the humanistic theory, by filling in the gaps. [3]

   You must choose a different term for each gap from the list below:

   free will   ideal self   self concept   self esteem

Humanistic theory says that everyone has a … *self concept* …which is how they see themselves. We also have an idea of who we would like to be which is known as the … *ideal self* … . The difference between the two is a measure of our … *self esteem* … . (3)

2. Give **two** criticisms of the humanistic theory of the self. [2]

It's unscientific. It's difficult to test. (1)

The candidate only gets one mark here as the answer is really one point – things that aren't scientific are difficult to test. You need to make two separate points to get two marks, for example, the point above plus it ignores other theories such as the biological suggestion that we may inherit our personality.

3. Explain how research into the self is used in counselling. [4]

Counselling is used on depressed people (1) and is based on unconditional positive regard. (1)

This answer is only just worth two marks. It is a very brief and basic response and does not really explain what the candidate means. A better answer would be:

A depressed person (1) may receive counselling to help them to self-actualise (1). This would rely on the depressed person being shown unconditional positive regard (1) which means that the counsellor will show them respect regardless of what the client does or says (1).

4. Describe Van Houtte & Jarvis' (1995) study into pet ownership. [6]

This question says describe so no evaluation is required.

The aim of the study was to look at the effects of owning a pet. American school children were asked about whether they had a pet or not and then they were measured to see if they were happy. The conclusions were that people who had pets were happier than people who didn't. The sample was not representative as they were American children and not everyone had a pet. (2)

This answer, which is worth 2 marks, is quite weak as it does not describe any of the study in enough detail. The study did not measure 'happiness' but was looking at measures of the self. The final point is an evaluation so it gains the candidate no marks. The answer below is much more developed and gives all the key features of the study.

The aim of the study was to look at the effects of pet ownership on self-esteem. American school children were asked to complete questionnaires which gave them a measure of autonomy, self-concept, self-esteem and attachment to animals. They were divided into pet owners and non-pet owners. They were also matched for marital status of parents, socio-economic status and number of siblings to make sure that these things did not make a difference to the way they felt about life. Van Houtte and Jarvis looked at the data they had collected and concluded that pets offer unconditional positive regard and that the children who owned pets had a higher measure of autonomy, self-concept and self-esteem although the age of the child had some effect on this. They didn't have a higher measure of attachment to animals as some of the children without pets said they were attached to animals too. (6)

SECTION TOTAL [15]

6 Research in psychology

Psychology is a science and, as such, uses what is known as the scientific method. This means that psychologists use the same research methods as the other sciences, but the trouble is that humans are not as predictable as metals or chemicals. Psychologists often try to work out what people are doing; however, people may lie or act in a different way to normal, or even do what they can to help psychologists to gather the information they think they want. As a result, the techniques psychologists use for research have to be well designed and carefully conducted.

Research methods used in psychology

Overview

As part of the OCR examination, you will need to have a good understanding of the techniques chosen by psychologists, and be aware of the strengths and weaknesses of each technique.

We will begin by looking at what you need to know about planning psychological research.

This will include giving you an understanding of the following topics:

● hypotheses
● variables
● experimental designs
● sampling techniques
● ethical considerations.

Then we will consider doing psychological research, which will include looking at the following techniques:

● experiments
● questionnaires
● interviews
● observations
● types of studies.

Once the data have been gathered, we will consider analysing research, considering the following:

● types of data
● descriptive data
● tables, charts and graphs
● evaluating findings
● sources of bias.

The final section focuses on planning an investigation for yourself. By the time you get to this part of the chapter, you should have a much better idea about how to carry out an experiment, questionnaire, interview and observation for yourself.

Planning research

Some techniques make it easy to keep a high degree of control, while others intend to study how people behave naturally. Some research generates data that we can analyse using statistics, while other pieces of research allow us to collect data that are more descriptive. You will soon understand how to choose the best method for different types of research.

When we consider carrying out research, it is because we have an idea that we want to investigate further. For example, we might be interested in looking at what helps people to remember lists of words. We might predict that by presenting words in some kind of hierarchical organisation (see Chapter 2, page 49), this will help people to remember more words than if they are just randomly presented with no organisation at all. In this case we have made a prediction of what we think will happen – we have made an educated guess as to the outcome of our study and this prediction or educated guess is our hypothesis.

DISCUSS…

Below is an organised list of words and underneath it is the same list but with no organisation.

Which list do you predict would be easier to remember?

Animals	Clothes	Colours	Furniture
Cow	Jeans	Pink	Stool
Pig	Socks	Green	Wardrobe
Bear	Skirt	Blue	Table
Horse	Sweatshirt	Yellow	Bed

Blue	Horse	Pink	Table
Cow	Skirt	Stool	Jeans
Socks	Wardrobe	Pig	Clothes
Furniture	Bear	Colours	Bed
Green	Sweatshirt	Yellow	Animals

We are going to use this example several times in this chapter – we will call it our hierarchical/random experiment. As a way of understanding this section, you might like to test the hypothesis for yourself, so think how you could do this before you read any further. Once you have decided how to do it, have a go and get your results – then read the rest of this section and see how many different aspects of the research you thought of for yourself.

There are two types of hypotheses: the null hypothesis (sometimes written as H0) and the alternate (research) hypothesis (sometimes written as H1).

Why do we have two hypotheses you may ask? Well, you have made the prediction that people will remember more words when they are presented in a hierarchical list, and because you have actually predicted a *difference* in the number of words recalled, this is a research hypothesis.

But what happens if there is no difference in the number of words recalled. The way round this is to make another prediction that there will be no difference in the number of words recalled between the two lists, or that any difference is just due to chance (which might include things like the time of day, the tiredness of the participants, the temperature in the room and so on). This way, you are really covering yourself!

So, we have the null hypothesis, which predicts that there will be no difference, and an alternative hypothesis (called the alternate or research hypothesis), which predicts that there will be a difference. This means that when you have completed your research and looked at your results, you will be able to accept one or other of the hypotheses.

The alternate hypothesis can predict a correlation as well as a difference.

▼ Table 6.1

Alternate (research) hypothesis	Null hypothesis
People who see a list of organised words will remember more words than people who see the same words listed in a random order.	There will be no difference in the number of words recalled, or any difference found will be due not to the organisation of the lists but simply to chance events.

In fact, you can have an alternate (research) hypothesis and a null hypothesis for any type of research.

If you start a null hypothesis with the words 'There will be no …', this may help.

HOMEWORK

Try to write a null hypothesis for each of the following pieces of research.

Alternate (research) hypothesis	Null hypothesis
Children who watch violent videos will hit a Bobo doll more often than children who have not watched violent videos.	
Scientists will be better than artists at remembering lists of technical words.	
Children who have strong attachments to their parents will have more friends at school.	

KEY CONCEPTS

The OCR examination requires candidates to be able to:

- distinguish between independent variables and dependent variables
- outline what is meant by an extraneous variable
- explain how extraneous variables can be controlled, including standardisation.

QUESTION

1. In the following pieces of research, see if you can identify the IV and the DV.
   - Researchers putting people in either noisy or quiet rooms to learn lists of words so they could compare the number of words remembered by the two groups.
   - Boys and girls being given lots of toys so researchers could see what toys they chose to play with.
   - Finding out if people who owned pets had lower heart rates than people who did not own pets.

Variables

Independent variables and dependent variables

When we have decided on our hypothesis, we will have predicted that something will cause something else to happen. The thing that we have predicted will have an effect is known as the independent variable (IV). The results it produces are known as the dependent variable (DV) because they depend on the independent variable.

A good way to remember this is as follows: The effect of things like television programmes, uniform, pet ownership and television commercials are all things that we can investigate. They are not dependent on anything – they are independent entities and we can manipulate them. On the other hand, the measured results they produce actually depend on them, because without them we would have no results.

If we want to look at the effects of sleep on memory we could manipulate tiredness by giving some people a good night's sleep, while others have to stay up or are woken after a couple of hours. We would then test their memory by measuring how many words the people will remember. So in this case the independent variable is the amount of sleep people get. The dependent variable is the number of words recalled.

With our hierarchical/random research, our prediction is that people who see a list of organised words will remember more words than people who see the same words listed in random order. Here, the thing we are manipulating (independent variable) is the way the words are presented. The measurement (dependent variable) is the number of words remembered.

Extraneous variables

Extraneous variables, or extra variables, are things that are likely to affect the results of the investigation because they have not been controlled by the researchers.

If a researcher is planning to carry out a piece of research, they will need to make sure that the IV has really caused the DV and that it was not caused by something else they had not thought about. Returning to our hierarchical/random memory experiment, if we find that there is a big difference in the scores between the hierarchical and the random lists, we will be able to accept the alternate hypothesis and reject the null hypothesis. However, we might suddenly realise that the participants who saw the hierarchical list were very different from the participants who saw the random list. In fact, although we did our best to make sure that they were all the same age and level of ability, we have just realised that most of the group who were learning from the random list had just arrived by bus. The bus was late and overcrowded and the participants arrived in a hot and stressed state. On the other hand, the bus carrying the hierarchical list participants was not crowded and arrived on time, so they were much happier when they arrived. In this case, the results of one group are going to be affected by the experiences they have had. On the other hand, if both groups had experienced the same difficulty with their journey, although it might not have been ideal, the differences between groups would still be due to the IV and not the bus journey!

We need to remember that extraneous variables may well affect the participants performance but if groups have the same experiences, then the extraneous variables will affect both sets of scores – actually cancelling each other out. The problem arises when only one set of scores are affected by extraneous variables.

There are a number of different extraneous variables that should be considered as far as possible to prevent this sort of thing from happening (although there may be others that you have not taken into account). An example might be to do with the physical environment where we have placed our participants, as this can unexpectedly affect their performance – perhaps it is too hot, too cold, too familiar or very unfamiliar and therefore frightening. It is necessary, as far as possible, to make sure that all these things are managed so that you know that the DV is due to the IV and not the result of something else.

Standardisation

Another issue that can produce extraneous variables is the way the experiment or study is conducted. It is really important to make sure that every participant has exactly the same experience; otherwise this could affect their performance. The procedure must be standardised so that each participant is treated in the same way, does the tasks in the same way, receives the same instructions, and so on. If one group of participants is treated in one way, having everything explained, for example, and the other group has someone shouting instructions and not explaining anything, the two groups of participants will probably perform very differently. One group may be happy to do their best, while the other group probably would not care.

Psychologists often use standardised instructions, where they say exactly the same words to their participants in order to prevent any

DISCUSS...

You are about to carry out your research into the hierarchical/random lists and all your participants are due to arrive. You have sorted out the lists of words for them to learn and have set out the paper on their desks for them to write down all the words they have recalled. In order to reduce extraneous variables as far as possible, work with a partner to write down standardised instructions to read to your participants, telling them what to do. Remember, you must not tell them much about the purpose behind the study because you might give the game away. Just remember to standardise the procedure they will need to follow.

extraneous variables occurring from the procedure itself. One way of ensuring standardisation is to provide written instructions, which should be simple and clear.

Experimental designs

When we are designing experiments, we need to decide the best way to investigate our hypothesis. For example, if we have decided to work with a group of 30 participants for our hierarchical/random memory test, we would need to figure out how to design this research. When we are thinking about experimental designs, we mean how we are actually going to test our participants.

- Are they all going to learn both lists? This is probably not a good idea because the same words are in both lists and this would mean that we would not know whether the way they were presented had any effect on their learning.
- Could half of the participants learn one list and the other half learn the other list? That would make more sense because at least we would feel more confident that the way the words were presented had affected the DV.

But what if the participants in one group were much more able than those in the other group (or much older, or did not speak English or could not read)?

Making these decisions and thinking about the strengths of each suggestion is what we mean by working out our experimental design.

Repeated measures designs

Let us think about the suggestions above. Are our participants going to take part in both conditions by learning both word lists (hierarchical and random)? This design is known as a repeated measures design because all participants take part in both conditions, so we repeatedly measure them.

Strengths:

- Because all the participants are taking part in both conditions, we know that any difference in our results will be due to the way the lists are presented rather than differences between the participants. Any differences would be cancelled out because if someone was much older and someone did not speak English, at least any poor scores they did produce would show up in both the random and the hierarchical lists.
- You will not need to find as many participants as you would if you used two different groups. After all, five participants in each condition would not give you very helpful results, whereas ten in each condition would be twice as good!

Remember, it is really important to think about who your participants are and why you have selected them. Are young children representative of the population? Would a group of male participants represent the population as a whole? You will need to be able to justify the selection of participants in the examination.

KEY CONCEPTS

The OCR examination requires candidates to be able to:

- distinguish between repeated measures and independent groups designs
- describe the strengths and weaknesses of a repeated measures design
- describe the strengths and weaknesses of an independent groups design.

Weaknesses:

The weaknesses are due to what are known as order effects.

● The participants may be tired by the time they come to learn the second word list.
● The participants will have had the chance to improve through practice what they have to do, so the second time they will probably perform better. They will also be less anxious, which may increase their scores further.

Independent groups designs

Are we going to divide our participants into two groups, so that half of the participants learn one list and the other half learn the other list?

This design is known as an independent groups design, as the participants take part in one condition each, so they are independent of each other.

Strengths:

The strength of this design is that it cancels out order effects because the participants only take part once.

● The participants will not be tired as they only learn one word list.
● The participants will not have had the chance to improve through practice.

Weaknesses:

● Because different participants take part in each condition, we cannot be totally sure that the difference in our results is due to the way the lists are presented; it might be to do with differences between the two groups of participants (perhaps all the participants in one condition were much older, while others may not speak English).
● More participants are required.

At the end of the day the choice is yours, as long as you think very carefully about which design is best for your particular piece of research.

Sampling techniques

When conducting any research, you have to consider what kind of person is relevant to your research. After all, if you were looking at the effects of gender on performance – for example, do men or women do better in memory tests? – it would not be very helpful if you only had male participants. You would need to look for both males and females to take part.

Target populations

The target population for your research would be the people you are interested in finding out about, so that by testing or observing or questioning some of them (your sample of participants) and finding out

Have you noticed that the advantages of one design are the disadvantages of another?

DISCUSS...

How many of these things did you consider when carrying out your own research on the hierarchical/ random memory test?

KEY CONCEPTS

The OCR examination requires candidates to be able to:
● distinguish between a target population and a sample
● distinguish between random sampling and opportunity sampling
● describe the relative strengths and weaknesses of random and opportunity sampling, with reference to representative samples and biased samples.

about their performance, you should be able to generalise your results to the target population as a whole.

Samples

The sample you select will be a group that is representative of your target population. If you chose people who were not relevant – for example, choosing men when you are interested in how pregnancy might affect women's memories – obviously you could not generalise your results to the population of pregnant women that you are interested in.

Further your understanding

Target populations might actually be everyone in the whole population but it might also be just men, just women, all children between the ages of 5 and 7, people living alone, insecurely attached children, heart attack victims, tall boys, teenage girls and so on.

DISCUSS...

Sometimes companies employ people to carry out research for them on whether or not they would use different products. Think of six different items you might find in shops and work with a friend to identify a suitable sample to ask about the products. Remember you need to think about your population first.

If you are interested in finding out more about random number tables, try this page from the Coventry University website: www.coventry. ac.uk/ec/~nhunt/meths/ random.html

QUESTION ?

2. Identify the target populations and samples in the following studies. Do you think the samples were representative of the target populations? (If you are unsure, give a reason for your answer.)

Study	Target population	Sample	Was the sample representative?
Bickman			
Haber and Levin			
Watson and Rayner			
Terry			
Piaget			
Yuki *et al.*			
Van Houtte and Jarvis			

Random sampling

Be warned, this may not be what you think it is – random sampling is highly controlled! To take a truly random sample, you have to make sure that every member of the target population has an equal chance of being selected. For instance, in a study with a target population of pregnant women, the names of all the pregnant women across the country would be collected. As each pregnant woman must have an equal chance of being selected, everyone's names could be written on individual slips of paper and put in a hat. To select 20 participants, the first 20 names taken out of the hat would comprise the sample, just as if you were drawing a raffle.

One way that researchers select random samples (if they do not have a big enough hat!) would be to use random number tables. Every pregnant woman would be given a number and the researcher would start at any point in the random number table and move either horizontally or vertically. You could then take the women who had been allocated those numbers as your sample.

Strengths:

- This method of selecting participants has the least possible bias and probably gives the most representative sample possible. It is more likely to give you a greater variety of participants than you would achieve by using some of the other methods available.
- Because the sample is representative, the results can be generalised to your target population.

Weaknesses:

- This method can be time-consuming because getting an accurate list of the names of everyone in your target population could be quite difficult.
- People may not agree to take part once they have been selected.
- You cannot use random sampling in some types of research, such as field experiments and questionnaires.
- A random sample can actually prove to be quite an unrepresentative sample. You may accidentally end up with a whole group of participants who, by chance, come from the same area when you were interested in investigating everyone from the UK – but that is what can happen when we do things truly randomly.

Opportunity sampling

Selecting an opportunity sample is quicker and easier than random sampling, which is why it is often favoured by psychologists conducting research. An opportunity sample consists of anyone who 'fits the bill', who is available and who agrees to take part in the research. An opportunity sample could be the members of a GCSE psychology class who are willing to take part, the teachers in a school or just a group of friends. It would also be possible to select a group of names from a telephone directory and ask if they would be willing to take part.

Some of the core studies have used students attending classes as their opportunity sample. This is both quick and easy, but is only representative of students!

If you were to select an opportunity sample of people who were walking down a street, would you choose the ones who looked least intimidating? Would you choose people who looked the same age as you? Often people who are selected by opportunity sampling have lots of characteristics in common, so would not be representative of the general population. This would make them a very biased sample.

Strengths:

- It is an easy and fast method.
- It is ideal for naturalistic and field experiments.

Weaknesses:

- The sample is very unlikely to be representative, so you would not be able to generalise to the population as a whole.

QUESTION ?

3. If you selected a group of names of people from a telephone directory, why would they not be representative of the population as a whole?

Ethical considerations

In the past, many psychologists got very excited about their ideas for research and designed experiments on humans and animals that actually ended up harming their participants, by deceiving them, embarrassing them or causing them pain and anxiety. You have read about the work of Watson and Rayner, who conditioned Little Albert to fear white rats. Although they found out how to create a fear in a small child, do you think this was fair on Little Albert? This experience may have affected him for the rest of his life. Although psychologists have expressed their concerns about past research, some people might believe that the ends justify the means, whereas others feel that we should not harm anyone in the course of research. In order to settle these dilemmas, psychologists agreed on a set of ethical guidelines that are used to guide any future research.

> *Ethics refers to the rules of conduct necessary to guard the welfare of participants when carrying out research.*

Further your understanding

To say that 'the ends justify the means' refers to the idea that if you need a specific outcome, it does not matter what you do to achieve this, as it is the result that counts. For example, people are often willing to take medicines in order to cure an illness, even if the drugs have horrific side effects. They would argue that the ends (a cure) justify the means (taking drugs that make them feel really ill).

> *If you want to read more about ethical guidelines, log on to the British Psychological Society website: www.bps.org.uk*

Ethical guidelines are the accepted rules and guidelines of conduct that are used when carrying out any psychological research today. Unethical work will discredit psychology as a discipline and the work of other psychologists, and this may prevent people from wanting to take part in research in the future. The guidelines that we follow in the UK are the guidelines drawn up by the British Psychological Society.

Informed consent and the right to withdraw

When participants are asked to take part in psychological research, they should be told what the research is about in order to allow them to decide whether or not to take part. After all, how can they give consent to take part without the researcher being honest about what they will be asked to do? If they know what the research is about and what they will be expected to do, they can give their informed consent. The trouble is that the results might be affected if the participants know exactly what the research is about, and this can present the psychologist with a dilemma. Therefore there are occasions when the participants are not always made aware of the aim of the study.

There are occasions when people are not able to give their informed consent – for example, if they are children and would not understand the purpose of the research. In cases like these, the parents of young people under the age of 16 have to give permission for their children to take part.

KEY CONCEPTS

The OCR examination requires candidates to be able to:
- discuss the issues of informed consent and right to withdraw
- discuss the issue of confidentiality
- discuss the issues of protection of participants, deception, and health and well-being.

One way to protect the welfare of the participants is to give them the right to withdraw from the research at any time, without being put under any pressure, even if they agreed to take part in the first place and were aware of what the research involved.

If we are observing people and we tell them that we are observing them, simply knowing we are watching is very likely to make them behave in a different way. If we then tell them what we are interested in during our observation, this is even more likely to make them behave in a different way, so that they do more (or less) of what we are looking for. This is an occasion when it is not helpful to get someone's informed consent. The way psychologists can get round this is to observe people where they are normally on public display, such as in the street or in a public park. It is not acceptable to put video cameras into someone's home or classroom without them knowing!

Confidentiality

Participants must be told that their identity and any data they provide will be confidential. This does not mean that their data cannot be shared, but it does mean that no one should be able to identify them from the information the psychologist has gathered. This is often done by giving each participant a number or letter, and then identifying them only by that number or letter in any research published. If the participant gives informed consent to sharing their data, however, then it is acceptable to do so, but the psychologist has to be sensitive about how the information may be used.

Protection of participants

Whenever participants take part in any psychological research, they should be protected to the best of the researcher's ability. Researchers must ensure that any equipment is safe to use, and that participants are not asked to do anything that is illegal or might affect their health or well-being. However, there are occasions when, despite the best intentions, participants may unexpectedly experience some distress from taking part in research. Special care should be taken with children, as they are much more vulnerable than adults, and may be unhappy or harmed by experiences that would not affect adults.

Use of deception

Participants should not be deceived. They should be told the true nature of the research, what they are going to be doing, and so on. As we said earlier, there are times when telling the participant the exact nature of the research will affect the results, but not doing so should only be considered if there is no other option although a great deal of thought must be given to their welfare.

DISCUSS...

- If the participants in Bickman's study had known that they were being watched to see if they followed the directions given to them, do you think it would have affected their behaviour?
- If Terry's student participants had been told the exact nature of the research, do you think they might have made more effort to remember the adverts in the middle of the commercial breaks?

Well-being of participants

Participants in any sort of psychological research should leave a study feeling as good about themselves as when they started it. This is why the research should be well planned and discussed with colleagues, to make sure that nothing has been overlooked that might cause the participants distress or embarrassment.

If they have been deceived in any way, they should be thoroughly debriefed, which means that the purpose of the study and the methods used are fully explained. The researchers must answer any questions the participants ask and do their best to reassure the participants in any way they need to. They should also tell the participants that the data they provided can be destroyed if that is what they want.

DISCUSS...

Discuss in class all the ethical guidelines broken in the following piece of research.

Molly and Peggy Brown, both aged 39, Mrs Jones, aged 42, and Mr Pearce, aged 48, all from Bradford, and Mr Smith, aged 51, Mr and Mrs Hill, both aged 36, and Mr James, aged 45, all from Tunbridge Wells, completed a memory test, although they were told they were participants in research into solving maths problems. They were asked to read a story and were then asked to write as much about the story as they could remember. Then they were asked to do some maths problems. They had been told that they story was intended to 'clear their minds' before they completed the maths task. Mrs Jones became quite upset as she found the maths problems really difficult, but the researchers told her she had to finish the page of problems before she could leave. Molly and Peggy Brown both laughed at her when she started crying, and afterwards they told her that she really was ridiculous crying over such simple maths problems. The researchers looked at what they remembered from the story and found that Mrs Jones had remembered 16 facts, whereas all the others had remembered fewer than 12 facts. The researchers published the research in a well-known journal and thanked all the participants individually by name. Mrs Jones became very depressed after the experience and was frightened to go out shopping again in Bradford in case anyone laughed at her.

QUESTION ?

4. Describe one ethical issue you would have to consider when investigating the effects of noise.

KEY CONCEPTS

The OCR examination requires candidates to be able to:

- describe the use of laboratory experiments
- describe the use of field experiments
- describe the strengths and weaknesses of laboratory and field experiments.

Doing research

Experiments

The experiment has been widely used in psychology because it gives the psychologist greater control over what happens than simply observing people or asking them questions, for example. This means they can look more closely at cause and effect and make deductions about why things happen and why people behave in the way they do.

Experiments are often chosen to investigate topics such as memory and perception, because the independent variables can be manipulated easily by the researcher, who can then measure the dependent variable and draw conclusions.

Laboratory experiments

In the laboratory experiment the researcher has a high level of control of the independent variable, as well as greater control over extraneous variables by using a standardised procedure, giving the participants the same physical environment (heat, light and noise) and generally protecting their welfare to the best of the researcher's ability. The problem is that people may respond to demand characteristics because they will be trying to work out what the demands of the experiment are. They may guess what they are supposed to be doing (and get it either right or wrong), and this will affect the way they behave.

The main concern about the results of laboratory experiments is that they may lack ecological validity, which means they will not be generalisable to the outside world. This is because the way that people perform in a laboratory may be influenced by the control and safety of the laboratory. In the real world, they are subjected to different pressures and experiences, which might change how they behave or perform.

Strengths:

● It is the best way of establishing cause and effect.
● It is easy to control extraneous variables using standardised procedures and controlling the environment.

Weaknesses:

● The results may lack ecological validity.
● Some people, especially children, may not always follow the instructions exactly, which may well affect the results.
● The participants may respond to demand characteristics.

Field experiments

In a field experiment the psychologist manipulates the IV, but the experiment takes place in a real-life setting, which means that there will be less control over other extraneous variables. Social psychologists tend to use field experiments as they are particularly interested in the behaviour of people in their natural environment. Bickman's study, which took place on the streets of an American city, is an example of a field experiment.

Strengths:

● In field experiments researchers can see how people behave naturally as a result of any manipulation.
● Field experiments have more ecological validity.
● Participants are less likely to respond to demand characteristics.

DISCUSS...

Do you think Bickman could have done his research in a laboratory?

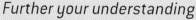

> ## Further your understanding
> ### Demand characteristics
>
> This study by Orne (1962) showed how participants taking part in a piece of research into compliance came to their own conclusions about the purpose of the research and acted accordingly.
>
> They were set the task of completing addition sums on separate sheets of paper. Each time they completed a sheet, they were told to pick up a card from a large pile, which would instruct them what to do next. Every card in the pile simply told them to tear up the sheet of paper they had just completed into a minimum of 32 pieces and go on to the next sheet of paper.
>
> This continued for several hours, with participants simply continuing to complete the sums and then tear up their papers, even though the task was totally pointless. When asked why they had continued, they said they had decided that the task was an endurance test – that is, they had made up their own minds about the nature of the experiment and acted according to what they thought the task demands were!

Weaknesses:

- It is much harder to establish cause and effect.
- It is much harder to control the extraneous variables that might affect the results.

KEY CONCEPTS

The OCR examination requires candidates to be able to:

- describe the use of questionnaires as a method of self-report
- distinguish between open and closed questions
- describe the strengths and weaknesses of questionnaires.

Questionnaires

Questionnaires as a method of self-report

In any sort of psychological research, the researchers are interested in gathering insight and an understanding into human thinking and human behaviour. The problem is that it is often difficult to get that information by watching or interviewing someone, whereas giving them a set of questions on a questionnaire, which they respond to either by writing their answers or responding to an administrator, is less personal. In fact, research has shown that people filling in online questionnaires often give more information than if they are interviewed. As a result, questionnaires are frequently used as a method of self-report within psychological research.

The questions can be closed or open-ended questions, depending on the kind of information the researcher wants.

Open questions are questions that do not allow people to give yes/no answers, but instead allow them to provide a lot of information. They are often used for in-depth research. An example of an open question would be, 'What do you think of your school?'

Closed questions require the respondent to provide a brief answer, such as yes or no – for example, 'Do you enjoy all your lessons in school? – Yes/No'. Respondents may actually want to answer, 'Well, it depends,' but because they are forced to choose yes or no, their answers may not reflect their real opinions.

> Respondents are the people completing the questionnaires.

As a kind of compromise, psychologists sometimes use rating scales that allow respondents to reflect their level of agreement. These still count as closed questions, but they provide more detailed information, which is still easy to quantify.

> *Questionnaires are quite difficult to construct because people often misunderstand the questions. When they are written, psychologists often ask people in a pilot study (a small-scale trial version of the main study) to give them feedback on the questions – checking whether they are clear and that they do not suggest to the person the way they should answer. The questionnaire may also be handed out to get an 'average answer', to help the researchers to understand if some of the responses are unusual.*

DISCUSS...

Have you ever completed a questionnaire with closed questions and felt really frustrated? Have you ever added another mark on a rating scale between two points?

Now imagine how difficult it is to score these ratings!

Please tick the box that applies to you where 1 = not at all and 5 = very much					
	1	**2**	**3**	**4**	**5**
Do you enjoy sports?					
Do you enjoy watching TV?					
Do you enjoy walking?					

Table 6.2 Example of a five-point rating scale used for a questionnaire

Strengths:

- Questionnaires are easy to administer.
- They can provide a large quantity of data.
- People may be more honest than if someone is actually asking them questions.
- All respondents have the same questionnaires to fill in, so there should be no extraneous variables affecting the information they provide.
- They are very easy to score if they have closed questions.
- They can gather rich information if they have open questions.
- It is possible to target a very large sample – for example, people in different areas can be sent questionnaires through the post or they can be put on the internet.

Weaknesses:

- The sample may be biased because it relies on people returning the questionnaires (they may be returned by people who have plenty of time or who have strong feelings about the topic).
- People may not give honest answers.
- People may not understand the questions if there is no administrator there to help them, so they may give inaccurate answers.
- Closed questions often hide really interesting information that can be provided by open questions.

Piaget used unstructured interviews.

- Open questions are really difficult to score or analyse.
- There is often a low return rate with postal questionnaires.

Interviews

Interviews, which are another type of self-report method, involve interviewers asking the interviewee questions in a face-to-face situation. There are two different types of interview: structured and unstructured.

Structured interviews

These consist of a series of questions that have been decided in advance and follow an identical format for each person.

Unstructured interviews

Unstructured interviews are more like spontaneous conversations. The interviewer will know what topics they intend to cover, but they do not have to cover them in any particular order, so the interview can be adjusted to suit the answers given by the interviewee.

Strengths:

- The interviewers can make sure that the interviewee understands the questions and can ask follow-up questions to clarify answers if necessary. This may provide more information than you could get from a pencil-and-paper exercise.
- You obtain rich and unique data from a person about their personal views or experiences.

Weaknesses:

- The method is very time-consuming.
- The respondents may give the answers they think the interviewer wants (socially desirable answers) rather than truthful answers.
- People may have difficulty expressing themselves.
- It is difficult to analyse these data and there is always a question about how much of the final report comes from the interviewer rather than the interviewee.

Observations

When psychologists want to try to understand the way people behave in certain situations, rather than ask them, they may choose to watch the participants and analyse their behaviour. Observations may be done either in laboratories or in people's normal settings, with the intention of seeing how they behave naturally.

Sometimes observations are carried out with two observers to make sure that nothing is missed. It also gives them a chance to agree on what they have observed and makes it less likely that the observers will see what they want to see (known as observer bias). Observations can be conducted as part of a bigger experiment if necessary.

> *Observer bias is when observers see what they are expecting to see (or want to see). Observer effects are where people behave differently because they know they are being observed.*

Overt and covert observations

If people know that they are being observed, this is known as an overt observation. If they are not aware that they are being observed, perhaps because the researchers are hiding, this is called a covert observation. Strengths:

> *The study by Bickman was an observational study.*

- Participants behave more naturally if they are in their normal environment, especially if they are not aware that they are being watched.

Weaknesses:

- Participants often know they are being watched, so they may behave differently to normal. If this were the case, you would say that the results may have been influenced by observer effects, and you would need to be aware that the results would be less valid.
- Observers can be influenced by observer bias.

Participant observations and non-participant observations

Participant observers become one of the group and join in their activities while observing them. In non-participant observations, the observer will watch from a distance.

Strengths:

- In participant research, the researcher gains a better insight into what is going on because they are interacting with the participants at the time of the study.

Weaknesses:

- In participant research, the researcher may not be as objective as they would be as a non-participant.
- Also in participant research, the presence of the observer may affect the behaviour of the subjects, changing it in some way.

Types of studies

So far, we have covered the most common methods used by psychologists when carrying out their research. There are occasions when they may need to use a different type of study, such as a case study or a study that looks for some kind of relationship between two variables. This is when other methods of investigation may be used.

KEY CONCEPTS

The OCR examination requires candidates to be able to:

- describe the use of case studies
- describe the use of correlational studies
- compare the use of longitudinal and cross-sectional studies.

> *Watson and Rayner and Diamond and Sigmundson both conducted case studies.*

Further your understanding

A very simple way to think about a correlation is to consider the following example: the taller the person, the faster they run. As one thing increases, so does the other, so there is an association or relationship between the two measures.

Case studies

The case study is an in-depth study of one person or a small number of people. It may include tests, observations and interviews of the person or persons being studied, as well as information from relevant others who may know about the participant's past or present experiences and behaviours. Researchers have to remember that retrospective evidence – that is, evidence that has to be remembered from the past – is not always accurately remembered. Case studies are often used for investigating people who show unusual abilities or difficulties.

Correlational study

If you want to look at how two factors are related in some way – for example, to see whether the amount of violent television watched is related to the amount of aggression demonstrated by different people – you would conduct a correlation.

Psychologists have to find an accurate way of measuring both variables and then analyse the data to show if there is any relationship between the two. In the example above of watching violence on television, you would need to ask your participants about their viewing habits, or find some way of monitoring their television watching and then either observing their aggressive behaviour or asking others to rate them. If the people who watched a lot of violent television were rated more highly for aggressive behaviour, we would conclude that one might lead to the other. (The important thing to note about a correlation is that is does not tell that violent television causes violent behaviour, only that people who watch more violent television are also more violent. There might be other reasons for the violence.)

▼ Figure 6.1

There are two patterns of correlation that can be plotted on a graph called a scattergram.

1. A positive correlation occurs when one variable increases as the other increases.
2. A negative correlation occurs when one variable increases as the other decreases.

If there is no upward or downward pattern in the scores, this suggests that there is no relationship between the two variables.

Longitudinal studies and cross-sectional studies

Longitudinal studies are used as a way of studying the same individuals or groups over a long period, in order to see any changes that may occur over time. The period of time involved could be from months to years,

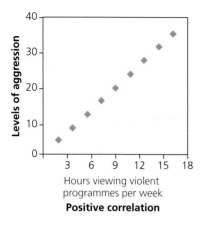

Positive correlation

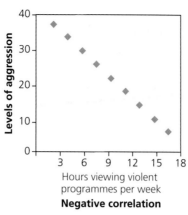

Negative correlation

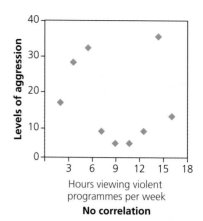

No correlation

▲ Figure 6.2 Patterns of correlation plotted on scattergrams

depending on what the researchers are interested in. This method is often used for case studies, studies of small groups or studies of cohorts (people with a common characteristic, such as a class of pupils). Researchers can chart the long-term effects of an experience or learn about developmental changes, for example, so it is ideal for the study of development in children.

One of the main problems with longitudinal studies is that the participants may no longer wish to be part of the research and drop out. Because it would be difficult to change the design of the study once it has been started, data that have been collected may end up being useless. In order to get over these difficulties, researchers may instead carry out a cross-sectional study, which also investigates how things change over time, but does so by comparing people who are at different ages or stages of development at one point in time.

Consider the examples in Table 6.3.

Table 6.3 Examples of longitudinal and cross-sectional studies ▼

Longitudinal study	Cross-sectional study
Psychologists interested in studying the development of a child aged between 3 and 15 years who has been in foster care	**Psychologists interested in studying the development of a child aged between 3 and 15 years who has been in foster care**
Study one child for 12 years	Assess fostered children aged 3, 4, 5, 6, 7, 8, 9, 10, 11, 12, 13, 14 and 15 years of age
Completed (hopefully) in 12 years if the child does not drop out	Completed in 1 month
Time-consuming, expensive and may be out of date by the time the study is completed, as circumstances may change for the child over the course of the study	Quick and easy to carry out, but raises the question of whether the children can really be compared with each other, as they may not all have been in foster care for the whole period. Are they comparable to the single child from the longitudinal study? Also, any differences between them may be due to their individuality rather than their fostering experiences.

Analysing research

Types of data

When you conduct research, you are going to collect data, which you will then need to analyse so you know what conclusions you can draw from your investigations, and whether or not you can accept your experimental or null hypothesis.

KEY CONCEPTS

The OCR examination requires candidates to be able to:

- explain what is meant by quantitative data
- explain what is meant by qualitative data
- describe data collected from investigations.

Quantitative data

If your participants produce scores that are either numbers or frequencies of occurrence, this sort of data is known as quantitative data. This sort of data can be analysed easily using statistical techniques.

> *In our investigation into hierarchical/random memory, each participant would receive a score for the number of words they remembered. This is quantitative data.*

Qualitative data

If your participants provide information that is descriptive and not numerical, such as information from an interview, this is known as qualitative data. It is more difficult to analyse qualitative data.

> *Quantitative data = numerical data or quantity data*
>
> *Qualitative data = descriptive data or quality data*

QUESTION

5. Complete the following table for the core studies, indicating with a cross what sort of data was collected in each case (hint: some may have both).

Study	Quantitative (numerical)	Qualitative (descriptive)
Diamond and Sigmundson		
Mednick *et al.*		
Terry		
Haber and Levin		
Hazan and Shaver		
Piaget		
Bickman		
Yuki *et al.*		
Watson and Rayner		
Van Houtte and Jarvis		

KEY CONCEPTS

The OCR examination requires candidates to be able to:

- use and interpret modes
- use and interpret medians
- use and interpret means.

Descriptive data

Modes, medians and means are often called descriptive statistics because they are helpful as a way of describing the data you have collected.

Modes

The mode is the most common score in a set of data. In Table 6.4 the mode is 26.

23	26	26	26	27	29	38	39	45	46	71

◀ Table 6.4 A set of scores from 11 participants in an experiment, put in order from lowest to highest

Medians

The median is the score that falls in the middle of a set of scores; the way you calculate it is to line up all the numbers in numerical order and find the one in the middle, just as the scores are in Table 6.4, where the median is 29. The reason it is useful is because if you have one unusual score, this will affect the average of all the scores, which could give you a false idea of what the results actually mean.

If you have an even amount of numbers, this makes it a little harder to identify the median. Take, for example, the following set of numbers:

23 26 26 26 27 29 38 39 45 46

In this case, you need to find the middle pair of numbers which are 27 and 29. You then find the value that would be half way between them by adding them together and dividing by two.

27 + 29 = 56

56 ÷ 2 = 28

Means

The mean is the numerical average score when you add up all the scores in one condition and divide them by the number of participants in that condition. The total of scores in Table 6.4 is 396, which, when divided by 11 (the number of scores), gives a mean of 36. The mean takes into account all the scores, but it is also affected by any extreme scores, such as the score of 71. If this score was not counted, the mean of the remaining ten scores would be 32.5.

Imagine you wanted to calculate the average age of the people in your classroom. All the students are aged 14 or 15, but the teacher is 56. Working out an average age would not give you an accurate idea of the average age of the class.

6. For the examination, you may be asked to work out the mode, median and mean from a set of data. Using the data below, from participants in an experiment, work out the mode, median and mean and answer the questions that follow.

Experimental condition	Control condition
23	14
26	15
26	15
26	16
27	17
29	18
38	19
39	19
45	19
46	22
71	24

- Calculate the mode for both conditions.
- Calculate the median for both conditions. Would the median be a useful descriptive statistic?
- Calculate the mean score for both conditions. Why are mean scores sometimes a good way to compare the two sets of results?

KEY CONCEPTS

The OCR examination requires candidates to be able to:

- use and interpret tables of data
- use and interpret bar charts
- use and interpret line graphs.

Tables, charts and graphs

Looking at a list of participant's scores often tells us little about the results we have just gathered, so when the data are collected, it is much easier to interpret them if they are presented in tables, bar charts and graphs.

Tables

You will see examples of tables in some of the core studies, including the Bickman study, where the frequency data for the civilian, milkman and guard, and the percentage of people who obeyed in each situation are presented in a table (Chapter 4, page 118). If this information had been presented using the raw data, it would have been very difficult to compare the results between the three conditions. Similarly, the table in Chapter 1, page 26, in the Mednick *et al.* study, shows the groups that were compared with each other and the relationships between them. This would have been much harder to interpret from the raw scores.

You need to be able to …
- Remember in the examination you will need to label each axis in any bar charts or line graphs you draw, and add a title.

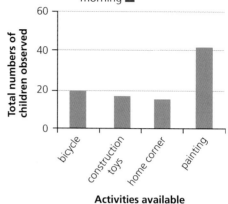

Figure 6.3 Example of a bar chart showing children's play preferences over one morning ▼

Bar charts

Bar charts show amounts or the number of times something occurs. Each bar represents a separate category. The bars can be drawn either horizontally or vertically. There are a number of bar charts in the Hazan and Shaver study (Chapter 3, pages 79 and 80) that show the percentage of participants in each category in a visual way.

Line graphs

It is possible to show the trend in scores and whether they go up or down using line graphs. Line graphs are also used to compare the trends in two different sets of scores, as can be seen in the line graph in Figure 6.4.

Evaluating findings

You have now read the core studies and considered their limitations. During your reading you will have realised that there are lots of things that can go wrong with psychological investigations, which is why it is really important to plan research carefully.

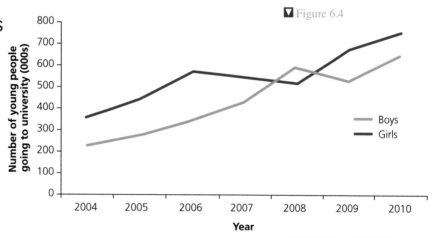

▼ Figure 6.4

You should also be aware of the things that can actually affect the results, and therefore the conclusions of any psychological research. You also need to consider that it is really important that any research can be replicated (repeated). This is either to make sure that the results are not just a 'one-off', or to see if the results change over time. This would be impossible if the research methods were not carefully documented, which is why the studies are written in the way they are.

Some of the key concepts you need to consider when evaluating research are detailed below.

Validity

We need to know whether the results actually assess what we want to assess. For example, if we are investigating aggressive behaviour in children

 KEY CONCEPTS

The OCR examination requires candidates to be able to:
- explain the concept of validity, including ecological validity
- explain the concept of reliability, including inter-rater reliability
- outline the problems of demand characteristics, observer effects and social desirability.

and we count one child chasing another child as an aggressive act, we would need to consider whether this really is aggression or whether they are just playing. If we counted it as aggressive behaviour, our results may not be valid because they might not be assessing what we want to assess (a game of tag is not aggressive!).

We first came across the idea of ecological validity in Chapter 2, page 40. Ecological validity refers to whether something is valid in the real world, rather than just valid in a laboratory.

Reliability

If we question whether the results of a study are reliable, what we really mean is whether they are consistent – if we replicated the study, would we get the same results again?

During observational studies, as we said on page 198, it is quite common to have more than one observer, to make sure that they do not miss anything. Having two observers also prevents one observer seeing what they want to see or misinterpreting the motives of the person being watched. Having two observers ensures inter-rater reliability, as they compare their observations and agree on the results.

Demand characteristics

Were the participants trying to work out what the researcher wanted them to do, and did this affect their behaviour? The study by Orne (page 196) explains demand characteristics well.

Observer effects

When participants are observed, do they behave normally or is their behaviour affected due to this observation? Most people are not natural when they are observed, which means that the results are not as valid as they might be.

Social desirability

Participants providing answers to interviews or questionnaires may lie because they feel that they have to say what they think the researcher wants them to say, rather than telling the truth.

Source of bias

Bias

If research findings are biased, this means that they are not objective and may be influenced by a researcher's beliefs rather than what is real. There are a number of possible sources of bias that might affect the results:

- Gender bias refers to the fact that the research is slanted towards either males or females. The research may involve materials that are easier for one gender over the other – for example, a memory test of the names of

football teams. Another example would be seeing all boys as aggressive, while all girls are seen as assertive. One famous researcher, looking into children's moral development, only used boys in his sample, suggesting they represented all children.

- Cultural bias refers to the fact that the research may be valid for one cultural group, but might ignore different responses that might be given by other cultural groups. Many of the more famous psychological studies used white, middle-class university students as their samples; this research is extremely culturally biased because it ignores other cultures completely, even though participants from these other cultures might have given very different responses.
- Experimenter bias refers to the fact that the researcher might interpret the results in the way they want to, rather than the way they really are. Most psychologists favour one school of thought over another, although it is really important in any research to keep an open mind. Experimenter bias occurs when a researcher favours one explanation over another, even though the evidence may not be that clear-cut.

Planning an investigation

Investigation and design skills

In order to make sure you have had some experience at carrying out your own research, you should be able to design your own experiment, design and use a questionnaire, conduct an interview and carry out an observation.

For each piece of research you will need to:

- state the hypothesis for an investigation
- describe and justify the sample used in an investigation
- describe the ethical issues involved in an investigation
- describe and justify how the variables are measured in an investigation
- describe and justify the control of extraneous variables in an investigation
- describe the procedure used in an investigation
- explain the strengths of the method used in an investigation
- explain the weaknesses of the method used in an investigation
- describe how data are analysed in an investigation.

You *must* discuss possible topics for research with your teacher and make sure that the ideas you have are both practical and ethical.

If you need some suggestions, the list below might give you some ideas. Remember that the research you carry out should be something you are interested in and something about which you can formulate a hypothesis.

Experiments

- Use the example of the memory experiment at the beginning of the chapter, with the hierarchical/random lists.
- Does noise affect task performance?
- Does using coloured paper increase scores on a maths test?
- Who has the better memory for names – males or females?
- Does the Necker cube change more in a minute for males or females? (You will need to look up the visual illusion of the Necker cube on the internet.)
- Test the capacity of short-term memory.
- Does music improve our ability to remember words in a memory experiment?
- Do people who eat breakfast get higher scores in a memory test?

Observations

- Do television adverts show gender stereotypes?
- Do men prefer to sit next to or opposite another person on the train or bus?
- Do women prefer to sit next to or opposite another person on the train or bus?
- Do infant boys and girls choose different types of toys to play with?

Questionnaires or surveys

- Do males or females show a higher level of conformity when told to turn off their mobile phones? (You could do this using a questionnaire or interview.)
- Which subjects do males and females prefer in school? Is there a gender bias to certain subjects?

Correlations

- Memory increases with age – the older you are, the better your memory.
- Is there an association between the size of someone's head circumference and their ability to do maths? (Get your tape measure and a maths test ready!)

Exam-style question – Research methods: Planning, doing and analysing research

These questions are taken from the OCR B543 Psychology paper, from May 2010. For more past and sample papers plus answer exemplars visit the OCR website. OCR have not seen or commented on the quality of the sample answers.

> **The Source**
>
> *A psychologist wanted to investigate whether there are gender differences in the levels of aggression shown by primary school children. He asked a primary school teacher to choose six girls and six boys from her class. The psychologist and two of his colleagues then spent five days observing the children as they played in the playground during their mid morning break.*
>
> *The observers recorded the number of verbally aggressive and physically aggressive acts shown by the children.*
>
> *The results are displayed below.*

Table 1 The mean number of verbally and physically aggressive acts recorded.

	Physically Aggressive	Verbally Aggressive
Boys	25	21
Girls	14	19

1. Give the aim of the study in the source. [1]

   To investigate whether there are gender differences in the levels of aggression shown by primary school children. (1)

2. State an alternate hypothesis for this study. [2]

   Boys will show more verbal and physical aggression than girls. (2)

   An alternate hypothesis must make a statement rather than just saying what the aim was. Two marks here because the candidate has shown that they understand a hypothesis predicts a difference (in aggression) and identifies both variables (boys and girls).

3. The psychologist used an opportunity sample.

   (a) Describe **one** weakness of using an opportunity sample for this study. [2]

   An opportunity sample might not give you a sample that is representative of the population as a whole as it might be biased. (2)

   (b) State **one** other sampling method the psychologist could have used other than opportunity sampling. [1]

   Random sampling (1)

4. Using the data in the source, give the mean number of physically aggressive acts that were shown by the boys. [1]

   25 (1)

5. State **one** finding of the study in the source. [1]

Girls weren't as physically aggressive as the boys. (1)

There were lots of possible answers to this question such as boys were more aggressive than girls, boys and girls showed similar levels of verbal aggression etc.

6. The psychologist used quantitative data rather than qualitative data. State what quantitative data is. [1]

Quantitative data is numbers. (1)

7. The researcher used an observation. One method he could have used is an interview.

Outline **one** weakness of the interview method. [2]

It's hard to analyse the results. (1)

This answer is not explained so the candidate only earns one mark here. The answer needs to give a more detailed explanation for two marks.

Is this a better answer?

Results may be hard to analyse because they will be words that were spoken rather than numbers which can be put into graphs. (2)

8. The study raises a number of ethical issues. Look at the diagram below. Draw a line to match each ethical issue to its correct definition.

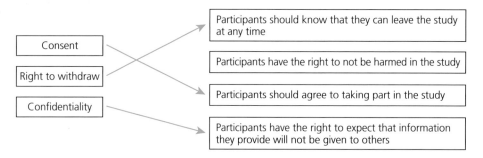

ETHICAL ISSUE   DEFINITION

Consent

Right to withdraw

Confidentiality

Participants should know that they can leave the study at any time

Participants have the right to not be harmed in the study

Participants should agree to taking part in the study

Participants have the right to expect that information they provide will not be given to others [3]

9. The psychologist carried out a covert observation.

Explain the difference between a covert and overt observation. [3]

Because this is a three mark question, you will realise you need to make three points – show that you understand the two terms – covert and overt – and explain the difference between them.

In covert observations, the participants do not know they are being watched (1) whereas in overt observations they do (1). If participants know they are being watched, they may act differently (1).

10. The psychologist used a non-participant observation.

Describe **one** strength of a non-participant observation. [2]

One strength of non-participant observation is that the researcher can record the behaviour as it happens (1). They are not actually part of the observation, they are just watching from a distance and can see more of what is going on (1).

Because this is a two mark question, the candidate has earned both marks by identifying a strength and explaining why it is a strength.

11. (a) Outline what is meant by the term inter-rater reliability. [2]

Inter-rater reliability means it is consistent or the same each time. (1)

This only gains one mark because although it shows the candidate has an understanding of inter-rater reliability, their understanding is not related to observations.

A better answer would be something like:

Inter-rater reliability is where all observers are watching for the same thing and recording them in the same way. (2)

(b) Explain how inter-rater reliability would have been achieved in this study. [2]

The observers could be trained before the experiment on what they are looking for (1) so they all record the same behaviour in the playground (1).

12. Explain what is meant by gender bias in research. [2]

Gender bias is where differences between men and women are exaggerated (1). Generally male behaviour is seen as the norm and female behaviour as inferior or abnormal when it is just different. It could also be the other way round, that women are seen as better and men inferior. (1)

QUESTION TOTAL [25]

Exam-style question – Research methods: Planning an investigation

These questions are taken from the OCR B543 Psychology paper, from January 2010. For more past and sample papers plus answer exemplars visit the OCR website. OCR have not seen or commented on the quality of the sample answers.

> You have been asked to use a **questionnaire** to investigate whether teachers are more stressed than other professionals. The theory is that teachers will report higher levels of stress than people doing other jobs.

1. (a) State a hypothesis for your investigation. [2]

There will be a difference (1) in the levels of stress reported by teachers and people doing other jobs (1).

Here the candidate could give either an experimental (alternate) hypothesis or a null hypothesis. The hypothesis could predict a direction or it could be non-directional like this candidate's answer.

(b) Identify which sampling method you would use for this investigation and explain why you would use it. [3]

I would use random sampling (1) because it would give me an unbiased sample (1) so I would put all my teachers' names in a hat and the first ten I pull out will be my participants (1). This sample may not be representative of the population as a whole as it's a small sample.

The candidate will get full marks but the last point is an evaluation and the question does not ask for an evaluation.

(c) Describe **one** ethical issue you would have to deal with when investigating stress. [2]

I would make sure none of my questions would upset the teachers. (1)

This answer does not explain how it applies to stress. By adding 'as they may not want to talk about how stressed they are' would link the answer to stress.

(d) Briefly outline how you would use a questionnaire to carry out an investigation into whether teachers are more stressed than people doing other jobs [3]

I would prepare a list of questions asking teachers and office workers how stressed they are. (1) I would then look for patterns in their answers and try to identify common things that cause them stress. (1)

This answer is only worth 2 marks because it does not explain the types of questions asked and suggests that the questionnaire would only look for common things that cause both groups stress. The question asked the candidate to find out whether teachers were more stressed than people doing other jobs and they have not explained how they had planned to look for a difference.

If the candidate had explained that they would first identify things that may possibly be stressful to teachers and other people (perhaps by asking one or two teachers and school admin staff before hand) and then asking participants to rate the stressful situations on a scale of 1 to 10. The candidate could then compare the two professions to see if there are common stressors or whether teachers are more stressed than other workers.

(e) Describe **one** weakness of using a questionnaire in this investigation. [3]

One weakness of using a questionnaire is that people may lie in their answers (1). Stress is a particularly sensitive area (1) and so people may not want to tell you how stressed they really are (1).

(f) Outline how you would analyse your findings. [2]

I would look at the results of my questionnaires and add up all the things that cause people stress and plot the teachers' and office workers' scores on a bar graph. (1)

This answer is only worth one mark.

Note here the answer to question (d) would affect how this question is answered. Although this answer has provided some possibility of analysing the results, the poor design of this candidate's questionnaire would make the results fairly meaningless when you consider what the candidate should have been looking for.

This answer is based on the example answer above which is why it is important to think your design through carefully.

I would look at the results of my questionnaires and look at the mean score for teachers and the mean score for office workers by adding up all the scores and dividing them by the number of participants in each group. I would plot these averages on a bar graph to show the difference. (2)

QUESTION TOTAL [15]

Answers

Chapter 1, Unit B541 Sex and gender, pages 2–15

1. The biological explanation as to why men are likely to be more sexually promiscuous than women is because men have millions of sperm, so can afford to be wasteful, whereas women have a limited number of eggs and therefore want to choose a good father to help them raise their children successfully.

2. If we accept Freud's explanation of gender development, children raised in one-parent families should have a poorly developed gender role (because they do not have a parent of each sex, or there is only a same-sex parent). Research indicates that this is not the case, and that these children develop gender roles as successfully as those raised by two parents.

3. There are several reasons that women give to change their breast size that are not always to do with feeling more feminine. Some women may think that having larger breasts make them look more feminine, others may decide to change because they want to look more like celebrities who are frequently photographed by the media. Fashion trends also change and this may play a part. Breast reductions are often done for practical or medical reasons.

4. Retrospective evidence is evidence given in retrospect (after the event has occurred). The trouble with retrospective evidence is that it is not always accurate, as we are not always very good at remembering things that have happened in the past.

5. John probably meant that the way he felt about himself, his feelings of being male and not female, the way he was able to behave (as a man, not as a woman) and the feelings he had in his body (probably his sexual urges) were now all in tune with each other.

Chapter 1, Unit B542 Criminal behaviour, pages 16–32

1.

Country	Age
Scotland	8
England, Wales and Northern Ireland	10
USA (some states)	6
Canada, the Netherlands	12
France	13
Germany, Austria, Italy, Japan, Russia	14
Scandinavian nations	15
Spain, Portugal	16
Brazil, Peru	18

2. People may choose not to report crimes for the following reasons:
   - inconvenient, as reporting crime takes a lot of time, for example, waiting around to be interviewed
   - embarrassing, especially with sexual crimes or if the person was not supposed to be where they were when the crime took place
   - they do not believe that the police will be able to do anything about the crime.

3. Examples of other types of vicarious reinforcement:
   - Seeing people dress in a certain way and receive praise and compliments may make you want to dress in the same way.
   - Seeing someone getting good marks and a reward for a good piece of school work may make you want to do work that is as good.
   - Seeing someone dancing in a certain way and getting admiring glances from the opposite sex may make you go home and practise dancing the same way in front of a mirror.

4. Any behaviour could be studied to try to understand if it is inherited or learned. We could consider whether being sociable is due to nature or to nurture. If someone was brought up in a family where they were quite isolated and had few visitors or friends, the child would probably find that being involved in social events such as parties would be very difficult. If the brother or sister or twin of that child was adopted and brought up in a family who had lots of visitors and were very sociable, the child might learn that being sociable is normal and then become very sociable themselves. The difficulty that exists is that it is actually impossible to be completely sure that there is not a 'shy' gene, because perhaps the sociable sibling (who was raised in the social household) would actually prefer to be quiet and on their own but has never had a chance to do so. Other examples of studies may look at aggression or phobias to see if they are innate or learned.

5. If they had been family members, they would probably share the environment of the children's original parents. This would mean that it would be impossible to work out whether nature or nurture was responsible for any criminal behaviour. This is what is known as a confounding or confusing variable (see Chapter 6, page 186).

6. If the researchers had used the data of the women who had a lower level of convictions, it would have 'skewed' the data. This means that it might have affected the results and made it look less like there was a genetic component to criminality. For example, if you had used a sample of 100 adopted men and 100 adopted women and only the men had criminal convictions, it would have appeared that only 50 per cent of the sample had the inherited criminal gene. On the other hand, if you only used the sample of 100 convicted men, it would look as if all of them had the inherited criminal gene.

7. Retrospective data are often inaccurate because we cannot always accurately remember things that have happened in the past (see Chapter 2). We may forget things that seem unimportant or get them confused with similar things. If we are anxious we cannot always remember things accurately. In this study, the retrospective data were in the form of numbers, so they were probably quite accurate.

Chapter 2, Unit B541 Memory, pages 34–51

1. Information processing is the way that information that enters through our senses is processed in stages so that it means something to us and we can either store it or use it in some way.

2. The stages of information processing are input, encoding, storage, retrieval and output.

3. **Input** – the information is input by typing it into the computer on a keyboard.
   Encoding – the information is put into a format that means the computer can store it.
   Storage – the information is stored in the computer's memory by saving it as a file.
   Retrieval – the information is pulled out of memory by opening the file.
   Output – the information is printed.

4. When talking about reasons why we forget information, to get the best marks in the examination, it is important to explain the reasons rather than just using one-word answers. See the table below for some of those reasons.

5. The following are different ways to prevent forgetting:

6. U-shaped serial position curve.

7. Present the words to the learner and get them to recall the words. Then jumble up the words and re-present them to the learner, who will learn and recall them again. Do this a third time or split the list of words into two shorter lists.

8. • Short-term memory
   • Long-term memory.

9. • **Iconic processing** – what something looks like (e.g. cat – all lower case)
   • **Acoustic processing** – what something sounds like (mat – rhymes with cat)
   • **Semantic processing** – what something means (cat – a furry animal with whiskers and a long tail that catches mice and likes curling up in front of the fire to sleep).

Chapter 2, Unit B542 Perception, pages 52–68

1. Any solid object can have shape constancy. For example, a mug will look different from different positions, such as above, alongside, looking at the bottom, the handle and so on. The same is true of a car or a house.

2. Four – height in the plane, relative size, superimposition and texture gradient.

3. Bottom-up processing.

4. Top-down processing uses information stored in memory to help us to recognise something. Bottom-up processing uses information that enters the eyes rather than relying on memory to make sense of what we see.

5. Recognising something like a building or an object.

6. Height in the plane, relative size, superimposition and texture gradient.

Type of memory	Why we forget	How we can improve memory
Sensory memory	The memory trace decays due to lack of capacity.	By paying added attention to incoming sensory information
Short-term memory	Short-term memory has a limited capacity (between five and nine pieces of information can be stored). Forgetting is due to displacement, where new information displaces the information already stored.	By rehearsal (keeping information in our awareness – for example, by repeating it over and over again)
Long-term memory	Information is forgotten due to decay because the information is no longer used or needed, or by displacement (where old information is overwritten by new information). It may appear to be forgotten but it may simply be inaccessible.	By making sure that the information is processed for meaning By using cues to try to access information: some information that seems to have been forgotten may still be there, but is difficult to access without retrieval cues, such as returning to where something happened or having the first letter of a word to help you retrieve the word from memory (see page 48 for more information on using cues to access memory)

Chapter 3, Unit B541 Attachment, pages 70–86

1.

Age of child	Response to separation	Response to a stranger
2 months	None	None
5 months	None	None
7 months	Upset and tears	Tries to get away

2. • **Privation:** Never having formed an attachment at any time.
   • **Deprivation:** Having an attachment figure and then losing them due to death, illness and so on.

3. Research suggests that privation is more serious than deprivation because if a child has experienced maternal deprivation, at least they have had experience of a positive relationship and may be able to rebuild another very strong relationship in the future. They are more likely to suffer from depression as an adult.

   The long-term outlook for children who have experienced privation is that they find it difficult to make relationships with anyone and this can often result in mental illness and personality disorders when they become adults. When they are children they find it hard to make friends or to trust anyone.

4.

Type of attachment	Behaviour of caregiver	Behaviour of child
Securely attached	Sensitive to child's needs; interprets and understands what they want; enjoys their company and is consistent with them	Happy to explore, using the caregiver as a safe base; secure and feels loved and valued
Insecure-avoidant	Aloof and cold; ignores or rejects the child's emotional needs or demands	Child becomes self-reliant and avoids displaying feelings or asking for comfort; child is good and helpful, but inside feels angry and anxious and doubts if they are lovable
Insecure-ambivalent	Caregiver responds inconsistently to the child's emotional needs and demands, sometimes being really loving and at other times cold and rejecting	The child never knows where they are with the caregiver and will hate them one minute and love them the next, not knowing what they really feel; the child is demanding, has tantrums, and behaves badly; the child feels needy and anxious, but will resist comfort when it is offered

Chapter 3, Unit B542 Cognitive development, pages 87–104

1. Universal means that all children go through the stages, irrespective of where they come from. Invariant means that they all go through the stages in the same order and never miss a stage – there is no variation in the way that children go through the stages, one after another.

2. Children might vary slightly in age when they go from one stage to the next, but Piaget gave approximate ages.

3. The things that might affect their progress will be their level of cognitive ability (level of intelligence) and the amount of stimulation and experience they have had while growing up.

4. By zone of proximal development, Vygotsky meant the difference between a child's achievements and ability when working on their own with no help, and their possible achievements when working with an adult or capable child who can show them what to do and how to do it.

5. The child will play with the bricks on the floor. They may manage to make a tower. If the adult or older child is there with them and shows them how to make a bridge or a stronger tower, they are likely to copy and learn the properties of the bricks more quickly. By sharing the task with the adult, the adult is providing scaffolding through that social interaction to allow the child to do things they would not have been able to do on their own.

Chapter 4, Unit B541 Obedience, pages 106–124

1.

Word	Explanation (try not to use the word itself)	Example
Obedience	Following a command, order or instruction that is given by someone in authority	Doing as you are asked when a teacher gives you an instruction
Defiance	Making the active choice to defy or go against what is being asked of you	Refusing to shoot someone if you are ordered to do so by your commanding officer
Denial of responsibility	Putting the blame for your actions onto someone else and saying it was their fault because you were acting as their agent at the time	As a soldier who has been told to shoot the enemy, saying, 'It was not my fault. I only did it because I was ordered to shoot.'

2. • **Power:** Doctors were seen as more powerful than nurses and they had the power to get the nurses into trouble. Nurses were frightened that if they did not obey, they might lose their jobs.

- **Setting:** The setting was a hospital, where there is a hierarchical power structure, with doctors at the top and ward nurses further down the chain of command. Within that setting, it was normal for nurses to obey the requests of doctors. The attire of members of staff also signified a chain of command. Doctors wore white coats and their usual clothes, while nurses all wore the same uniforms. The nurses of the day also wore starched aprons, which might also give a signal of subservience (their role was serving others).
- **Culture:** The culture was one of obedience and order, with little opportunity to question higher authority. Doctors gave instructions and commands to nurses on a regular basis within a hospital, so it would be expected that they would be asked to carry out tasks for the doctors.

3. • Milgram's study: Participants were not told what the research was really about. They had been told it was a study of learning, not obedience. They did not give informed consent to take part. The participants were led to think that they could not withdraw from the procedure. They became distressed during the procedure and many of them were upset once it had finished.
   • Hofling *et al.*'s study: Participants did not know they were participants, so they were not able to consent to take part. They were also deceived. The nurses may have been worried and distressed about what the 'doctor' had asked them to do.

4. Some psychologists believe that situational factors can explain obedience, whereas others believe that dispositional factors are a better explanation. Dispositional factors are things about the disposition of the person, such as their personality traits or their individual characteristics. This means that obedience is more to do with upbringing than the situation you find yourself in.

5. This was to ensure that there were no differences in the appearance of the 'authority figures', because if one had been physically much larger than another, this might have affected people's willingness to obey.

6. Research has shown that people are more likely to disobey an order if they are with someone else, as they diffuse the responsibility between them. So the experimenters chose people walking on their own as they were more likely to obey.

7. It is likely that the participants would have changed their behaviour if they had realised they were taking part in research (see demand characteristics in Chapter 6, page 196).

Chapter 4, Unit B542 Non-verbal communication, pages 125–45

1. • Christian's facial expression – bowing his head but looking upwards towards the teacher – a submissive expression

- Christian's body language – bowed head, shoulders rounded and hands down by his sides
- Bobby's facial expression – mouth turned downwards with a staring look
- Bobby's body language – head to one side and arms folded, legs slightly apart.

2.

Feature	Facial expressions	Body language
Arms folded		✓
Frown	✓	
Crossed legs		✓
Eye contact	✓	
Open palms		✓

3. Social learning theory states that non-verbal communication starts when a child **observes** other people using non-verbal signals. The child then **imitates** these signals by performing them themselves. If the signals help them to communicate, these are **reinforced** and they use them again. However, if the signals do not work or the children are **punished** for inappropriate use, they are less likely to use them again (OCR Jan 2010).

Chapter 5, Unit B541 Atypical behaviour, pages 147–63

1.

Subject	Typical	Atypical
Crossing the road	Looking both ways and listening as you cross	Walking out without looking for any oncoming traffic
Sitting an examination	Being quiet and sitting at the desk, waiting for the exam papers to be given out	Shouting out to the examiner to hurry up and then talking to your friends
Meeting someone new	Being polite and either shaking their hand or greeting them	Going up and hugging them and talking over the top of them
Finding a spider in the bath	Trying to get it out, either by picking it up or by coaxing it into a cup or other receptacle to throw it out of the window	Running screaming down the stairs and refusing to go into the bathroom ever again

2. To begin with, salivation, **the unconditioned response**, occurred with the presence of food, **the unconditioned stimulus**. After pairing the bowl, **the neutral stimulus**, and the food together many times, the dogs became conditioned to salivate to the empty bowl. This empty bowl is therefore the **conditioned stimulus**, and salivation is now called the **conditioned response** because it occurs with the conditioned stimulus.

3. • **Consent and deception:** Although Little Albert's mother gave her consent to him taking part, we do not know if it was informed consent. Watson and Rayner should have explained what the study was about. If they had, would she have let her little boy be frightened as he was?
   • **Confidentiality:** The study is known about and Little Albert has been photographed and named. Perhaps he should have been called something different and no photographs taken.
   • **Conduct:** Participants must be protected from harm. They should also leave the experiment in the same mental state as they entered. Little Albert left with a phobia of rats and other furry things. In order to get round this, if Albert's mother understood the nature of the study, she would have realised how important it was to let Albert stay to be 'deconditioned'.

Chapter 5, Unit B542 The self, pages 164–81

1. • family position – first born, middle child, youngest
   • gender – boy or girl
   • family structure – one parent, two parents, step-siblings, grandparents
   • parenting style – harsh or too easygoing
   • social class and educational opportunities
   • cognitive ability – level of intelligence
   • any sort of learning difficulty (dyslexia)
   • any sort of physical disability (hearing impairment)
   • physical appearance – height, weight, hair colour
   • personality – introvert (likes being quiet and prefers the company of one or two people rather than a crowd) or extrovert (outgoing, sociable type who likes noise and lots of people)
   • life experiences – where you live, type of school, type of teacher
   • religious beliefs
   • culture and ethnicity.

2. Humanistic theory says that everyone has a **self-concept**, which is how they see themselves. We also have an idea of who we would like to be, which is known as the **ideal self**. The difference between the two is a measure of our **self-esteem**.

3. Being nice to someone regardless of what they say or do, and showing love and support without expecting anything in return.

4. Pre-adolescent pet owners and non-pet owners were interviewed and an assessment was made of their self-concept, self-esteem, autonomy and attachment to pets.

5. • Depression: When feelings of sadness and misery are completely out of proportion to an event, or when they go on for a very long period of time and stop a person from functioning properly (eating, sleeping and socialising).
   • Self-actualisation: To achieve one's potential.
   • Unconditional positive regard: Accepting someone for who they are without judging them or disapproving in any way.
   • Empathy: Seeing and feeling something from someone else's perspective.

6. Counselling can help people who are depressed. The counsellor will show empathy and unconditional positive regard, which would help the client to feel better about themselves. The counsellor will listen to the client and will reflect the client's thoughts back to them. The counsellor is non-directive and will allow the client to make their own decisions about the future.

Chapter 6, Unit B543 Research methods used in psychology, pages 183–213

1.

IV	DV
Noisy or quiet rooms	Number of words remembered
Boys and girls	Toys chosen
Pet owners and non-pet owners	Heart rates

2.

Study	Target population	Sample	Was the sample representative?
Bickman	All pedestrians	People in New York	Possibly, but unlikely as people in a New York street are unlikely to represent the population as a whole.
Haber and Levin	The population	Students	No
Watson and Rayner	The population	Little Albert	No
Terry	The population	Students	No
Piaget	Children between the ages of 2 and 7 years	17 children between the ages of 4 and 6 years	Probably not, as we were not told enough about the sample and no young children took part

Study	Target population	Sample	Was the sample representative?
Yuki *et al.*	Japanese and Americans	Students	Probably
Van Houtte and Jarvis	Pre-adolescent children	Pre-adolescent children from one school	Unlikely, as they would have been from one area, which may have had little social diversity

3. • Not everyone has a telephone.
   • Even people with a telephone might choose to be ex-directory.
   • They would be people living in one area only.
   • They may all be related (if you chose people with the same name), so would have shared experiences.

4. Ethical guidelines say it is important to protect participants from harm. Noise could be very painful to participants' ears and damage their hearing.

5.

Study	Quantitative (numerical)	Qualitative (descriptive)
Diamond and Sigmundson		X
Mednick *et al.*	X	
Terry	X	
Haber and Levin	X	
Hazan and Shaver	X	X
Piaget		X
Bickman	X	
Yuki *et al.*	X	
Watson and Rayner		X
Van Houtte and Jarvis	X	

6.

Experimental condition	Control condition
Mean 36	Mean 18
Median 29	Median 18
Mode 26	Mode 19

The median would be a useful descriptive statistic because there is one 'rogue' or extreme score in the experimental condition that has affected the mean score. The median score gives a better idea of the difference between the two sets of scores.

Mean scores are sometimes a good way to compare the two sets of results because they take into account every score.

Index